The Caregiving Ambition

The Caregiving Ambition

What It Is and Why It Matters
at Home and Work

JULIA B. BEAR

AND

TODD L. PITTINSKY

OXFORD
UNIVERSITY PRESS

Oxford University Press is a department of the University of Oxford. It furthers
the University's objective of excellence in research, scholarship, and education
by publishing worldwide. Oxford is a registered trade mark of Oxford University
Press in the UK and certain other countries.

Published in the United States of America by Oxford University Press
198 Madison Avenue, New York, NY 10016, United States of America.

© Oxford University Press 2022

Library of Congress Cataloging-in-Publication Data
Names: Bear, Julia B., author. | Pittinsky, Todd L., author.
Title: The caregiving ambition : what it is and why it matters at home and work /
Julia B. Bear, Todd L. Pittinsky.
Description: New York, NY : Oxford University Press, 2022. |
Includes bibliographical references and index.
Identifiers: LCCN 2021049879 (print) | LCCN 2021049880 (ebook) |
ISBN 9780197512418 (hardback) | ISBN 9780197512432 (epub) |
ISBN 9780197512449 (digital-online)
Subjects: LCSH: Goal (Psychology) | Caring. | Success.
Classification: LCC BF505.G6 B43 2022 (print) | LCC BF505.G6 (ebook) |
DDC 158.1—dc23/eng/20211202
LC record available at https://lccn.loc.gov/2021049879
LC ebook record available at https://lccn.loc.gov/2021049880

DOI: 10.1093/oso/9780197512418.001.0001

9 8 7 6 5 4 3 2 1

Printed by Sheridan Books, Inc., United States of America

CONTENTS

9. Lessons for Living Ambitiously 168

Conclusion: Caregiving as the Passion Project 188

ACKNOWLEDGMENT

We began this book before anyone had heard of COVID-19, but ended up writing much of it in the midst of the global pandemic. We would like to acknowledge the frontline workers, first responders, as well as the too-often-forgotten responders: the caregivers for the young and old, family and friends, who did the work of caring through such a critical time. At Oxford University Press, we gratefully acknowledge the thoughtful editorial assistance from our editor, Abby Gross, as well as assistant editor, Katharine Pratt. Finally, this book benefited from countless conversations with friends and family who shared details of their ambitions, caregiving and career, as did the many individuals who made time to share their experiences and perspectives as participants in our research—thank you.

Introduction

Caring Ambitiously

Ambition is enthusiasm with a purpose.

—FRANK TYGER[1]

Whom would you call "ambitious" or, for that matter, a "big success"? Someone who starts their career in a good mid-level job and, over the years, works their way up to CEO and a seven-figure salary? An actor who keeps plugging away with bit parts in commercials and local theater but eventually becomes an A-list Hollywood star with a luxurious Hollywood lifestyle?

What about a mother of two who also cares for her aging father and makes it possible for him to pass away peacefully at home, as he wished, because she is determined not to leave him to die hooked up to IVs and beeping machines in a hospital? Or how about a single father working hard to make a good living, earning promotions along the way, who is also profoundly devoted to his children? These are admirable people, but do you call them ambitious? Do we, as individuals and as a collective society, consider them successful? Should we?

In a global study funded by the US National Science Foundation, 7,000 people from 27 countries were surveyed about "what matters most to them."[2] In countries as diverse as Australia and Bulgaria, Thailand and

The Caregiving Ambition. Julia B. Bear and Todd L. Pittinsky, Oxford University Press. © Oxford University Press 2022.
DOI: 10.1093/oso/9780197512418.003.0001

Uganda, a unifying thread was found: The majority of respondents reported that caring for family members was their *top* priority. The study's senior researcher, Douglas Kenrick, summarized the findings: "Everybody cares about their family and loved ones the most, which, surprisingly, hasn't been as carefully studied as a motivator of human behavior."[3]

And it's good they care that much. This research also found that people who rate family caring and long-term relationships as the most important features of their lives also report the highest sense of well-being. The researchers concluded that people "really . . . are happiest taking care of the people they already have."[4] Other studies have confirmed that, under the right circumstances, caregiving helps not only care recipients but also caregivers, who experience reduced stress, increased social connectedness, and even increased overall happiness.[5]

Caregivers also generally report high satisfaction, sources of which include personal growth, feelings of giving back, knowing loved ones are getting excellent care, and increased meaning and purpose in life. A study by the National Opinion Research Center found that 83% of caregivers believed it to be a positive experience.[6] To put that figure in context, a 2019 Conference Board Study found that just 54% of US workers were satisfied with their jobs. And that 54% was a two-decade high point![7]

Further, caregivers often report feelings of great self-worth, accomplishment, and joy in caring for loved ones. More intense caregiving relationships also often lead to closer family bonds between the generations. As Kim, a 41-year-old wife, mother, and caregiver to her own mother, explained, caregiving takes her relationships to a "different, deeper level."[8]

Beyond benefits to any individual caregiver or beneficiary, caregiving is essential for maintaining the social fabric and building human capital. The quantity and quality of caregiving in a society are therefore much better indicators of that society's quality of life than its gross domestic product or any stock index. Former US first lady Rosalynn Carter astutely observed, "there are only four kinds of people in the world—those who have been caregivers, those who are currently caregivers, those who will be caregivers and those who will need caregivers."[9]

Still, in contemporary US culture, caregiving is commonly construed as a duty, an obligation, or a responsibility. Yet many people don't experience it that way at all. They don't go through all the work of raising their children or helping raise their grandchildren or taking care of their elderly parents simply because they have to, even if they recognize that they have to. Nor do they do so simply out of instinct, although they might agree that it can feel instinctive.

Rather, they do it because it is an *ambition*. They want to do it—and do it well—for its own sake. They don't just want an older relative in need of care to be bathed, fed, and rotated; they want them to be cared for as well as possible, and they want to be the ones providing that care or at least a large portion of it. Ambition is "enthusiasm with a purpose."[10] As Vince, a father of two, shared, "For me, it is a passion more than just an obligation. I'm certainly aware of societal expectations for parenthood, but I also have a deep desire to provide a good, safe and happy childhood for my kids . . . above and beyond what I 'must' do." Asia, a mother of four, recognized the obligation but, like Vince, explained her personal passions and ambitions for caregiving as more than an obligation: "For me, it's an obligation, of course, but much more, caregiving is something I desire to do very well."

Oftentimes, caring ambitiously is part and parcel of loving someone, but it doesn't have to be; many people are driven by a strong *caregiving ambition*, "an individual's aspirations to nurture and care for others above and beyond any obligation."[11]

Unfortunately, caregiving ambition in our society is seriously and systemically undervalued. That goes for both paid and unpaid caregiving. As individuals, we know, for example, that doing our best for our children is probably the finest thing we'll ever do. And at points, most of us are profoundly grateful for the care we might receive from a nurse, doctor, social worker, or member of the clergy or even from a stranger who gives us directions and offers to lead the way if we're lost and late. But at the collective level, many aspects of contemporary life—the frantic pace, workplace policies, unequal access to healthcare, and much more—push in the direction of undervaluing caregiving, placing value mainly on careers and material well-being.

This undervaluation has deep historical and economic roots. The separation of work and home that we take for granted is an artifact of the Industrial Revolution. With the rise of factory production, caregiving and work were separated not only by location but also by gender, which served the new manufacturing and economic model that prioritized industrial output—the result of so-called men's work—over the economically unquantifiable activities of caregiving—so-called women's work.

The undervaluation of caregiving leads naturally to the undervaluation of the caregiving ambition. This, in turn, has great social consequence, including the co-opting of the work–life "revolution" by corporations and other workplaces. The work–life movement, in general, has sought to help individuals experience less conflict between their work and life and sometimes, even more ambitiously, perhaps to find synergies between different domains. Efforts have been made to help workplaces evolve to be more supportive of employees' non-work ambitions, such as focusing on their relationships with family and friends, becoming meaningful members of their communities, and simply having time and energy to do things they enjoy.

Still, many continue to experience work–life conflict and, more specifically, work–care conflict. Jobs and careers are at odds not just with favorite hobbies or pastimes but with the very ability to care for loved ones. In work–care conflict, the demands of work interfere with the demands of caregiving and vice versa. Simply put, the work–life movement's efforts to help workers reduce work–care conflict are not focused on people who are ambitious about their caregiving—instead, they are designed to advance the bottom-line interests of corporations.

The social imperative to fully and ambitiously pursue career ambition while merely managing caregiving leaves many people feeling stuck. It is not that they can't meet basic caregiving obligations while aggressively pursuing their career ambitions—that's certainly a struggle, but it can be done. Rather, they cannot aggressively fulfill career ambitions while also fulfilling caregiving ambitions. The more society tries to categorize—and limit—caregiving as an obligation rather than as an ambition, the more it rings false and the harder it becomes to fulfill either type of ambition.

Women, in particular, often feel they are battling themselves, trying to balance their career ambitions and caregiving ambitions, while their employers and their governments only recognize the former, which helps explain the persistently low representation of women in business and political leadership. As more and more men—millennials, in particular—seek to be more to their families than just the breadwinner, they find themselves in a similar battle.

The work–life movement and the bevy of human resources managers, researchers, and consultants who are part of it will remain stuck in place—as will the gender gaps in leadership—if we don't take people's caregiving ambitions seriously. This goes for men as well as women. Society has loosened up somewhat with respect to men as caregivers. Yet there is a long way to go toward recognizing not just the obligations of, say, a single father, but his caregiving ambition, which may equal or even surpass a very strong career ambition.

Caregiving ambition is a general characteristic of humanity. Most of us have seen how caregiving can powerfully inform our own and others' lives and decisions—the "lived experience" of caring ambitiously for others. Yet we have become so cynical about caring for others that those who do can be objects of satire and ridicule. Consider the crazed "tiger mom" stereotype or the trope of the father loaded down with expensive baby paraphernalia, well intentioned but ridiculous. Understanding and honoring caregiving for what it truly is—an ambition—is the ambitious goal of this book.

AMBITION, NOT JUST OBLIGATION

Society's failure to acknowledge caregiving as an ambition has created real consequences, including a troubling lack of caregiving for each other, stubborn gender gaps in leadership, and widespread dissatisfaction with life.

Career advice books—for women, in particular—rarely acknowledge that many people have aspirations for how they care for others. These relationships are all cast as attachments and anchors, dead weights to what we're told should be our sole ambition: soaring careers. Such books tell only half the work–care story and leave many readers still struggling to pursue a caregiving ambition that the world around them insists is only a chore.

This book is different. We push beyond the "mommy wars" that divide women by how they care, uniting them instead on why and how much they care. And we provide a more honest account of today's working fathers and sons: men with career ambitions, yes, but also ambitious in their parenting and other human connections.

Through our firsthand quantitative and qualitative empirical research and the wealth of research we have reviewed, we bring together psychological theories and cutting-edge management research to recognize the existence and importance of caregiving ambition—a recognition that can make our individual and collective lives more humane and caring.

About the Authors

This book is a collaboration of two researchers who have studied career and organizational dynamics for decades. Though we certainly do not think identically, we both felt that our work–care stories and challenges were being overlooked in the common framing of caregiving as a duty, not as a passionate ambition. The book is informed by a range of personal and professional experiences and activities.

Past Research

Our past research set the stage for this book. Julia's has focused on gender differences in negotiation and on gender gaps in organizations. Time and again, she has been struck by the extent to which what we think of as gender differences in career experience can be explained by differences in caregiving roles. Julia has done this work first as a doctoral student in organizational behavior at Carnegie Mellon University and now as associate professor at Stony Brook University (State University of New York [SUNY]) in the College of Business.

Todd's research has focused on positive social relations at work and on the latent possibilities for more positive experience in groups and organizations. He has a long-standing interest in the work–care nexus; indeed, his first research position was at the New York Families and Work Institute, and he later co-authored *Working Fathers*, one of the earlier studies of men's experiences as caregivers. Todd studied organizational behavior at Harvard University, taught there for 10 years, and now is a professor at Stony Brook University (SUNY) in the College of Engineering and Applied Sciences.

Research for the Book

Together, we conducted research specifically to examine caregiving ambition, involving surveys, which were then analyzed quantitatively; interviews, which were then analyzed qualitatively; and a review of archival data.

Conversations with and Observations of Friends, Family, Co-Workers, and Neighbors

We've also been talking about this topic with anyone and everyone—friends, family, co-workers, neighbors—and we have found that people like to discuss it. Through these conversations we observed points of consensus and disagreement, which have also informed this book (see the Appendix for details of the caregivers whose reflections are included in the book).

WHAT DO WE MEAN BY CAREGIVING IN THIS BOOK?

If caregiving ambition is the ambition to give care as excellently as possible because one wants to, rather than satisficing out of rote duty or obligation, what do we mean by caregiving?

Caregiving, by any definition, is the social, emotional, spiritual, and/ or physical care of another. In our definition, it involves not only tending to the needs or concerns of another person but also an emotional attachment and suggests a long-standing relationship. Caregiving is alternatively—and sometimes simultaneously—exciting, exhausting, ennobling, frustrating, stressful, tiring, rewarding, and taxing. It strains our bodies and our minds and—most caregivers will say—our patience, too. Sometimes it pushes too far; the needs of the care recipient can exceed the capacity of even the most devoted and skilled caregiver, which makes caregiving so challenging in general and even more so when one does it ambitiously.

In our usage in this book, a "caregiver" is generally an unpaid caregiver, caring for others in their family and/or social network. We recognize— and know full well from our own experience—that paid caregivers are often ambitious caregivers, giving love as well as care.

While they share characteristics, it is important to think too about the differences between paid and unpaid caregiving. Unpaid caregiving does not require any formal certifications, training, or degrees. Unpaid caregivers have a higher degree of autonomy. There is some risk here of being incompetent, but in most cases, the bulk of what makes up caregiving is well within an ordinary person's ability to figure out or to learn informally from someone who already knows. Caregivers developed their own styles of caregiving in response to their own experiences, their own abilities and orientations, the particular care recipients, and their own social and economic context.

In our society, unpaid work is less visible than paid work. People who take on unpaid care—especially women, on whom emotional caregiving often disproportionately falls—can be taken for granted. Family and friends may not grasp how time-consuming or stressful the care is.

So, while at points we will discuss paid caregivers, our primary concern is unpaid caregivers and the policies (social, corporate policies) that can help those engaged in non-caregiving occupations also be ambitious caregivers.

WIRED TO CARE

Caregiving is central to who we are as individuals and as a society. Evolution itself plays a role in this centrality. Human infants are helpless for much longer than those of other species, and they take much longer to mature fully. With very few exceptions, we humans cannot survive alone. For hundreds of thousands of years, therefore, we have lived in groups. Those who were good at forming and keeping relationships and at caring for one another were more likely to survive—securing food was a collective activity—and pass their genes on to the next generation.

Humans developed mechanisms to ensure that caregiving can be emotionally pleasurable, including a natural capacity—a desire, even—to care for others. This capacity now extends beyond one's own children to include other family members, friends, acquaintances, and sometimes even strangers. So, we do not just "give care"—we care for others with intention, investment, aspiration, and diligence.[12]

Overwhelming evidence shows that humans have a need to belong to a social group.[13] The ability and willingness to care for others are certainly advantages, and often necessities, for group acceptance. Such acceptance is, in turn, good for us. Many studies have confirmed that parenthood, marriage, and social integration—all of which involve caregiving in some form—are "robustly associated with greater longevity."[14]

Recent neuroimaging studies have also demonstrated how specific brain regions are more active during caregiving. In one experiment, some participants held a romantic partner's arm while the partner endured a series of uncomfortable shocks. Those who provided emotional support showed increased activity in the neural regions associated with pleasure

and reward.[15] Other neuroscience experiments have found increased activity in the neurochemistry of happiness when people give money to
help others rather than win money for themselves.[16] In an experiment
conducted by Tristen Inagaki and Naomi Eisenberger at the University of
California–Los Angeles, participants were asked to write either a caring,
supportive note to a friend in need, or about a neutral topic. Participants
who were asked to help out a friend, through the note, experienced a significant reduction in stress.

When we feel excluded from a group, we become stressed. Socially isolated young men occasionally become not only stressed but angry and
even violent. A study of deadly school shootings in the United States
found that 13 of the 15 shooters experienced chronic rejection by peers
and felt profound social isolation.[17]

A GLOBAL CORONAVIRUS CRISIS
DISRUPTS CAREGIVING

In the late winter and spring of 2020, a novel coronavirus, COVID-19,
turned life upside down in most parts of the world. And it had a profound
effect on the ways, and even degrees, to which we could care for each
other. As this public health crisis transformed into a battle, established
patterns of caregiving became collateral damage. For example, as coronavirus cases in eldercare facilities surged, some made the difficult decision
to bring their loved ones home—to care for them in person as best they
could rather than leave them professionally cared for but isolated—even if
doctors felt they weren't ready to be discharged.[18]

In the meantime, more and more of us became unsettled due to social distancing restrictions—parents unable to visit their children,
grandparents unable to visit their grandchildren, home health aides unable to visit those they cared for. Employees who could work from home
now had to both care for and educate their children. Many parents who
already found it hard to juggle parenting and work were now spending
a lot more time parenting. Partners and families of those infected with

coronavirus needed to self-quarantine, physically isolating themselves from their loved ones, just when they most needed companionship and comfort.

Yet we also saw so much caregiving above and beyond the call of duty, from supermarket workers to parents to medical personnel, keeping the world working as well as it could. If one has to find a silver lining amid all the heartbreak and exhaustion of the first wave of the COVID-19 pandemic and its aftermath, it might be how it pushed caregiving into the headlines and public conversation—not just the fact of caregiving as central to society but how important caring for others, and being cared for, is in our lives, how it helps us feel "right" and well in the world. In a culture that, on its surface, celebrates material, career success above all else, this was profound. For a moment, at least, we could see caregiving as not simply an obligation but a powerful ambition, leading us to rethink and revalue how we care for others. How specifically?

First, we may (finally) re-evaluate our paid caregivers, such as child care providers and home health aides—some of whom are given so little in remuneration, benefits, or insurance—economically. Second, we might also see greater flexibility in—and more acceptance of—working from home. While companies love to tout flexibility to help workers both work and care, the reality before the COVID-19 pandemic was usually quite different. Research finds that people who ask for flexible schedules are sidelined (and, yes, they tend to be overwhelmingly women with young children) and that flexibility policies tend to be underused. The pandemic made telecommuting necessary, so using these policies may now be viewed more widely as a way to simultaneously fulfill one's caregiving and career ambitions. It turns out that being seen with a baby on your lap during a Zoom meeting is not the career-killer it was once portrayed to be. In fact, during the pandemic, videos of children interrupting their parents' work often went viral.

Third, people may have a harder time now pretending that jobs and careers alone are paramount. This virus has shown us something basic and true about ourselves: Our families and dearest friends are the most important people in our lives, and we need to act like it. We might take care of each other more now that we've seen how admirable and possible that is, while also recognizing what it's like to suddenly lose our caregiving capabilities, whether directly or indirectly. Many people—probably most—will be glad to turn teaching and nursing back over to teachers and nursing homes as soon as possible, but there may also be an increase in homeschooling and in-home eldercare. We might begin leaning toward a more caring society.

But regardless of how we collectively respond to COVID-19's long-term effects, one thing will not change: Many people will still be ambitious in their caregiving. And if the pandemic has taught us anything, it's that caregiving needs to be valued and that caregivers need to be supported.

THE TRUE COST OF CARING

The forces of capitalism and feminism—not normally seen as jointly responsible for anything—have unwittingly combined to force caregiving into its current devalued and too often stigmatized position. As sociologist Joan Acker observed, employers "assume a disembodied and universal worker." The closest thing to this ideal is a mythical "male worker whose life centers on his full-time, life-long job, while his wife or another woman takes care of his personal needs,"[19] including children, aging parents, or other dependents. The corporate point of view has always been that workers should find the most efficient way to get caregiving done—often via outsourcing to others—without letting it affect their paid work.

The entry of greater numbers of women into the paid workforce in the 1960s provided a new talent pool, adding a new dimension to the ideal mythical worker. Since then, it has become advantageous to employers to acknowledge women's long-suppressed career ambitions, while categorizing childrearing as simply an obligation to be outsourced. The drive to create more equality for women in the working world has not been matched by a drive to create greater participation among men in caregiving or a drive more generally to fulfill the caregiving vacuum that has ensued.

Thus, as individuals and as a society, we are left woefully unprepared for the reality of caregiving ambition. There is no generally accepted frame of understanding for caregiving as an ambition that can hold its own—legally, economically, and politically—with financial and professional success.

Ambitions generally come at great personal cost, and caregiving ambition is no exception. For example, there is often a financial strain. Taking care of someone needy—or hiring others to do so—can be expensive to the point of bankruptcy. In addition to direct expenses, there is the income lost by working fewer hours, taking a leave of absence, forgoing extra education, or even turning down a promotion or relocation. Lost career opportunities may in turn cause losses in health insurance, retirement savings, and eventual Social Security earnings.

In addition, many people feel—and may well be—ill-prepared for their caregiving responsibilities. Unless we specifically pursue one of the caring professions, we are never formally taught how to take care of others. If we're lucky, we've had a good example in our own family; but that is more likely an example of character—patience, resolve, good humor—than of specific skills, such as administering injections or figuring out what a person with dementia is trying to say.

Of course, many ambitious caregivers come to feel stressed or overwhelmed, even those with professional training and experience. Those who are giving care on top of their other responsibilities often feel they don't have enough time in the day to get everything done—certainly not to do it all as well as they intend. As Crystal, a mother of one, explains, "I believe that it [my caregiving] is a passion . . . but of course sometimes I just feel overwhelmed, too"

Ambitious caregivers may find it hard to also take care of themselves, with consequences that can range from annoying to life-threatening. Ambitious caregiving is likely to make it more difficult—or impossible—to keep up certain relationships with friends and even with family members. Despite the fact that, as we mentioned, caregivers generally report being happy and satisfied with their roles, it's no wonder that research finds that caregivers are more susceptible to depression and anxiety than non-caregivers.[20]

CAREGIVING: PROFOUNDLY CHALLENGING, DEEPLY
REWARDING, AMBITIOUSLY DONE

It would be dangerous and wrong to interpret a discussion of caregiving ambition as an effort to romanticize something that is, in the end, profoundly challenging. Caregiving has good days; it has many bad days as well. It has beautiful moments but also heart-wrenching and even horrific ones. But it is just as dangerous and wrong to tolerate the notion that our careers are the most meaningful activities in our lives. It's simply not true that our roles and experiences as caregivers are less meaningful than our roles and experiences as moneymakers.

But the central concern of this book is not to arbitrate which sphere is more important. Our concern is to stop, once and for all, the silly and sometimes harmful notion that caregivers are just "doers" who go about their caregiving with no particular standards, passion, verve, or agency. People do not give care with apathy—they care ambitiously.

A NOTE ON DIVERSITY AND THE UNIVERSALITY
OF CAREGIVERS AND CAREGIVING

Different types of caregiving are experienced differently. When we speak of caregiving in general, we are discussing child care primarily and eldercare secondarily, though of course there are many other varieties, such as caring for those with chronic illnesses and disabilities. Child care is often pursued with a future life in mind, while eldercare is often pursued with the end of life in mind.

Caregiving, as a central human experience, transcends specific cultural and economic forces but is also inevitably, and powerfully, shaped by them. Race, class, ethnicity, religion, gender, sexual orientation, and family formation (such as nuclear, single, or extended) all play powerful roles. An African American single father will have very different caregiving experiences from a White single father. A lesbian White mother will have different experiences from a straight Latinx one. Though different circumstances change the nature of caregiving, *they do not change the ambition caregivers bring to it*. Simply put, we believe—and have found in our research—that caregiving ambition is widespread.

To be sure, one of the most profound differences in caregiving experiences is found in socioeconomic class.[21] We discuss a range of occupations in the book, but we focus on white-collar work. The demands of blue-collar work and their implications for working and caring are quite different. Economic class informs the discussion because it dictates not only the kind of work one is likely to do but also the kinds of support and the benefits available. Class also informs approaches to combining working and caring. Women from working-class or lower-middle-class backgrounds, for example, traditionally have not had the option to radically question how they integrate working and caring.

Throughout the book, we introduce you to a diverse cast of people caring and working. We hope this book will spark future research that will directly examine the ways caregiving ambition is common across groups, as well as surface the ways it is experienced uniquely in different identity groups and by individuals living at the intersection of different identity groups.

ROADMAP FOR THIS BOOK

Before we move on to Chapter 1, let's take a quick look, chapter by chapter, at where this book is headed and what it has to offer you.

Part I, "The Caregiving Ambition" (Chapters 1–3), is a deep dive into the widespread but seldom acknowledged phenomenon of caregiving ambition.

Chapter 1, "An Abundance of Ambition," shows that the defining problem of working people with dependents, whether children, spouses, parents, or others, is not insufficient devotion to one's career. Instead, for most, the problem lies in an abundance of ambition: plenty of career ambition but just as much—or even more—caregiving ambition. We delve into the psychology of ambition and consider how broadening our view of ambition to include caregiving and relationships can also lead to greater valuation of caregiving.

Chapter 2, "Why Work–Life Won't Work," explains how and why the work–life movement claims to be about supporting caregiving yet manages to sidestep caregiving ambition. Within the professional field of work–life, and among those who focus more specifically on work–care programs, caregiving is conceptualized only as an obligation. Not surprisingly, these programs have not moved the dial significantly on work–care conflict. We discuss how recognizing caregiving ambition can shed light on the limitations of this short-sighted work–life agenda.

Chapter 3, "Providing, Not Just Provisioning," clarifies two modes of caregiving. Caregiving can be provided directly or provisioned—that is, arranged for someone else to provide. Both modes have their places, and people have ambitions concerning both. Moreover, it is important to clarify the distinction between the two—and the key role of ambition to provide care directly—to understand the challenges of managing working and caring. In fact, we delineate how this distinction is at the heart of work–care conflict and the tough choices that parents, in particular, face about child care and fulfilling caregiving ambition.

Part II, "Why Care?" (Chapters 4–6), makes the case that, as a society, we need to address the implications of caregiving ambition now. We are already suffering some of the consequences of having ignored this ambition for so long, and the resulting problems will only get worse the longer they go unresolved.

Chapter 4, "Careless," gives a stark picture of the world we face if current trends continue. There is less and less emphasis on caregiving. We neglect caregiving for children and older adults and, indeed, among all of us, as evidenced in the growing epidemic of loneliness and isolation.

Chapter 5, "The Stubborn Caregiving Gaps," delves into how caregiving, not gender, underlies gaps between men and women in pay and career advancement. We review extensive research on these gaps, which reveals that conceptualizing caregiving as an ambition can help achieve gender equality, whereas treating it as an obligation will not. Right now, caregiving ambition is central to why women don't get ahead. This obstacle can't be removed until it is given proper attention.

Chapter 6, "The Robots Are Coming," examines a caregiving "solution" that is rising up all around us, though many of us are still hardly aware of it—artificial intelligence–powered robots. Robots can—and already do—have their uses in caregiving, but they are far from a "solution" to the "problem" of caring. Though there are a number of issues inherent in this type of care, one of the underlying problems is that using robots entirely bypasses the particular resources that people bring to caregiving.

Part III, "Taking Care" (Chapters 7–9), looks constructively to the future. Where should we go, and how can we get there from here?

Chapter 7, "A 'Freedom-To' Work–Care Agenda," shows how corporate policies prioritize only one category of response to work–care conflict and proposes new and different policies to address caregiving ambition. Work–life policies and programs are based on categorizing caregiving as an obligation, not as an ambition, and therefore focus on helping employees provision care, not provide it directly, even if this is what many of them want to do. This unnecessarily narrow approach is woefully insufficient and perpetuates an already unsatisfactory status quo. At its core, the work–life movement's efforts to reduce work–care conflict are aligned with the employer, who has a much easier time arguing for accommodations that afford freedom from caregiving than for those that afford freedom to be an ambitious caregiver while also being a valuable employee.

Chapter 8, "The Case Against the Business Case," debunks the so-called business case for work–life, demonstrating how it paradoxically undermines progress. In fact, the business case is not new. Historically we have seen it played out from the company towns of the Industrial Revolution to the spike in women's employment during World War II (with government-sponsored child care to boot) to the corporate benefits programs that cropped up in the early 1980s. Yet the business case rests on a category error, namely that supporting caregiving is, and must be (to be justified), good for the bottom line. The chapter then argues for putting an end to the business case and replacing it with a humanistic case.

Chapter 9, "Lessons for Living Ambitiously," offers our advice on how to live ambitiously both for one's caregiving and for one's career. We offer four principles and three options for fulfilling one's ambitions across these domains. Our suggestions are based on our research, interviews, and observations.

Finally, the Conclusion, "Caregiving as the Passion Project," invites the reader to consider how, in an age in which we are constantly told to find and pursue our passion projects, the most obvious one—organizing a life in which our natural caregiving ambition is given full scope—is still hiding in plain sight.

We provide this roadmap with the hope that you will use it in your own journey through the book. We encourage you to direct your attention to chapters that are most engaging to you now. You may read a few chapters and put the book down but then return to it as your work and caregiving journey changes.

You will notice that each chapter—including this Introduction—ends with a few "Defining Questions." Don't worry, they don't constitute a quiz, and you probably can't answer them right off the bat. Rather, these are some of the really big questions about our society's values that we want you to consider as you read the book. As a society, we rarely discuss them, but we have written this book to help you think about them. We call them "defining questions" because your own individual answers define who you are and your relationships with others. At the same time, how we answer them as a society shapes our collective well-being. We encourage you to think about these questions and to discuss them with your co-workers and your friends. Only then can we begin the process of becoming collectively more ambitious about caregiving.

DEFINING QUESTIONS

- When you think of your caregiving for others, do you believe you have provided care with ambition or only out of duty or obligation?

- Whom do you remember more, your role models at work or those who have cared for you?
- As you start reading this book, what do you most hope to gain from it?

PART I

The Caregiving Ambition

An Abundance of Ambition

America has historically been and continues to be a nation driven
principally by ambition.

—W. C. KING[1]

WHAT IS AMBITION?

When people hear the word "ambition" they typically think of striving
for some type of professional achievement—and they're not necessarily
wrong to do so. Defined as "a strong desire to do or achieve something,"
ambition is associated with motivation and undergirds people's goals.[2]
Ambitious people tend to display certain personality traits, including
extraversion, conscientiousness, and emotional stability.[3] People with ambition also tend to display certain types of behaviors. For example, they
are typically assertive and achievement-oriented.[4] Not surprisingly, they
are more likely to achieve success in terms of education level, career pres-
tige, and income than their less ambitious peers.[5] So, ambition and professional achievement are, indeed, closely linked.

It's therefore not surprising that when thinking about ambition,
someone like Bill Gates is more likely to jump to mind than, say, Mother
Teresa or the chair of our local Parent–Teacher Association. However, it
is puzzling that we tend to think about ambition solely in terms of career
if we take a more holistic perspective on life. People are motivated toward

The Caregiving Ambition. Julia B. Bear and Todd L. Pittinsky, Oxford University Press. © Oxford University Press 2022.
DOI: 10.1093/oso/9780197512418.003.0002

goals and success across a variety of domains in which they find meaning, not just at the office or on the job site. According to Freud, there are two fundamental sources of meaning, the first of which is work. The second source, however, is love.[6] And it's possible to see how love manifests itself in adulthood through our desire to take care of those whom we love. We find this desire in our daily actions but also in popular psychological models and theories.

For example, Erik Erikson's model of the stages of human development outlined the two primary stages of adulthood—intimacy and generativity. Both stages involve goals and aims concerning caring for others.[7] Erikson's intimacy stage is broadly defined as forming intimate and loving relationships with others, and the generativity stage is broadly defined as leaving a legacy through caring for and nurturing the next generation. The former becomes prominent in early adulthood, and the latter becomes prominent in mid- to late adulthood. Generativity is fulfilled across a variety of domains, including work and family but also community engagement. Erikson shows that forming and maintaining relationships are paramount to the adult experience.

Another example comes from the prominent early 20th-century psychologist Abraham Maslow, who created a five-level hierarchy of needs as a way to explain what motivates people, with relational needs on level three and self-actualization on the highest level.[8] Although lacking in empirical support, Maslow's hierarchy remains widely popular because of its intuitive logic—it rings true with people. More recently, however, evolutionary psychologists have questioned the placement of self-actualization and relational needs in the hierarchy. They argue that procreative goals, such as finding a partner and having children, should be at the top, *not* self-actualization, stating "the top of our hierarchy is defined by taking care of others—not pursuing that which gives one idiosyncratic pleasure [self-actualization]."[9] This rethinking of Maslow's hierarchy conceptualizes caregiving—in the context of reproductive goals and childrearing—as a central life goal.

Other psychologists likewise have recognized belongingness and attachment to others in relationships as central human needs people seek to fulfill, just as they seek to fulfill needs related to work and professional goals.[10] Gilbert Brim, psychologist and author of *Ambition: How We Manage Success and Failure Throughout Our Lives*, discusses how ambition, in fact, relates to various life domains: "We have a basic drive for growth and mastery that is expressed in a variety of specific ambitions. The goals we seek [through ambitions] may be diverse—health, creativity, money, intimacy, helping others, doing good, and many more—but we are propelled by the same operating energy that is distinctive of humanity."[11]

Note that Brim doesn't even mention work, something that many of us likely assume would get top billing in a definition of ambition. However, for the most part, today ambition is studied and considered in the professional domain. As a society, we also reward ambition at work and in our careers. Interestingly, however, the tendency to laud ambitious individuals and their career successes is a relatively recent phenomenon—competitive, achievement-oriented, and hard-working go-getters with big plans weren't always seen in the same positive light that we tend to shine upon them today. Historically, ambition was viewed negatively more than virtuously.[12]

How Are People Ambitious About Caregiving?

As discussed, ambition results in part from a human need for growth and achievement. Developing relationships and creating connections with others are also fundamental human needs. If people so strongly yearn for connection, they must also want to behave in ways that create connections. But these connections do not appear out of thin air: They are built and nurtured via the act of caregiving. Therefore, it's logical that to fulfill our specific human needs, people must have aspirations and goals about how they give care.

Thus, although some people are so ambitious about their work that they view it as central to their identity, many are equally ambitious about their caregiving, considering it one of the most meaningful parts of life. Indeed, people around the world rate "taking care of a child/children" and "spending time with and helping parents, siblings, or other relatives" as their most important life goals, more so than professional status.[13] Moreover, for some, caregiving, and raising children in particular, is not to be taken for granted. As Alicia, a mother of one, explained, "It [caregiving] is a passion because I worked hard to get my child. I went through IVF and that was work just to have and care for my own child."

In a study of life goals among college students, relationship goals received the highest mean importance rating, higher than career goals. Social and religious life goals also were rated as highly important.[14] Thus, even by late adolescence, people have developed goals beyond just earning money or career advancement. When we asked hundreds of undergraduate students to envision their lives in 10 years and describe their goals for caregiving, they listed a variety of ambitions, including taking care of their future spouse and children, parents and grandparents, friends, siblings, and pets.

In a separate survey, we also asked several hundred adults about their life ambitions. Among respondents, 68% reported that their ambitions concerned both family and career. A smaller percentage reported ambitions only about career (30%), and a much smaller percentage reported ambitions about family only (2%). When asked directly if caregiving is more of a duty or more of a goal, we found that almost two thirds of respondents rated their caregiving as a goal. The bottom line? Most people are ambitious about both their families and their career.

Caregiving ambition, as we mentioned in the Introduction, is defined as the desire and aspiration to nurture and care for others above and beyond any obligation. Caregiving ambition has distinct emotional, cognitive, and behavioral components. Caregiving ambition is felt on a visceral, emotional level; and these emotions are a fundamental part of the desire to care for others. Although people talk about the drudgery of changing diapers and performing chores, they also recount the joy and meaning that their caregiving brings.[15] Jamal, a father of one, put it this way: "Caring for my children can be defined by so many statements that some seem to be understatements at times. . . . I love seeing my children happy, providing for them what they want and allowing them [to] live a good life, that alone gives me much happiness." From a cognitive perspective, people report thinking a great deal about and planning how to fulfill their caregiving ambition. From a behavioral perspective, caregiving ambition is fulfilled through both direct and indirect caregiving (more about that in Chapter 3).

To be clear, caregiving ambition is not just caregiving, in the same way that career ambition is not just the equivalent of going to work and climbing up a career ladder. Ambition more broadly involves the desire to achieve. Just as career ambition is a motive with emotional, cognitive, and behavioral components involving feelings, thoughts, and behaviors concerning advancement and achievement in one's career, caregiving ambition also involves feelings, thoughts, and behaviors all related to goals and aspirations about taking care of and nurturing others. The quotes in this chapter help to illustrate how people feel, think, and act in terms of caregiving ambition.

As mentioned in the Introduction, we surveyed diverse adults from across the United States about their caregiving ambition.[16] By far the most popular topic that respondents raised for their caregiving ambitions was caring for their children, but they also described their goals in caring for their parents, as well as their friends and neighbors. Here's a representative sample of what people had to say.

CAREGIVING AMBITION FOR CHILDREN

Most of the descriptions of caring for children concerned both emotional care and physical expressions of that care—such as cooking and cleaning—with the aim of nurturing their kids:

- "I plan on being around long enough to make sure my daughter makes it through high school and on into college with the tools and ambition she needs to succeed. Every day after school, she and I talk about her day. She writes down a short summary about each class, and we plan out her homework. This should give her a proper work ethic, and a way to be able to manage her time appropriately." (Michael, father of one)

- "I want to be the best mother I possibly can. There is nothing more important to me than my children. I want them to be well fed, clothed, and to be able to have fun activities. When they're happy, I'm happy, and that is how it should be. Being a mother is very important to me and there is nothing I would ever do to change that. Making sure that my kids are well taken care of is a huge part of my life. And it will always be, even when they are out of the house." (Jessica, mother of four)

- "I am a working Mom to 5 children. 4 girls between the ages of 13 and 5. I also have a 3 year old son. My goals are to show them strength and a hardworking spirit. . . . I also hope to start spending more individual time with each of them. I do all the emotional labor with regards to child rearing and I want to have a special connection with each of them." (Diana, mother of five)

- "I hope to teach my children to be strong and independent. When it comes to my kids and my husband, I want to give them good meals, a clean house and a place they know they are always welcome and loved. I want my kids to know their friends are always welcome here. When it is a holiday I like everything to be 'just so.' I want everyone to have their favorite dishes, and I make sure to continue with their favorite traditions. I guess I am trying to give them the best of everything. Raise them to be smart and independent, but know home is a place they will always feel secure." (Michelle, mother of two)

- "I am homeschooling my children. I am hoping to have success and not have to put them in a school where I worry all the time for their safety. My son has special needs, so I need to work with his therapist and learn the best ways to care for him to give him the best chance at a successful, productive life." (Sarah, mother of four)

Caregiving Ambition for Parents and Older Relatives

Those respondents who mentioned ambitions concerning eldercare described focusing on making their older relatives' and parents' lives easier and emotionally richer. Some reported relocating to give care, as well as intentionally trying to keep their relatives at home rather than using institutionalized care:

- "I hope that my mother . . . feels well cared for, loved, important, and that she has an advocate always on her side in all circumstances. I hope she is aware of how much I love her and does not feel like she is a burden but understands that it is something I want and love to do." (Lydia)
- "My parents are getting old and having a harder and harder time functioning. I recently moved in with them to care for them as their health starts to have issues. My goal would be to make their lives a little easier in their golden years." (David)
- "My wife's father is ill. . . . We spend a lot of time taking care of him, and making sure our 16 month old daughter, his only grandchild, spends a lot of time with her grandpa. I just want them to bond now while they can." (John)
- "Right now we are caring for my grandfather. I hope to keep him happy and healthy for as long as possible, and to try to keep him out of a nursing home." (Susan)
- "My grandmother is getting on in years, so I am preparing myself to take on full care-giving responsibilities fairly soon. My ambition in this regard is to make sure my grandmother is as comfortable as possible in her final time on this Earth. I hope to achieve this through giving her constant attention and near round the clock care." (Jared)
- "It's really quite amazing, as I start to assume more responsibility for my mother, she continues to care for me. Helping her to maintain her independence is a lot of work, but also peppered with times of great joy and laughter." (Yaacov)

CAREGIVING AMBITION FOR FRIENDS AND COMMUNITY

People often immediately think of family when it comes to caregiving, but those respondents who reported ambitions about caring for their friends or other people in the community were, at times, just as passionate about their commitments as those who focused on their children, parents, and older relatives:

- "I am helping my friend . . . who is in stage 4 breast cancer. I take her to appointments, I run errands when she is not feeling up to it, and I take her on errands when she does feel like it. I recently stayed overnight with her in the hospital for several days. Her children that are here in town both work but they do their fair share. Thankfully, I am retired and have the time and desire to lend a hand. I hope to continue to be of service to her until she no longer needs my help." (Tom)

- "I am not young, but I have friends that are 15–20 years older than me. They've been a God-send when I've needed them through knee surgeries. I plan on being there for them 100% if they need me in any crisis that may arise, such as health or in any other way." (Aaliyah)

- "My best friend was diagnosed with leukemia two weeks ago. She has been in the hospital for a week receiving chemo. When she comes home in three weeks, I will be providing care for her . . . helping her with all her daily needs including running errands for prescriptions and groceries until she is able to do so herself which will be quite some time. I have done this for others so I will do my best to provide her with comfort and a positive attitude on my part to get her well again." (Lauren)

When it comes to caregiving, people have well-articulated, thoughtful goals. They are ambitious. We read response after response along these lines. Though most respondents describe fulfilling their caregiving ambitions primarily in the context of their families, many also do so in the context of friends and community as well. People who are ambitious about giving care in one aspect of their lives are likely ambitious to give care in other areas. Respondents also brought up caring for their colleagues and co-workers in various ways and volunteering for community organizations. Simply put, as found in our research and that of others, there is no shortage of caregiving ambition. That said, how we give care and how others receive it are not always cut and dried.

Fruits of Caregiving Ambition

While often influenced by a variety of external factors, career ambition is defined and measured within a single individual. Caregiving ambition, on the other hand, does not involve just one person—it can only be expressed and fulfilled through another, a care recipient. Although caregiving and career ambitions involve similar processes—such as effort and time spent pursuing goals—caregiving ambition is different. This ambition more directly involves other people, rather than just individual goals and aspirations. The results of caregiving ambition are dependent not just on the caregivers themselves but on the people they're giving care to as well.

Someone who is high in caregiving ambition likely seeks out opportunities to care for others and spends a great deal of time engaged in related activities, often doing so in diverse ways. In general, most of us would expect that effort to lead to better outcomes for those being cared for, but outcomes do vary depending upon the needs and wants of the caregiving recipient. Moreover, it's not uncommon for caregivers to have concerns that aren't shared by the caregiving recipients.

Independence is a particular case where needs and wants of caregivers and recipients diverge.

Indeed, in caregiving, there are also attempts by recipients to be independent from their caregivers. Yet, by definition, there is some degree of dependence between the two, which may lead to tension.[17] For example, as any parent of a toddler or a teenager knows, during these stages, the caregiver needs to facilitate their child's independence while simultaneously keeping them safe, within certain limits. This issue plays out slightly differently later in life in terms of eldercare: Older adults often bristle at limits placed on their independence—driving, in particular, can become a hot-button issue as people age.[18]

With the juxtaposition of caregiving ambition with the needs of caregiving recipients, the best outcomes require a delicate balance. This balance must reflect the caregiver's aspirations and the caregiving recipient's desires and needs. If caregivers' ambitions lead them to behave in ways inconsistent with what the caregiving recipients actually need, then these ambitions can manifest in non-constructive ways. If caregiving ambition becomes too self-referential—reflecting the caregiver's aspirations more than the caregiving recipient's needs—or if the caregiver aspires to fulfill only the recipient's needs and wants and becomes overly indulgent, negative outcomes are likely to occur. In short, the caregiving thus becomes more about the caregiver, not the care recipient.

When considering the fruits of caregiving ambition, it is not as simple a calculation as those of career ambition. Fulfilling caregiving ambition is more complicated than moving up a rung on an organizational ladder or earning a higher salary; it involves aspirations to give care, as well as the needs and wants of those who receive that care. Becoming a caregiver is therefore only a partial fulfillment of caregiving ambition—the effects on the care recipient are important outcomes as well.

AMBITIOUS WOMEN

Let's again consider the question first posed in the Introduction about whom you would consider a "big success" but from a different angle: Is the person who comes to mind a man or a woman? Several decades ago, researcher Virginia Schein famously coined the phrase "Think manager, think male," describing the fact that people are more likely to associate managers with men than with women.[19] Today, career ambition is still often associated with, and encouraged in, men more than women. Furthermore, supporting a family was used historically to buttress men's work ambition.[20] Not surprisingly, people are now more likely to associate ambition with professional goals and with men.

Although gender differences in career ambition have been found in some studies, with women reporting lower levels compared to men,[21] these differences are far from clear-cut. First, not all studies on the topic find different levels of career ambition between genders—many researchers report no gender differences whatsoever. For example, Professor Gary Powell, a prolific researcher of gender issues, along with Professor D. Anthony Butterfield investigated career aspirations among male and female MBA students. They found that men and women did not differ in their aspiration for top management.[22] Also, in some studies gender differences vary depending upon the specific measure of ambition that the researchers used.[23] In some other cases still, gender differences in ambition disappear after taking into account other variables.[24]

It's also hard to know how to interpret gender differences in self-reported ambition found in some studies, due to how men and women approach the topic: Expressing professional ambition is more socially acceptable for men compared to women. Psychiatrist Anna Fels, author of *Necessary Dreams: Ambition in Women's Changing Lives*, argues that expressing ambition is actually taboo for women.[25] She maintains that this taboo serves as a form of modern discrimination: "The elimination of the barriers that have historically kept women from mastering a subject . . . has brought women a long way toward realizing their ambitions. But the pressure on girls and women to relinquish opportunities for recognition in the workplace continues to have powerful repercussions."[26]

Similarly, a study by economists of MBA students at an elite university revealed that single women, as compared to married women, are more reticent to express career ambition in surveys about career preferences. The researchers concluded that this reticence comes from a concern that expressing such ambition could hurt single women's prospects of getting married, at least in the heterosexual marriage market. The authors explain: "single women avoid actions that would help their careers because of marriage considerations [which] . . . may be an additional explanation for gender differences in the labor market."[27] (By the way, this paper was published in 2017—not the 1950s.)

When gender differences in levels of career ambition do emerge, they are affected quite a bit by situational factors. For example, young women's role models shape their professional goals; the extent to which they envision themselves working outside the home is influenced by their parents' beliefs about gender stereotypes and work.[28] Partners also exert a fair amount of influence on women's career aspirations. Although career-oriented women report a preference for mates who are also career-oriented, women who anticipate being breadwinners report greater preferences for mates who will be caregivers.[29] Likewise, in studies conducted among heterosexual, young adults, researchers have found that women's expectations for themselves in non-traditional roles are associated with how much caregiving they believe future male partners will provide.[30]

Women's career ambitions are also shaped by their experiences in the workplace, which subsequently influence their estimated likelihood of future career advancement. In a study of employees at a major consulting company, there were no gender differences in career aspirations among recent hires to the company. Gender gaps in aspirations for top management emerged, however, among employees who had been working in the company for more than 2 years, with women expressing lower aspirations than men.[31] So it appears that gender gaps in ambition are not a given but crop up depending upon many circumstances that sometimes send messages to women, unwittingly or not, that they shouldn't be, or that it's not worth it to be, overly ambitious.

Moreover, men's and women's considerations when forming and cultivating ambitions may differ. For example, research shows women value non-career-related goals to a greater extent than men.[32] Women report having greater interest than men in the "helping occupations," such as in education and healthcare.[33] And women also are more likely than men to anticipate work–family concerns when formulating their future career goals.[34] Therefore, any gender gaps in career ambitions may also be driven by a greater variety of aspirations, as well as more complicated considerations, including balancing work and care, when planning for the long term. In sum, women's ambitions are powerfully influenced by at least six primary factors: (1) socialization by parents and society at large based on beliefs about women and work, (2) expectations concerning (future) partners, (3) anticipated work–care conflict, (4) the nature of the work itself, (5) working conditions such as the extent to which a job offers flexibility, and (6) the salience of other life goals.

With apologies to Schein, as shown, "think ambition, think male" appears to be inadequate. Gender differences in career ambition are highly sensitive to circumstances, which too often send messages to women about the viability of their professional ambitions. And balancing multiple life goals is not a simple matter, leading to tough choices about which ambitions are worth pursuing.

Lean In: To What?

Sheryl Sandberg made a huge splash in 2013 with her bestselling book *Lean In*, in which she critiqued women's propensity—or lack thereof—to give their all to their careers.[35] A highly successful professional, who achieved fame as chief operating officer of Facebook, Sandberg highlights her observations of the numerous ways in which women are reluctant to "lean in" and behave assertively at work. In the book, she exhorts women to take their place at the table, not to leave organizations too early in their careers, and to inspire and mentor other women to follow the same approach. Many of her arguments are quite logical, and when the book was released, they resounded with many women (and men). Resulting Lean In circles—in which women and men met and discussed the book and the issues it raised—spread throughout the country and across the globe.

Yet, in an interesting twist toward the end of her book, Sandberg describes her mother, who was a stay-at-home mom and devoted community volunteer. Despite having just written an entire polemic on why women should lean in to the workforce, Sandberg lauds her mother's achievements, arguing that through motherhood and tireless volunteer work, her mom had "leaned in" throughout her life too. And by all the evidence in Sandberg's account, her mother had leaned in ambitiously—to caregiving and to her community. But according to Sandberg's book, with leaning in defined narrowly in terms of work, her mother hadn't really leaned in at all. Sandberg seems to backpedal as a way to justify her mother's life path, which was so vastly different from her own.

So what should women—and men, for that matter—lean into? Why are women, who are often leaning in heartily at home and in their communities, not recognized for their ambitions? What about leaning into life more generally—including work, family, and community? Why can't we recognize and honor the different ways that men and women lean in broadly—to work, to caregiving, to homemaking, to their communities? By broadening not only the ambitions that we seek to fulfill but also the ambitions that we honor, society and humanity will be only the better for it.

BROADENING OUR VIEW OF AMBITION

When conceptualized solely in terms of professional success, mixed findings on gender and career ambition highlight the traditionally narrow and limiting view of achievement and ambition. Psychologist Jacquelynne S. Eccles argued that this limited view of achievement has influenced, in turn, the research questions asked and the discoveries made on the topic:

> Defining achievement itself . . . is a value-laden enterprise at best. Evaluating the meaning and consequences of gender differences on any particular criterion of achievement is equally value-laden. . . . As a consequence, very little systematic, quantitative information has been gathered regarding more stereotypically female-typed achievements.[36]

The same can be said for ambition.

Other life ambitions appear to take precedence for highly ambitious, professionally successful women who leave full-time work for an extended period of time, a decision often referred to as "opting out." Mothers who opt out report devoting time to their children, especially academic and extracurricular pursuits for school-age children; community and volunteer work; and overall organizing and carrying out family life. But these noble pursuits are often not valued according to traditional achievement referents.

Critics use terms like "intensive mothering"[37] and "concerted cultivation"[38] to refer to raising children ambitiously. They tend to argue that such motherly ambition has as much to do, if not more, with social class gatekeeping as it has to do with providing tender, loving care.[39] Indeed, some parents' goals are related to social class, such as gaining admission to certain elite colleges and universities. However, these same women who are criticized from a class perspective typically describe their caregiving experiences as driven by ambitions for their families and as highly meaningful. As Gwen, a high-achieving mother of four who is currently employed part-time, explained, "I would have loved to become a world-renown researcher, or speaker, or even a highly respected (and highly paid!) consultant. But, those roles would involve a level of time and travel that I simply do not have. . . . I wanted a big family (I have 4 children) and have a husband with a very demanding job, so I felt more limited. . . . I made the tradeoff willingly and consciously."

Life ambitions are diverse and much more varied than a simplistic focus on a job or profession. If women balance a wider range of ambitions to a greater extent than men, that may explain the gender gaps that are sometimes present in reported career ambition. Nonetheless, clearly a dearth of ambition is not the problem: An abundance exists, in both career and caregiving and for both women and men.

DEFINING QUESTIONS

- Do you consider yourself ambitious? Why or why not?
- Are you more ambitious about your career or your caregiving or both equally? Have these respective ambitions changed over time?
- How would reframing ambition to include caregiving have positive effects on society's respect for caregiving?

Why Work–Life Won't Work

We're all the sum of our experiences, and raising children plays an enormous part in making us who we are. For some of us, perhaps the largest part.

—Jennifer Senior[1]

THE PERPETUAL ANGST

Work–care conflict is a common challenge; a Google search on the term yields almost half a billion results. In fact, work–care conflict is rampant in the United States (and around the world), a struggle that both men and women describe as straining and pulling them in multiple directions.[2] While at work, they feel guilty for neglecting their families; when they're with their families, they feel guilty for neglecting their work—it's an endless, perpetual, negative cycle. A frequent experience, especially among mothers, is the sense that one is never doing enough in either domain, despite the fact that mothers report spending significantly more hours both on paid work and on child care compared to previous decades.[3] Among fathers, according to the Pew Research Center, 63% report spending too little time with their children, with work obligations cited as the main reason.[4] A reader may note we use the term "work–care" and not related terms like "work–family" and "work–life." This is intentional. Caregiving is a critical,

The Caregiving Ambition. Julia B. Bear and Todd L. Pittinsky, Oxford University Press. © Oxford University Press 2022.
DOI: 10.1093/oso/9780197512418.003.0003

underlying dimension of these related and overlapping constructs. It is so consequential that it must be understood and addressed on its own terms.

Not surprisingly, the Families and Work Institute, one of the leading work–life research centers, has found that work–care conflict, also referred to as "work–family conflict," has increased over the past several decades, particularly for men.[5] Work–care conflict is, of course, unpleasant—disappointing others you care about, feeling stressed and ineffective. More importantly, it can negatively affect mental and physical health, causing stress and physical strain and hurting job performance.[6] For blue-collar and pink-collar workers, the further demands of shift work, in particular, often conflict with family life, incurring the same negative effects.[7] In the meantime, organizations suffer: Absenteeism due to family-related caregiving creates billions of dollars in losses for American businesses.[8]

Perhaps even more concerning than the mental and physical health consequences is how the anticipation of this conflict constrains people's family and career goals. A survey of undergraduate students conducted in 2012 by Stewart Friedman, a pioneer in the work–life field, found that they were half as likely as an earlier cohort, surveyed in 1992, to say that they plan to have or adopt children. The main reason? It wasn't that they didn't want children—rather, they didn't see how they feasibly could have them given their anticipated long working hours.[9] The students surveyed hailed from the University of Pennsylvania, an elite institution, so one could argue that the sample was not particularly representative. True enough, but by the same logic, these young people should have more resources to cope with work–care conflict. In fact, their concerns are consistent with national trends. According to data collected in 2018 from the General Social Survey (GSS)—a national, representative survey of Americans conducted every 2 years, people report having, on average, 1.86 children despite reporting an ideal number of children closer to 3.[10]

Concerns about potential work–care conflicts decrease career goals as well, especially for women. Anticipating work–care conflict lowers women's career ambitions even among young college-age students who are years, sometimes decades, away from starting families.[11] And, by the way, women have not been advancing in their careers at nearly the rates one might expect given the push for their greater labor participation. The gender pay gap, a topic discussed in depth in Chapter 5, is almost non-existent for young adults but continues to balloon once men and women reach age 35,[12] not surprisingly, the age by which most adults engage in extensive caregiving.

THE STATE OF THE WORK–CARE AGENDA

So work–care conflict is up, family formation is down, and the gender gap in career advancement is more or less stagnant. Does this mean that organizations are neglecting these issues? Surprisingly, no. There is no doubt that the United States lags behind other countries in terms of policies that support caregiving, such as paid family leave, often to a mind-boggling extent.[13] Yet, it is inaccurate to say employers have completely neglected the issue. Many large companies have actually invested extensively in work–life and work–care programs.

For example, some leading US companies offer both paid maternity and paternity leave after birth or adoption, phase-back programs for new mothers returning to work, back-up child care (child care in the case a parent's usual arrangement falls through), and back-up care for sick children (child care in the case that children are sick and parents cannot use their usual arrangement).[14] Many other companies offer a subset of these benefits. Although these companies may be outliers in terms of the range and extent of benefits offered, the Society for Human Resource Management reports that the percent of companies offering paid caregiving leaves—beyond what is covered by state law or short-term disability—continues to increase, albeit slowly (for example, 26% of companies in 2016 to 30% of companies in 2017).[15]

Likewise, there are renewed efforts on the federal level to support caregiving. Republicans generally support programs involving tax cuts to try to incentivize a greater number of private sector employers to provide paid leave, whereas Democrats generally support programs to directly subsidize the leaves. But despite the varying tactics, there is (finally!) agreement on both sides of the aisle that paid family leave is important. Moreover, at the end of 2019, federal workers were granted paid parental leave.[16] In the spring of 2021, President Biden announced the American Families Plan,[17] which includes paid family leave, subsidized child care for low- and middle-income families, and a universal prekindergarten program, among other programmatic proposals. The lack of a comprehensive pro- gram, notwithstanding, states, cities, and counties have implemented paid family leave programs. Currently, only California, New Jersey, New York, the District of Columbia, Washington, and Rhode Island offer paid family leave after birth or adoption; but more and more states' local counties and cities are following suit.[18]

Still, as mentioned, the United States significantly trails the rest of the Western world in support for combining work and caregiving. The struc- tural and financial support offered by these other countries, particularly in western Europe, include paid maternity and paternity leave, subsidized child care, and financial benefits for caregivers.[19] In countries with such structural child care support, mothers report greater levels of happiness.[20] Moreover, the lack of structural support in the United States typically hurts the most vulnerable, particularly non-professional, non-unionized workers, many of whom are not employed by corporations that offer pri- vate programs or by government branches that offer extensive family- friendly benefits.

Retail and food service workers are especially subject to wildly un- predictable hours that are completely inconsistent with caregiving and family life. Employees at fast-food restaurants and similar establishments like Starbucks are often informed of their work schedule a day or two in advance—undermining their ability to manage work and caregiving.[21] In 2017, New York City passed the Fair Workweek Legislation, giving re- tail and food service workers within the city limits the right to a predict- able schedule.[22] Other cities, including Chicago, Philadelphia, Seattle, and San Francisco, have passed similar legislation.[23] Still, even with these steps forward, contrast this system with employees at McDonald's in Sweden, where they are informed of their work schedule a month in advance.[24]

For the employees who do have access to work–care benefits in the United States, you might think their situation is enviable—relative to non-skilled workers without benefits, perhaps, but the picture is a bit more complicated. Research has shown that these benefits often remain on the books and unused because employees are apprehensive about actually taking advantage of them.[25] And rightly so, in many cases. Employees often incur penalties for taking advantage of work–life benefits, such as being seen as less committed to work or being "mommy-tracked"—put on a slower career path with a limited trajectory—by their employers. In fact, research has shown that organizations use work–care benefits as a way to reward and retain valued employees as opposed to as a humane benefit available to all employees to facilitate working and caregiving.[26]

Despite the obvious deficits, there is a work–care agenda, along with a burgeoning government agenda, that should benefit at least a subset of the population. Yet work–care conflict is only increasing. What's going on? The answer may lie in how we define the problem in the first place.

Solving Company Problems, Not Parent Problems

In the winter of 2019, the Bill and Melinda Gates Foundation rescinded its widely hailed and celebrated 52-week paid family leave program. Citing the organizational challenges of providing such a generous amount of leave, the management decided to cut the leave offered by half. Instead, employees now have a 26-week leave and receive $20,000 to spend on outsourced caregiving—still a very generous policy, especially compared to what is standard at most organizations. However, the implicit message in the policy is clear: Find hired help, and get back to work. What's most surprising about this rollback is that the foundation is an extremely well-funded organization with the public mission of helping people lead better lives, with a focus on advancing women's well-being in particular.[27]

The Results-Only Work Environment, or ROWE, is a highly celebrated work–life program that was created by two human resources managers, Jody Thompson and Cali Ressler, at Best Buy headquarters. The program was subsequently implemented in other organizations such as the Gap corporate headquarters. ROWE eliminated the notion of "face time"—a focus on hours spent in the office—and instead shifted the focus to the actual results employees produced. The policy removed specific working hours, sick days, and paid vacation, instead giving employees total autonomy over their time. This new, unique system entailed a radical job redesign that went beyond just flexible working hours.[28] In 2013, however, in the midst of reduced financial performance for Best Buy, a new chief executive officer (CEO), Hubert Joly, abruptly removed ROWE, despite evidence that it had improved employee productivity, well-being, and work–life balance, while also reducing turnover.[29]

RECOGNIZING CAREGIVING AMBITION IN THE WORK–LIFE AGENDA

Unfortunately, the policy retractions at the Gates Foundation and at Best Buy are not unusual—many work–life programs that entail comprehensive work redesign, rather than merely window dressing, often do not endure (more on this point in Chapter 8). Typical work–life programs operate with the intention of keeping employees at work and their personal lives at bay rather than really redesigning how people work to facilitate both work and caregiving. Generally speaking, work–care programs are aimed at facilitating outsourced child care, and in some cases eldercare, to make sure workers can remain focused on their jobs. Take, for example, back-up care for parents when their kids are ill. Though this benefit is pragmatic, albeit unusual, most parents would likely prefer to provide the care to their sick children (more on this point in Chapter 7).

There are, of course, challenges inherent in working and organizing around employees who take leaves for caregiving. But these challenges are far from insurmountable. Entire professions have even adapted to these needs. Medicine, for example, has become much more family-friendly.[30] While some fields of medicine are less flexible, such as surgery, in certain specialties, career and caregiving are being combined in a healthy, successful way.

Furthermore, a completely work-centric work–life movement is simply shortsighted. Even with greater governmental support, which is sorely needed, a view of caregiving as something to be outsourced so that everyone can get back to work misses the larger point that many of us do not believe caregiving is just a duty, nor do we want to wholly outsource our caregiving in the first place.

Indeed, caregiving is, of course, a major duty and obligation—we would never argue that it's not—and people's lives are often defined by and organized around caregiving needs. Children need care. Aging parents, relatives, and spouses often need care. The need to give and receive care is indisputable. Yet, for many people, the experience of caregiving entails a larger sense of purpose and provides a deep source of meaning. Thus, for many people, caregiving is not just a chore. And if it is to be outsourced, then people have very specific ideas about how they want it done. In other words, people have goals and ambitions for caregiving, above and beyond taking care of their loved ones simply out of necessity so that they can work unhindered by their close relationships.

Furthermore, people who report high caregiving ambition also tend to report high career ambition. When asked to rate their caregiving ambition and their career ambition, people's responses to the two scales are positively correlated.[31] In other words, it is not the case that these ambitions are mutually exclusive; on the contrary, people who are ambitious in one area tend to be ambitious in the other. Thus, it behooves organizations to consider both ambitions in the work–care agenda, not just the work side of the equation. Specifically, if organizations seek to hire and retain the people who are most ambitious about their careers, then they need to realize that high career ambition and high caregiving ambition often go hand in hand.

Stereotypes and Reality: Helicopter Parents, "Tiger Moms," and Choice

Caregiving ambition could be scoffed at as further evidence of overly intensive parenting— mothering, in particular—that has become common among upper-middle-class families in the United States and closely associated with maintaining or improving social class, at least according to some academics[32] and various media sources.[33] Indeed, in her book about middle-aged, Gen X mothers, journalist Ada Calhoun highlights how Gen X parents may overcorrect for the lax parenting they themselves experienced: "Gen Xers helicopter over our kids because we have too vivid memories of what happened—or could have happened—to us when our parents didn't hover."[34] There's also no question that a more competitive economic landscape during recent decades has helped fuel a preoccupation with children's educational and professional success, particularly among middle- and upper-middle-class parents (more on that in Chapter 3).

But what's wrong with being ambitious, especially as a parent? Why do we vilify intensive parenting? Most other types of intensive activities—work, exercise, travel, rock climbing, computer programming, you name it—are admired and celebrated. Why not taking care of children and others?

Today, a lot of media attention is paid to what seems like the outer limits of mothering—from the neurotic "helicopter moms" or "snowplow parents"[35] to "tiger moms," who are stereotyped as nearly psychotic. Many reacted with shock and horror to Amy Chua's portrayal of herself in *Battle Hymn of the Tiger Mother* as a mother who is as determined to raise "successful" children as any CEO is to boost the company's market share. Chua's unabashed trumpeting of a regime of strictness was understandably controversial, but one can only wonder if some of the ferocious anger directed at her was provoked by her daring to declare her high ambitions as a mother. She was determined "not to raise a soft, entitled child—not to let my family fall."[36] Is that so horrible—or so different, for that matter—from the hopes of many other parents for their children and family? Or the ferocity that we celebrate when manifest for one's career?

It should be possible to be ambitious, and publicly ambitious, about caregiving for your children—to want more than anything for them to be happy and successful—without being cast as a maniac or social pest. According to the Pew Research Center, more than 11 million parents in the United States, almost 20% of parents, stay at home full-time. The number is even higher for parents with children under age 5. The primary reason cited for this arrangement is to "care for home or family."[37]

Many sociologists who study gender issues argue that this "choice" to stay home is not really a choice at all given the lack of family-friendly workplaces, and there is certainly evidence supporting that argument.[38] Framing decisions around work and family as purely personal choice obfuscates the dearth of societal support for caregiving, the extremely high cost of child care, and the gendered decision-making processes that often lead to women making the "choice" to stay home. However, based on our discussions with parents around the country, there is also the truth that many mothers and fathers prefer to stay home or cut back on work hours while their children are young, giving them the opportunity to care for their children themselves when they have that option. Jim, a father of two who cares for his children at home full-time, explained to us, "It is very important for me to personally provide care to our children. I chose to be a stay-at-home dad when our daughter was born and have continued in this role to the present. I want to be home during these early years and am grateful that it is an option for us."

When asked to choose the best way to organize family life with under-school-aged children, only 12% of parents chose the option of both parents working full-time. The remaining 88% preferred one parent either working part-time or staying at home full-time. When asked to choose the worst way, 36% chose the option of both parents working full-time. Moreover, 56% reported a preference for family members over institutionalized child care for children younger than school age.[39] Thus, it does not seem accurate to say that parents who stay at home with children do so only because of societal constraints. As individuals, the vast majority of us seem to believe in providing care directly to our own children; but as a society, we see caricatures of caregivers, cartoons of "helicopter parents" or "tiger moms" cast as too involved in their children's lives and too ambitious in their caregiving.

To be clear, we, of course, by no means advocate reverting back to the stifling, traditional gender roles that have been prevalent throughout history. Quite the opposite: Caregiving is so important to both men and women that we want all genders to be more empowered to work and care. Yet today the societal focus on careers over caregiving perpetuates an overvaluing of careers and an undervaluing of caregiving, both personally and professionally.[40] Primary caregivers who aren't employed outside the home are typically characterized as incompetent, as opposed to admirable, for their caregiving roles. Fathers, in particular, who want to focus on their families or who request family-friendly benefits are more likely to be stigmatized[41] (an issue that we discuss in Chapter 5). According to a Pew Research survey, respondents reported that most Americans value men's contributions at work to a much greater extent than their contributions at home. In contrast, the majority of respondents reported valuing women's contributions at work and at home equally, with a smaller portion reporting valuing their contributions at home more so than work.[42] Thus, the upshot of the past few decades is increased valuing of women in the workplace without the concomitant valuing of men in the caregiving arena, or valuing of caregiving, unpaid and paid, more generally.

So, yes, some parents today may hover and helicopter too much. Gen Xers, in particular, may have overcorrected for some of the lax parenting of their youth. But let's not throw the proverbial baby out with the bathwater. Critiques of intensive parenting too often sound, or operate, like another backhanded way to devalue caregiving, even though parents—mothers and fathers—agree on its importance and want to be involved. Unfortunately, the value of caregiving, and the role of caring for one's family, is often diverted to divisive "wars" that began as women further entered the marketplace in the 20th century, that is, the so-called mommy wars, wars which still rage on today.

An End to the "Mommy Wars"

The media seems to delight in pitting mothers who are employed outside the home with those who are not. A classic example is the 1992 brouhaha that erupted after Hillary Clinton famously quipped, "I suppose I could have stayed home and baked cookies and had teas, but what I decided to do was to fulfill my profession," during her husband's campaign for president.[43] The media pounced on this quote, what today would be considered "clickbait," and her comment hit a major nerve, particularly with homemakers. Not only did Clinton backpedal on her statement, she subsequently engaged in a cookie bakeoff sponsored by *Family Circle* magazine with Barbara Bush, the wife of the Republican candidate, George H. W. Bush. In fact, the bakeoff and images of candidates (and their spouses) making cookies remained a fixture of US presidential elections until it was suspended indefinitely in September 2020.

Clinton's quote set up a false dichotomy, however, namely that staying home and baking cookies is antithetical to fulfilling an ambition, that the two options are mutually exclusive. The contrast between pursuing a profession and full-time caregiving implies that the former involves ambition but the latter does not. As discussed, though, many people are ambitious about and engage in both. Interestingly, these pernicious, so-called mommy wars may be put to an end by a stronger recognition of caregiving ambition, a valuable side effect that could further change how we handle our work–life commitments. For example, Yaacov, whose experience with eldercare appeared in Chapter 1, is a professor and a father of one. He describes joyfully baking with his son on the weekends as a ritual between them, which he is quick to point out in no way contradicts or detracts from his professional ambitions. Given that most women, and men for that matter, are engaged in both work and caregiving throughout their lives, these "wars" create a false dichotomy, to say the least.

It is time to puncture the myth that ambitions about work and ambitions about care are mutually exclusive. In reality, parents who work outside the home and those who stay at home both share ambition. As caregiving ambition in particular is further recognized, it can then be valued with or without professional ambition. Eric Clapton plays one instrument very well; Stevie Wonder plays several. Without a doubt, both are top musicians.

BRINGING LIFE BACK INTO WORK–LIFE

We laud career success in the United States, a country infused with the Protestant work ethic and a belief in the free market system. However, there is also a clear consensus that caregiving should be supported and valued. In a national US survey, the majority of respondents (82%) said there should be paid leave for childbirth and adoption, with more than half recommending between 6 and 12 months of leave.[44] There is also consensus on the growing need for caregiving, specifically eldercare, which is ballooning with the aging boomer population.[45]

Still, under the patina of concern for employees, employers offer policies that, in their essence, support work, not caregiving. In a country based on capitalism and the triumph of the bottom line, caregiving ambition is not recognized or valued. The work–life and work–care programs offered have become part of a "theater" of a corporate agenda as opposed to an actual movement to value and support caregiving and caregivers specifically.

Later in the book, we propose solutions for how caregiving ambition can be, and should be, incorporated into work–care programs (see Chapter 7), along with a dissection of the business case for work–life more specifically (see Chapter 8). In the meantime, however, we propose a more fundamental question: What if ambition about caregiving was lauded in the same way that ambition about careers is lauded?

It's one thing to be stuck between two responsibilities but quite another thing to be stuck between two ambitions. This is the place most workers find themselves in today. Are we really content with our society telling women it's finally acceptable to be ambitious in one's career and great in one's paid work but only if they're going to settle for being unambitious in their caring and simply "obliged" and duty-bound as a mother? And what kind of society tells men to be more ambitious as fathers but if and only if they don't reveal that involvement at work and if it doesn't get in the way of their career ambition?

DEFINING QUESTIONS

- Is your work–care conflict increasing, decreasing, or stable? If it is increasing or decreasing, why?
- Have you had to modify your career and caregiving ambitions because they came into conflict, and if so, how did you modify them?
- How do cartoonish portrayals of "tiger moms" and "helicopter parents" undermine everyday caregivers' experiences of caregiving ambition?

Providing, Not Just Provisioning

Caretakers of both sexes, wet-nurses, even "daycare"—none of these are uniquely human, nor particularly new.

—SARAH HRDY[1]

HERE'S THE WRINKLE

Heather, a mother of two, grew up in the 1980s with certain work and family ideals, especially concerning motherhood and gender gaps in the workforce. She studied US history and was interested in the leap in women's employment during World War II, a time during which the government provided child care so that women could work in factories to support the war effort. Heather firmly believed a similar model could be applied in the 1980s and 1990s and that public child care would subsequently solve gender gaps in employment and earnings. She also extensively critiqued her own mother for staying at home with her and her siblings when they were young, instead of joining the workforce.

Then Heather had her first child. All of a sudden, her reality and her ideals clashed: Although she still strongly supported public child care as a policy, she realized that many parents would not necessarily want someone else taking care of their children. Heather found that she was one of the many people who wanted to care for their babies themselves, especially in their children's early years, despite how difficult this can be in the

The Caregiving Ambition. Julia B. Bear and Todd L. Pittinsky, Oxford University Press. © Oxford University Press 2022.
DOI: 10.1093/oso/9780197512418.003.0004

United States given the lack of paid leave in so many professions. Her view of her own mother shifted as well, and she felt remorse for criticizing her decisions concerning work and family. She felt she understood far better the complexity of her mother's decisions and why she had made them.

Heather had run up against the distinction within caregiving ambition between *providing* ambition—the ambition to directly give care and personally meet the needs of family and other loved ones—and *provisioning* ambition—the ambition to indirectly ensure that the needs of family and other loved ones are met by procuring quality care for them.[2] Providing and provisioning are the two dimensions of behavior that make up caregiving. We provide care when we nurse a sick child or partner back to health. We provision care when we hire a babysitter to watch a sick child or take someone to the doctor.

These dimensions are consistent with attachment theory—a prominent theory of the psychology of close relationships originally conceptualized by John Bowlby, a British physician and psychologist, and further developed in collaboration with Mary Ainsworth, an American developmental psychologist. According to this theory, caregiving is defined in terms of (a) giving help and protection to someone who is in need (providing) and (b) fostering growth and development (provisioning). Bowlby and Ainsworth originally formulated the theory as a way to understand the key role of maternal–infant relationships in psychological outcomes. They emphasized the centrality of the bond between mother and child, as well as the potential negative consequences when that bond is severed.[3] Over time, the theory has evolved to encompass a diverse array of familial, work, and community relationships beyond just mother–infant attachment, such as those that develop between children and caregivers other than their parents.[4]

Secure attachment, or feeling secure bonds with adult caregivers, is essential for human development. This secure base enables infants to explore the world while knowing their caregiver is still close by and available when needed. When an adult caregiver does not or cannot provide this security early in a child's life, the result is an insecure attachment. Insecure attachment is characterized by either anxiety, known as an anxious attachment style, or detachment, known as an avoidant attachment style. In anxious attachment, infants display insecurity by being overly clingy; in avoidant attachment, infants show insecurity by being detached and dismissive.[5] In other words, a lack of security leads infants to compensate to one extreme or the other, a pattern that often gets replayed throughout childhood and in close relationships in adulthood.[6]

Furthermore, according to attachment theory, caregiving serves as an evolutionary adaptation to foster the survival of close kin.[7] Research has shown that across cultures caregiving behaviors are markedly similar, including, for example, using a soothing voice and touch.[8] Caregiving behaviors therefore include both a direct, emotional, and interpersonal component—expressing affection and relieving another's distress—and an indirect component—facilitating another's development and exploration in the world by provisioning support and resources. These two components map onto providing, the former, and provisioning, the latter.

Intuitively, it makes sense that caregiving ambition encompasses both providing and provisioning dimensions. Creating a warm home environment, for example, involves both indirect material resources, such as a physical space, and direct personal caring, including nurturing and meeting emotional and physical needs. One dimension without the other is, by nature, incomplete.

People, however, may vary in terms of their ambitions on each dimension—some may be high on one and moderate on the other or vice versa.[9] In other words, people may have high providing ambition only, high provisioning ambition only, some combination of the two, or low ambition on both. Often, how we experience our desire to provide or provision care relates to where we are in our lives and the situations we face.

PROVIDING AND PROVISIONING AMBITIONS

Where our providing and provisioning ambitions lie may depend on both context and our life stage. For example, infancy and toddlerhood often involve intense physical needs and closeness between children and their caregivers. Providing ambitions for children at this young age aim to fulfill these needs by spending time together, with parents feeding, nurturing, and soothing their infants and toddlers. Provisioning ambitions in this stage may involve aspirations to procure quality care by others, such as a grandparent, babysitter, or child care center.

In contrast, older children and teenagers may have less intense physical needs (though this, of course, varies) but more intense emotional needs. Providing ambitions with children of this age are likely to involve parents caring for their kids' emotional development, through direct advice and support, and their cognitive development, such as helping them with homework and other educational or learning activities. Provisioning ambition may also become more prominent as children get older and enter their teens. These ambitions often involve issues similar to those of providing ambitions, but they are handled with a different approach. In the case of emotional development, parents may have a mentor or relative give their children advice on certain topics and then find tutors or sign them up for other enrichment activities to help them with cognitive development. Other provisioning ambitions may involve facilitating activities that promote independence, like encouraging them to volunteer or trying to support their studies, or assisting them to find their first job.

In terms of eldercare, providing ambition may involve directly helping older parents with daily tasks when needed. Provisioning ambition in this case may come in the form of procuring care by others, such as a home healthcare aide or nurse, or through institutional care, like an assisted living or skilled nursing facility. According to the Pew Research Center, the most common type of care that adult children do for their parents involves errands, housework, and help with house repairs, consistent with providing ambition.[10]

It is important to note that burnout and exhaustion are genuine risks, especially for those high on providing ambition. Extensive research has shown the very real effects of *caregiver burden*, which is defined as the toll that caregiving takes on caregivers' functioning across multiple dimensions, including mental and physical health.[11] Caregiving in-home for spouses and parents is associated with depressive symptoms and limited physical functioning among women,[12] although not when the caregiving recipient does not live at home.[13] Caregiver burden is particularly associated with eldercare and is more likely in the context of providing care for someone with a chronic illness, such as dementia.[14] Providing child care can also be demanding and exhausting. Parents of children with disabilities, in particular, report caregiver burden.[15] Thus, it is important to acknowledge the very real demands and risks of burnout and exhaustion associated with a high level of providing care.

Nonetheless, whether caring for young children, adolescents, or elderly relatives, providing and provisioning come into play. Most parents and caregivers do—and have ambitions for—both. Moreover, even for those high on providing ambition, caregiving has always involved at least some degree of delegation to balance between the care recipient's demands and the care provider's needs and circumstances, typically financial ones.

Challenges of Ambitious Providing

Parents who are high on providing ambition seek to care for their children directly. They care ambitiously with specific goals in mind, often with an emphasis on the amount of time spent together. For people high on providing ambition this latter goal—time together—is often crucial. Nina, a mother of four, recalled the importance of having a great deal of time with her children when they were younger:

> When my first son was a year old I put him in a new daycare to go on a job interview. I was completely preoccupied during the interview and couldn't wait to finish and pick him up. It was definitely harder for me than it was for him. After that episode it was probably another year before I ventured to work again. I worked very part time . . . a few hours a week and my (ex) husband's grandmother watched the baby. . . . My career—speech therapy—allowed for enough flexibility that . . . I could pretty much work when I could coordinate child care or for a few hours or when the kids were in preschool/school.

Consistent with Nina's experience, and as discussed in Chapter 2, parents often experience intense conflicts between caring for their children and breadwinning, a dilemma that poses a particular challenge for those with providing ambitions. Economists such as Harvard professor Claudia Goldin talk about "greedy jobs," or those jobs that require, and reward, working extremely long and demanding hours.[16] (This type of job and its concomitant requirement of near complete work devotion are discussed in Chapter 5.) Many greedy jobs with unstable and unpredictable hours essentially remove the ability to provide, forcing parents to almost fully provision.

Interestingly enough, however, not everyone, even those very ambitious about their careers, takes this provision-only route. Although popular culture includes many extreme stereotypes of either the career woman with no time to provide (think of Miranda Priestley in *The Devil Wears Prada*) or the career mother-turned-stay-at-home mother (such as Madeline Mackenzie in *Big Little Lies*), many parents—mothers and fathers—work hard to blend providing ambition and breadwinning through various arrangements. For example, Amy Berman Jackson, a distinguished federal judge, took a 5-year leave to raise two children in the midst of many prestigious career milestones.[17]

History gives some perspective for these modern-day challenges. Before industrialization, the divide between work and home was not nearly as demarcated. Historian Stephanie Coontz explains, "Throughout most of human history, mothers have devoted more time to other duties than to childcare and have delegated substantial portions of childrearing to others. But there are new conflicts between women's work and family responsibilities today, since they take place in mutually exclusive locations and times."[18] These mutually exclusive locations and times for work and care make fulfilling providing ambition more complicated and create added stress, especially for those high on providing ambition, contributing to work–care conflict.

Breastfeeding also illustrates particularly well the tension between providing ambition and breadwinning. Although many women wish to breastfeed, it can be especially difficult to combine with working outside the home. Lactation rooms, where women can pump milk at work, thankfully have become much more common[19]; but it still may be difficult, especially in jobs that require long hours, travel, and constant interaction with co-workers or others, such as patients and clients, to find the time to pump breastmilk. Lily, a fashion stylist, recalled pumping breast milk under rolling racks of clothes in the middle of conducting shoots with models. Although infant formula is a useful modern development, many women wish to nurture their children with breast milk; and breastfeeding, which also involves physical and emotional closeness, has important emotional and relational caregiving dimensions consistent with providing ambition.

In sum, given the nature of providing ambition, this ambition may be difficult to fulfill along with breadwinning. Many parents, especially those high on providing ambition, may experience mental and physical anguish while coping with modern life's demands that interfere with that ambition. When they're faced with provisioning care for their children, they want to ease this anguish by ensuring that their kids receive the best care possible. Parents often first aspire to provision from family members or their immediate community.

Challenges of Ambitious Provisioning

Studies of caregiving around the world reveal how common—and often preferred—it is to use relatives to help care for children. As Jorge, a father of two, responded when asked about his provisioning ambition and preferences for caregivers, "One of the most important things is that they are relatives. It is hard to trust other people. Family members are the most trustworthy and I feel very comfortable with a relative looking after my children." Grandparents, in particular, often play a central role in provisioning care. For example, according to national surveys from Taiwan, grandparents often serve as primary caregivers for their grandchildren.[20] According to a study of child care arrangements in the United States, approximately 20% of employed mothers with children under 5 report that grandparents serve as their primary source of child care.[21] Not only are grandparents a preferred mode of provisioning but their availability appears to have a positive association with mothers' employment rates. In that same study, the researchers also found that the availability of child care by grandparents was associated with a 9-point increase in mothers' participation in the labor force, particularly among minority, single, and unmarried mothers.

Research has shown that historically grandmothers, in particular, play a role in helping with childrearing, a phenomenon known as the "grandmother hypothesis."[22] This hypothesis posits that the long post-menopausal phase of life that women have relative to other mammals enables the very useful role of grandmothers in assisting their daughters to care for their grandchildren. Research (based on data from 11 European countries) has also shown that as grandfathers age, they become more involved with their grandchildren, especially when they have a healthy spouse with whom they can jointly care for their grandchildren.[23] Moreover, in many households in the United States, grandparents are the primary caregivers for their grandchildren, a trend that continues to rise.[24] Still, one study found that, although approximately 75% of parents surveyed reported that provisioning child care to a partner or a relative is their preference, only 40% of those same parents reported child care arrangements that match this preference.[25] Thus, the challenge around provisioning becomes more difficult when grandparents or other relatives are uninterested or unavailable to provide care.

Despite the strong preference for provisioning by relatives, it is not always feasible or necessarily desirable for many parents. More often than not, grandparents do not live close by; according to a report by the American Association of Retired Persons, over half of grandparents have at least one grandchild living farther than 50 miles away.[26] And grandparents are not necessarily available to care for their grandchildren, especially if they work full-time. While some grandparents may wish to be involved and even heavily involved in caring for their grandchildren, many grandparents cannot, or simply do not want, to take care of their grandchildren all day, every day. Such a situation often causes people—at least those who can afford to—to provision care using nannies and child care centers, as well as tutors and therapists, outsourcing a variety of care to compensate for a lack of extended family support.

People high on provisioning ambition seek out high-quality and enriching care for their children, often investing a great deal of time and effort in finding and securing caregiving arrangements, as well as educational and enrichment opportunities. Indeed, according to the National Association for the Education of Young Children, high-quality child care should include ten components related to positive relationships among children, their families, and their caregivers, educational goals, and a safe and healthy environment."[27] However, finding a trustworthy child care provider with whom parents feel comfortable provisioning such care is not a given. On top of that, affordability of quality child care is a challenge, both psychologically and economically. Tuition for a quality child care center for one child alone can represent as much as 30% of median income in some areas.[28] Other people prefer a caregiver at home, rather than a child care center, while their children are young. An at-home nanny may allow flexibility for parents who work more hours than a standard workweek, who travel frequently, or whose days, hours, and shifts change from week to week. That said, just like enrolling kids in a child care center, the expense of at-home care can be exorbitant.

In response to potentially cost-prohibitive care, some parents decide to form or join a child care co-op, an organized rotation among a group, where members take turns as care providers, or use group or individual child care in another member's home. These arrangements may be informal—just a few hours a week in the short term—or more structured—involving multiple families and running over a longer time period.

For those with high provisioning ambitions, a high-quality child care center or an excellent in-home caregiver offers many benefits for both parents and children. Parents are freed up to work and/or have time for something other than child care. Children benefit from forming bonds with adults other than their parents, as well as socializing with, and learning from, other children, particularly in the case of child care centers.[29] Indeed, provisioning care often involves more than just the actual care—it is also a way to fulfill ambitions related to educational goals and life experiences for one's children.

For example, Priya is a mother of two, and both she and her husband work demanding jobs, sometimes involving travel. They also both take provisioning very seriously. To find a nanny, they interviewed several candidates to get the right fit. In addition, their nanny is a native Spanish speaker, which was important to Priya because her husband is also a native Spanish speaker, and they aspire for their children to grow up learning Spanish. The nanny has worked for the family for over 7 years now. Priya reports that the arrangement has worked out very well, including for the two children, who benefit from having another loving adult in their lives.

Still, no matter the method or price tag, outsourcing caregiving can be stressful, prompting parents' guilt and worry about the care itself and the caregivers. The stress of provisioning may also be compounded by the vulnerability of some care recipients, who are, by definition, dependent and thus often unable to communicate about the care they receive. Infants in day care cannot report how their caregivers behaved throughout the day, nor can older adults with dementia. This vulnerability means that people place tremendous trust and faith in professional caregivers, whether at home, in day cares or nursing homes, or at institutions for children and adults with disabilities.

Clearly, caregiving ambition becomes complicated when considering providing and provisioning ambitions. Providing ambition often clashes with other life tasks, such as breadwinning. Provisioning ambition creates less conflict with breadwinning but is typically difficult to fulfill in the way many people aspire to, especially when they have a dearth of extended family support. A crux of the challenge of work–care balance, this issue has been fodder for the conservative critique of feminism, both during and following the second-wave feminist movement.

SECOND-WAVE FEMINISM, PROVIDING,
AND PROVISIONING

Whether to provide or provision child care became a central question at the heart of many of the flash point issues of the second-wave feminist movement in the United States. Long before "work–life balance" became common parlance and, at least ostensibly, part of the corporate agenda, feminists advocated for a range of policies that would support to differing degrees both provisioning and providing.[30] Second-wave feminists' proposals for federally subsidized child care sought to support those who needed, or wished, to provision care for periods when they were employed outside the home, given that relying on grandparents and other relatives was often not a feasible and/or stable means of child care.[31] Other proposals by second-wave feminists sought to support providing care and included calls for financial remuneration for primary caregivers and homemakers.[32]

Many of the proposals seemed radical for the time. Some still seem radical today—such as the availability of 24/7 child care, 365 days a year. But far more of their proposals included policies that are now considered mainstream (e.g., access to family leave, pregnancy discrimination protections). Their calls for a more involved role for fathers in child care, attention to quality day care and preschool, and equitable divisions of labor in heterosexual marriages are no longer fringe but rather primary concerns and expectations for many men and women. Many of the benefits and accommodations feminists championed, such as greater flexibility in work hours and greater access to paid leave, have not come to fruition.

As with most movements, a countermovement quickly and strongly emerged. Critics of second-wave feminism focused on certain proposals that, not surprisingly, rubbed some members of middle- and working-class America the wrong way, subjecting second-wave feminism to the "anti-family" label. The conservative critique of second-wave feminist efforts, led by Phyllis Schlafly, together with a host of social, cultural, and political factors, effectively shut down proposed work–family policies being considered in Congress. On December 9, 1971, despite having originally supported the bill, President Richard Nixon vetoed the Comprehensive Child Development Act (CCDA), which included, among other things, federally funded child care centers around the country.

The failure to ratify work–care policy at that time, in the early 1970s, highlights the complexity of the providing–provisioning distinction when raised in the public sphere. Many people have ambitions about caregiving. Sometimes these ambitions entail both providing and provisioning care. Sometimes people focus on one (i.e., providing care ambitiously) or the other (i.e., provisioning care ambitiously). When translated into the political space, and political movements and countermovements, it can be explosive. When caregiving ambitions are threatened or critiqued, public opinion becomes polarized quickly and fiercely, especially when leaders engage in stereotyping the other and deploying scare tactics. Our personal caregiving ambitions are that defining.

Since Nixon's veto of the CCDA in 1971, many policy proposals have languished, leaving those with both providing and provisioning ambitions in, oftentimes, difficult situations. Child care and eldercare remain framed primarily as "private problems," as opposed to a societal issue (discussed further in Chapter 8). Though society presumably cares about people's well-being, it is still largely up to individuals and individual families to find their own solutions to the work–care dilemma, while also living up to their own caregiving ambitions.

MODERN PARENTING STEREOTYPES: PROVIDING AND PROVISIONING

Why do we as a society seem to be so obsessed with others' caregiving arrangements? The choices we all make about many other day-to-day tasks and issues aren't much of a concern. For example, some people wash their dishes by hand, while others use a dishwasher; but we don't feel a need to come to some broad social consensus about how people should wash their dishes. In fact, we care a lot more about caregiving than we do about dishwashing. Caregiving is a high-stakes endeavor, and the choices that people make along the providing and provisioning dimensions are either enormously affirming or profoundly challenging to our personal choices and identities.

Indeed, our national obsession with how to raise children and arrange for their care—and the haste with which we judge how others do so—reflects our underlying providing and provisioning ambitions. The myriad of caricatures and stereotypes of caregiving, particularly with mothers, reflect this national obsession. These stereotypical styles range from the free-rangers to the hoverers.[33] Yet, in fact, undergirding these caricatures, which have become part and parcel of the mainstream discourse about parenting, are parents' desire and ability to provide and provision. Let's take a few examples of the most popular stereotypes— which generally criticize, and less commonly compliment, modern parents—and see how they map onto the providing and provisioning dimensions.

Helicopter parents are cartooned as hovering over and micromanaging their children constantly, to ensure safety from injury and to foster academic and career success. They would classify as high on providing ambition as well as high on provisioning ambition. On the providing side, they have high aspirations for spending time with their children, particularly in terms of directly keeping them safe and engaging with them in activities related to their children's future success. On the provisioning side, they have high aspirations for procuring care for their children, also particularly in terms of activities related to their future success. Aside from being high on both providing and provisioning ambitions, helicopter parents typically are portrayed as having the time and financial resources to fulfill both ambitions.

Economic pressures have grown over the years, and the stakes for child-rearing have become higher, due to growing income inequality, as well as greater returns on a college education (particularly in certain fields) in most Western countries. As economic opportunities have contracted and the value of a college education has substantially grown, it's no wonder parents' focus on children's educational achievement has ballooned since the late 1970s, along with the rise of intensive parenting, especially among middle-class and upper-middle-class families in the United States and, to an increasing extent, Europe.[34]

Attachment parents are stereotypically characterized by breastfeeding their children until age 4 or older (for the mothers), sleeping with their children until elementary school (sometimes well into elementary school), and generally professing admiration for attachment parenting experts like Dr. Sears, who emphasize a parenting approach based on responsiveness to and closeness with one's children.[35] They would classify as high on providing as they have high ambition to directly provide care and invest a great deal of time and effort into fulfilling this ambition. These parents tend to have relatively low provisioning ambition. Provisioning does not really fit into the attachment paradigm, particularly when children are young. In fact, provisioning care before children are of school age runs counter to the paradigm. These parents' high providing ambition typically overrides career ambition, at least for one partner, who is typically the mother.

Tiger parents are characterized, often lampooned, as being incredibly high on both providing and provisioning ambition, with an often intense focus on their children's academic and career success in particular. High providing ambition takes the form of high aspirations for direct, personal parental involvement in their child's academic endeavors (the parents are closely engaged as tutors) and being deeply, personally involved in their child's choices, from friends to clubs. These parents, the stereotype goes, are also very ambitious provisioners of care for their children, manifest in procuring high-quality teachers, tutors, coaches, and other educational professionals to help their child to excel and in extensive research (and devotion of family resources) to co-curricular experiences like science camps, sports clinics, enrichment programs, and the like. Unlike helicopter parents, tiger parents are cast as having no intention of shielding children from difficulties, at least in the domain of academic achievement. Quite the opposite, in fact—tiger parents consider challenging lessons learned from hours of practice and drilling highly valuable.

Free-range parents are stereotyped as letting their kids "run wild," with high aspirations for them to explore the world freely and independently, with great autonomy. Though they ostensibly have low caregiving ambition, free-range parenting actually suggests high provisioning ambition and low providing ambition. Not to be confused with negligent or absent parenting, as they're described in the media and popular culture, free-range parents cherish independence of children as an overarching goal and ambition. These parents have high provisioning ambitions in terms of creating opportunities for exploration of the world for their children, a world that is increasingly sheltered and structured.

The rest of us parents? The vast majority of parents, let's face it, are not easily categorized into any of these boxes or social stereotypes. They do not neatly fall into any one of these caricatures. A quick scan of these types of parents may result in the feeling that one has some aspects of all of them yet is perhaps not well captured by any one of them specifically. Children and specific life situations complicate parents' ambitions. Parents regularly feel tugs in multiple directions with conflicting ambitions: While they may be drawn to "tiger parenting" because they aspire for their children to succeed, they may not want to take that approach to the extreme. And though some parents appreciate the virtues of "free-range parenting," they may recognize constraints of the modern world, and their particular place in it, that may make it riskier for their children to "roam freely." In fact, the inability to categorize individual parents in this simplistic way further speaks to the fact that most parents have both providing and provisioning ambitions that influence how they raise their children, even if those ambitions can be challenging to fulfill.

Furthermore, childrearing is also dynamic. A loving preschooler becomes a surly adolescent. A difficult preschooler becomes a kind, easygoing adolescent. A shy elementary school student who might have needed coaxing transforms into a confident, affable young adult. And different children, even within the same family, respond to different approaches. Parents worry about one issue yet report often finding themselves confronted by another, which they did not anticipate. While providing and provisioning ambitions influence raising children, the reality of the experience likely diverges from their original plans and ambitions.

Still, these ambitions remain central to the decisions people make about their professional and personal lives.

PROVIDING AND PROVISIONING: AT THE HEART OF DECISION-MAKING AROUND WORK AND FAMILY

Many like to dole out advice about managing work and care (ourselves included—we offer ours in Chapter 9). Yet blanket advice is difficult to do honestly and well because personal feelings about providing and provisioning ambitions lie at the heart of these decisions. Moreover, socioeconomic class and financial constraints (or the lack thereof) play a role in which options, if any, people have when it comes to work and family. These ambitions also depend on age and stage: Some, for example, report higher providing ambitions as their children get older and lower providing ambitions with infants, whereas others report the exact opposite.

Indeed, many parents describe falling in love with their infants instantaneously and not wanting to delegate that time or care to anyone else while their children are young, even if they had previously planned on doing so. In other words, their providing ambition skyrockets after their children are born. Recall that Heather, from the beginning of the chapter, found this to be the case when she gave birth to her first baby. Nicole, a mother of two also described her change of heart: "Prior to having children I thought we would hire a nanny. Once I realized that I was missing imperative moments of engagement, while allowing someone else's opinions and values to influence my children, I decided that I would be the one to care for them. The daily interactions we have with our children shape who they will become and I was not going to give that privilege to anyone else." Alicia, a mother of one, also discussed in Chapter 1, described her strong urge to provide care directly in a similar vein: "It is very important for me to personally provide care to my son myself because I feel that no one will take care of him the way I do and they will not love him as I do."

Still others balance providing and provisioning in particular ways due to financial circumstances or other priorities. For example, Tracy, a mother of two, explained that, "It was important for me to be involved and for me to have high quality care for my children and my mother. Due to life circumstances I was not always the one providing the direct care." And Vince, a father of two first described in the Introduction, stressed his personal priority of exposing his children to a variety of experiences, reflecting his provisioning ambition: "There are certain experiences that it seems every parent 'must do' such as the Disney theme parks— I have intentionally skipped those, focusing instead on unconventional experiences I feel are critically important, such as Bob Dylan concerts, that I made sure my kids did." In contrast, Rodney, a father of two, described a similar ambition to expose his children to new experiences but explained that he has not yet fulfilled this ambition due to limited resources: "I have goals and desires to care for my children that I have not been able to fulfill as of yet. I want to be able to expose them to different people, places, and things. I have not been able to do so because of the lack of resources, namely time and money." In other cases, life circumstances tilt individuals not toward provisioning but instead toward providing—a lost job may leave a couple with less money for child care, and a parent who was once employed now devotes themself fully to caregiving.

Other parents described fulfilling their providing ambition through adoption. Nina, whom we heard from earlier in the chapter (see Challenges of Ambitions Providing), told us how she had always dreamed of both having biological children and adopting:

> From a young age, I felt that adoption was an attractive option for building a family. I felt that the world was overpopulated and that, as a person who wanted a large family, I could produce one or two humans fewer and provide a loving home for a child who may otherwise have grown up without a family. . . . When I found out that I was carrying a third boy, I turned to my then-husband and said, "We always talked about adoption—let's adopt a girl to complete our family." Four was always the vision. And once I had four, I was pretty overwhelmed, but also very satisfied.

The calculus between providing and provisioning has many variables—not only an individual's own ambition but for those in relationships the ambitions of their partner, values (above and beyond their ambitions), plus a variety of circumstantial factors such as finances or a child's mental and physical health needs. It's important to think about ambitions in terms of both providing and provisioning and to take a long-term perspective, despite the many short-term demands. That topic is explored further in Chapter 9. Understanding your providing and provisioning ambitions can give insight into your own personal feelings and preferences. To that end, let's explore where you currently fall on providing and provisioning ambition.

Know Thyself

We have developed a measure of providing and provisioning ambitions that we use in our research with caregivers, a version of which appears in Table 3.1.[36] Take the following survey and add up your scores. Then check the descriptions after the table to see where your ambitions fall and what that may mean in terms of your caregiving and career. Rate each item on the following scale:

    1 = Strongly disagree
    2 = Disagree
    3 = Neither agree nor disagree
    4 = Agree
    5 = Strongly agree

If you scored in the 16–20 range on providing and in the 16–20 range on provisioning, you're high on providing ambition and high on provisioning ambition. When you provide care, you likely push yourself to be engaged as a caregiver as wholly as you can; when you provision care, you likely are very concerned with vetting and monitoring the care. When you are doing one, your concurrent high ambition for the other may lead to

Table 3.1 Providing and Provisioning Ambition

Dimension	Items	Rating (1–5)
Providing	1. Directly providing care is one of my highest goals in life.	
	2. I aim to have as many hours as possible in the day to care directly for those I love.	
	3. I am constantly on the lookout for new ways to be a better caregiver.	
	4. I am driven to provide direct care for the others in my life.	
	Total for providing	
Provisioning	1. When I look for caregivers, I aim to find the very best caregivers in the world for those I love.	
	2. I am driven to make sure that those I love have the very best experience of everything.	
	3. Whenever I make caregiving arrangements for those I love, I take the task seriously.	
	4. When I delegate caregiving for those I love to another person, I am picky.	
	Total for provisioning	

feelings of "what if" and wondering if it wouldn't be better if you provided care (when you're provisioning) or provisioned care (when you're providing). Your caregiving is likely dynamic and may change throughout the life span of your children, with a stronger focus on fulfilling your providing ambitions when they're younger and a stronger focus on fulfilling your provisioning ambitions when they're older. You likely will use, or have used, a mix of child care—both providing directly and provisioning care. You also likely fall into the classic bind of combining caregiving and work, especially given your high providing ambitions.

If you scored in the 16–20 range on providing and in the 4–8 range on provisioning, you're high on providing ambition and low on provisioning ambition. You have strong ambition to provide care directly, and you have little desire to provision care. When you provide care, you are in your element—fully engaged and attentive to your loved ones' needs. A stay-at-home role or part-time work may suit you well and enable you to fulfill your high providing ambition to give care directly, if it is feasible financially. You may also gravitate toward a caregiving career such as in healthcare or education. You are less likely to provision, but when you have to, you probably prefer that a relative or family member provides care rather than a hired caregiver.

If you scored in the 4–8 range on providing and in the 16–20 range on provisioning, you're low on providing ambition and high on provisioning ambition. You are likely drawn to finding high-quality caring experiences for your loved ones that nurture them in quality ways. You are likely to explore many options for the care and not simply go with the most readily available option. You may personally be well suited to a traditional breadwinner role, as long as you are able to provision high-enough-quality care to fulfill your provisioning ambition. You will likely be comfortable with a partner with a similar profile, or you may find a good fit with a partner who is high in providing ambition. It may take time to arrange the caliber of provisioning care you aspire to, but once you find a way to do so, you will be comfortable.

If you scored in the 4–8 range on providing and in the 4–8 range on provisioning, you're low on providing ambition and low on provisioning ambition. Caregiving is likely not an animating concern of your life or your career. You're well suited to a traditional breadwinner career if you desire one. If you decide to partner with someone, you may opt to couple with a partner who has high caregiving ambition (providing and/or provisioning) or someone with low caregiving ambition (providing and/or provisioning). You may prefer not to engage in a caregiving role at all above and beyond what you feel obliged to do and may focus on fulfilling career and other life ambitions.

If your scores added up to 12 on either ambition (or both), then you are in the mid-range on that dimension. Being in the mid-range means that your ambitions are moderate, which gives you flexibility as you navigate work and care. If you are in the mid-range on one dimension but high on the other dimension, you would likely be more driven in your choices by the higher of the two.

As you can see, providing and provisioning ambitions influence our work–care lives (our choices, yes, and our satisfaction with our circumstances) in a myriad of ways. Unfortunately, as we will see in greater detail in Chapter 7, workplace policy typically revolves around enabling provisioning rather than providing. Though in our research we've found that many people report high providing ambitions, such ambitions are not honored and valued in our society by mainstream institutions. By recognizing and distinguishing between providing and provisioning ambition, we also hope to clarify some of the confusion at the policy level and, more ambitiously, to forever change the conversation about work and care.

DEFINING QUESTIONS

- Have your providing and provisioning ambitions changed or been stable over time?
- Are your providing and provisioning ambitions different depending upon the care recipient? How do your scores change when you think of different care recipients when answering the questions?
- Have you provided care when you preferred to provision care or vice versa? If so, how did that feel? In what ways was the experience better, worse, or about what you had expected?

PART II

Why Care?

Careless

Americans now face a caring deficit: there are simply too many demands on people's time for us to care adequately for our children, elderly people, and ourselves.

—Joan C. Tronto[1]

NOT CAREFUL

Imagine you have a friend you admire for delivering a free lunch every day to a house just outside of town. Each day, the box has a sandwich, a cup of soup, an apple, and some cookies. That's nice, isn't it? Then one day, you get a glimpse inside the house. There's a family with two parents, four young children, and two old grandparents. Though your friend may have done her best, it falls way short of the need. It's not that she's not caring enough, but the care she can give just isn't enough. Americans can be generous; in fact, international surveys find they tend to be more generous as individuals (i.e., more likely to help a stranger, to donate money, to give time to charity) than their counterparts in other countries.[2] But as a society, the United States is shocking in the degree to which it does not take care of the young, old, poor, sick, and lonely. Our public programs are amazingly unambitious in comparison to those of similarly well-off countries and to the needs themselves staring us in the face.

The Caregiving Ambition. Julia B. Bear and Todd L. Pittinsky, Oxford University Press. © Oxford University Press 2022.
DOI: 10.1093/oso/9780197512418.003.0005

Today, governments in the United States (federal, state, and local together) all spend to support our children's education, care, nutrition,
health, and other services. Yet that spending is dramatically skewed toward older children. Government spending per child is markedly lower
for younger age groups than older. This approach is precisely the opposite
of what might be hoped for: greater investment in children during the
earlier years.

Meanwhile, America faces a looming crisis for which it is completely
unprepared: a surge of aging without proper planning. According to the
Pew Research Center, 16% of the US population is 65 or older, and that
number is expected to almost double by 2050.[3] Far from planning economically for this long-foreseen trend, US citizens and politicians sit
around arguing about how not to cut Medicare and Medicaid too much.
Then there's the shocking lack of eldercare, the defunding of elder centers,
and the dismal state of our nursing home infrastructure. Perhaps most
troubling is the isolation: Many older Americans find themselves without
meaningful family contact and community interaction.

No matter our age, connection to others is widely considered a fundamental human need, yet the United States has always been more interested
in meeting its citizens' material needs than in meeting their fundamental social ones. The situation in this day and age is no different: A
great paradox of our current hyperconnected society is that we seem to
feel less connected—and we suffer from it. As Massachusetts Institute of
Technology professor Sherry Turkle has observed, we are increasingly
connected and increasingly alone, expecting more from our technology
but less from direct contact with other people.[4]

Individual experiences of caregiving ambition and caregiving are
embedded in social and political contexts. The degree to which a society
supports—or alternatively devalues—caregiving more broadly matters
profoundly. In this chapter we explore the broader, societal context in
which individuals' caregiving ambition and unpaid caregiving occur. We
review a more expansive terrain of the caregiving context in this chapter
to illuminate the broader devaluing of caregiving in which individuals
with high caregiving ambition find themselves.

Whether considering children, older adults, or even each other—friends, neighbors, community members—caregiving in America consistently falls short. To get a better idea of how, where, and why, it's important to understand the major issues and factors at play. Thus, in this chapter, we review the various policies related to caregiving in the United States. Only after recognizing and coming to terms with our country's mistake in not prioritizing caregiving on a policy level can we hope to improve, both through individual efforts and as a society.

CARELESS TOWARD CHILDREN

Over the past 200 years, the US federal and state governments developed a hodgepodge of programs to improve education and care for children. These investments ranged from universal part-time—and then universal full-day—kindergarten through twelfth-grade education to preschool and after-school care, nutrition services, and healthcare. These efforts were designed not only to boost individual welfare but also to create a highly skilled workforce and thus a stronger nation.

Historically, US spending has focused and still focuses on older children—those who will be entering the workforce sooner—with an eye for investments that will yield short-term economic gains. A recent report by the White House Council of Economic Advisers finds that national spending levels are lowest for children under age 5.[5] Yet research clearly shows that a person's contribution to the economy is largely shaped by their earliest environment.

Preschool Years

On every level—local, state, and federal—this country invests too little in its children during the first 5 years of their lives. According to a 2019 report, the United States ranked 41st among developed economies in pre-primary-school and primary-school enrollment for 3- to 5-year-olds.[6]

France, New Zealand, Denmark, Norway, Sweden, and other countries spend more than 1% of their gross domestic product (GDP) on early-childhood programs, while the United States spends less than half that.[7] The consequence of our collective lack of investment in public preschool is massive in loss of human potential in general, and in particular for children from the country's highest-need communities.

The research finds that early-childhood programs are among the very best investments a government can make; they boost children's health and educational outcomes. For over half a century, academics, advocates, and politicians from both major parties have called for more investment in these programs, yet the pace of change has been glacial. Only a small percentage of children from low-income families—who research shows will benefit the most from preschool—attend center-based preschools (as opposed to one based in a home). Only about 44% of children of low socio-economic status starting high school in 2020 had attended a center-based preschool, compared to 69% of children with high socioeconomic status and 54% of their middle-class peers.[8]

The lack of focus on early childhood education and care is due in part to outdated assumptions that more mothers will stay home with their young children—while presumably a father goes to work—than is actually the case.[9] This assumption is hardly realistic now and, in fact, was never the case for many women, especially women of color.

Creating appropriate facilities in which all preschool children can learn and play would not be cheap, but the return on such an investment could run as high as $7.20 for every $1 spent.[10] Though studies of subsidized preschools like Head Start have produced mixed results—some find beneficial effects, while others find no effects or effects that do not last—even the biggest skeptics concede that the benefits of preschool for a child, their family, and the wider society increase significantly the higher the quality of the preschool experience.

Lack of availability of high-quality preschool amplifies the challenges of simple affordability. Most parents pay out of pocket for some portion, if not all, of their child care costs, including preschool or pre-kindergarten. Publicly funded programs in the United States that do offer free care reach only a fraction of their targeted populations. For example, Head Start reaches less than half of all of the preschool-aged children eligible for its services. Early Head Start, for infants and toddlers from families with the lowest incomes, reaches less than 5% of the children eligible.[11]

Unfortunately, the negative effects of the lack of investment in our youngest children are compounded by the fact that parents of young children tend to have lower-than-average salaries, lower-than-average savings, and less access to credit than parents of older children and teenagers.[12]

Child Care Quality and Affordability

Child care remains unaffordable for many American families—not just those with low incomes. Even middle-income families have great difficulty affording such care. Child care costs are some of the largest expenses in a family's budget, largely because child care and early education are labor-intensive, requiring a low student-to-teacher ratio.[13]

Still, child care is particularly expensive for low-wage families. The US Department of Health and Human Services (HHS) considers child care affordable if it costs 7% of a family's income or less.[14] But even using a less stringent bar—a 10% threshold—there are only two states in which infant care is "affordable" for all families: South Dakota and Wyoming.[15] And that's affordability for families overall—parents earning the minimum wage are priced out of most formal care options without subsidies and/or scholarships. For example, a parent earning the minimum wage living in South Dakota will have to spend 31.8% of annual earnings to afford infant care. In contrast, that would be 103.6% of annual earnings for parents earning the minimum wage in Washington, DC.[16] This expense moves even further out of reach for families with more than one child requiring care. Massachusetts has one of the highest center-based infant care costs in the nation; costs there fail the affordability test of the HHS for over 80% of families.[17] In a study of child care expenses, the Care.com platform found that 55% of families report spending $10,000 or more per year on child care—which exceeds the national average annual cost of in-state college tuition.[18]

Overall, the child care workforce is strikingly low-paid: child care workers are paid 23% less than demographically similar workers in other occupations.[19] The US Bureau of Labor Statistics reports that, for 2019, the median hourly wage for child care workers was $11.65.[20] Other research has found that the pay for child care workers is 39.3% below the median of other occupations requiring similar credentials.[21]

Multiple child care quality studies have shown that the strikingly low compensation for most child care work contributes to the low training of this workforce and the high turnover, which together undermine quality.[22] Continuity in care provider and the degree of past experience of care providers are two key ingredients that influence the quality of early child care over time.[23]

For those families tied to non-standard work schedules—evening work and overnight work in a range of industries such as healthcare, safety, production, and 24-hour retail—the options are even more limited—the more so because such workers' schedules often change weekly. According to a 2018 analysis, only 8% of center-based providers are open at any time during evenings, overnight, or weekends.[24] Parents with irregular work schedules may qualify for child care subsidies, but they often have problems accessing the child care itself due to policies that are structured for parents with standard work schedules. Further, parents who face irregular work schedules must find providers who are flexible about when children can use the care or who allow parents to pay only for the care they use.

Education of School-Aged Children

There is evidence of a lack of caring for our older (i.e., school-aged) children too, particularly in their education. Does the United States care about educating all its children? Increasingly, it seems the answer is no. According to the most recent global study by the Programme for International Student Assessment (PISA), presented in December 2019, despite this nation's wealth, its students overall performed only slightly above average in reading (ranked 14th) and science (ranked 19th) and slightly below average in mathematics (ranked 38th).[25] The lackluster average performance of US children compared to their international peers has been largely steady for decades.

America has long thought of its schools as powerful engines of equality. Yet the "poverty gap" in educational attainment is larger today than it was a generation ago.[26] This gap is, in part, a result of a common US practice of linking school funding to property taxes, ensuring that children from families with greater economic resources have more educational resources than children from families with fewer economic resources. As is the case in most countries, the most recent round of PISA testing for the United States found socioeconomically advantaged students dramatically outperforming disadvantaged students in reading, mathematics, and science.[27] Only 4% of disadvantaged students in the United States, compared to 27% of advantaged US students, were top performers in reading (that is, students who attained one of the two highest proficiency levels).[28]

A recent Children's Defense Fund (CDF) research study found that the differences in educational opportunity by family economic income start early and are powerful.[29] Lower-income children are significantly less likely to enter school ready to learn. In fact, CDF's research found that less than half of the children from the families with the lowest economic resources are ready for school at age 5. In contrast, 75% of their wealthier peers are ready.[30] Fourth- and eighth-grade public school students from families with the least economic resources are almost twice as likely to score below grade level in reading and math as their higher-income peers. Fast forward to high school graduation: Only 62% of children who spent half their childhoods in poverty completed high school by age 20 compared to 90% of children who never experienced poverty.[31]

Medical Care and Nutrition

Though the shortcoming of education is a major issue in the country's child care deficit, it's not the only one, and it's related to many others. For

example, our infant death rate is twice as high as in similarly wealthy countries. Premature births and low birthweight are common, causing lifelong
and even intergenerational effects. For every 100,000 live births in the
United States, 28 women die in childbirth or shortly thereafter, compared
to just 11 in Canada.[32] Within the United States, racial disparities abound.
A powerful point of evidence is the fact that Black women are three times
as likely to die during or shortly after childbirth as are White women.[33]

A lack of health insurance is also a major problem. The US Census Bureau
finds that, in 2018, roughly 4.3 million children did not have any health insurance.[34] That limits their access to, among other preventive measures,
vaccinations. Obesity among American children is also now described
as an "epidemic"—about 13.7 million children and adolescents (18.5%)
are clinically obese.[35] At the other extreme, in 2018, 13.9% of households
with children were food-insecure at some time during the prior year.[36]
According to a 2019 report by the US National Child Abuse and Neglect
Data System, a project of the HHS, on average, nearly five children die
every day—and 1,720 children die annually—from abuse or neglect.[37]

And when the government does provide family-friendly tax benefits,
food stamps, health insurance, and the Women, Infants, and Children
program to qualified individuals, the United States still spends less of its
GDP on programs and benefits for families than all other Organisation for
Economic Co-operation and Development (OECD) countries, aside from
Mexico and Turkey. We spend less than half as much as Denmark, Sweden,
and the United Kingdom. In France, a household (dual-income or single-
parent) that earns less than $48,000 a year receives a cash payment of $1,100
for each child born.[38] Parents at the lowest income levels in France also receive 3 years of monthly payments to help cover new child–related bills.[39]

Families with the Lowest Incomes

The United States does not insure the welfare of even its most impoverished
families. Indeed, the Temporary Assistance for Needy Families (TANF)
program has reached only a fraction of families with children living

below what the federal government considers "austere poverty."[40] And the trends are in the wrong direction. In 1996, TANF reached more than 8 in 10 of those families.[41] Since 1996, after adjusting for inflation, benefits have fallen by 20% or more in 33 states.[42] Nationwide in 2018, just 22% of families with children in poverty received TANF assistance.[43]

The United States has a higher child poverty rate than nearly all other OECD countries. In 2020, the CDF reported that children are the poorest age group in the United States: Nearly 1 in 6 children live in poverty—some 11.9 million children nationally.[44] The child poverty rate (16%) is nearly 1.5 times higher than that for adults aged 18–64 (11%).[45] Our child poverty rate is 2, 3, or even 4 times as high as that of nations with comparable per-capita income. Despite being one of the richest countries in the world, the United States is about on par with Mexico in its rate of childhood poverty.

As many as 1.5 million families—with 3 million children in their midst—live on less than $2 per person per day cash income, excluding other forms of subsidies or gifts. Race and ethnicity, sadly, have a lot to do with the rates of poverty in the United States: 1 in 9 White children live in poverty, but a staggering 1 in 3 Black and Native American children do as well, along with 1 in 4 Latinx children.[46] The negative results of such poverty ripple far and wide.

What about the two major federal programs intended to offset employment-related child care costs for families in need? We have the child and dependent care tax credit, which is a tax benefit for people provisioning child care for their dependents. And we have the employer-provided child care tax exclusion, a tax benefit to try to incentivize employers to provide child care support for employees. But due to income eligibility limits, copayments, and waiting lists, neither comes close to meeting eligible families' actual needs.

All New Parents

The United States is the only OECD country that has no federal paid maternity leave and no paid parental leave. Hungary, for example, offers 160 weeks of paid parental leave. Many American mothers have to return to work mere days after giving birth. Under the Family and Medical Leave Act, the United States guarantees just 12 weeks of unpaid parental leave after the birth or adoption of a child—and only for those who work at a company with 50 or more employees. Many companies also stipulate that the employee must have worked there for 12 months before receiving this benefit. In contrast, all German workers have up to 58 weeks of paid parental leave.

Expanding guaranteed parental leave to all wage-earners in the United States would help parents better nurture their infants. It would reduce the amount of paid child care needed as well since it would reduce the time period between the end of leave and the child starting school. As discussed in earlier chapters, a small but significant step in the right direction came in late 2019 when federal employees were granted up to 12 weeks of paid time off for the birth, adoption, or foster-caring of a new child. But this act only applies to the federal workforce.

Rates of Child Homelessness and Foster Care

Based on calculations by the American Institutes for Research, using data from the US Department of Education and the US Census, 1 in 30 children in the United States—2.5 million children in total—are homeless in any given year.[47] Research has long shown how homelessness puts great stress on children and families and is a significant risk factor for the healthy development of multiple dimensions of a child's life—physical, emotional, educational, cognitive, behavioral, and social. According to the most recent data from the federal government, there are approximately half a million US children living in foster care.[48] Racial inequalities are pervasive. Many experts argue that our collective extraordinary tolerance of child poverty in the United States is a significant driver of family separation.

In short, the United States offers its children a combination of carelessness and unambitious caregiving across the board. And, as evidenced earlier, our carelessness toward children is, not surprisingly, woefully skewed. The class divides in the time and money parents are investing in their children have widened, and these investments are one way that economic advantage is transferred from generation to generation.[49] Meanwhile, increasing income inequality has resulted in more money at the disposal of higher-income families and less money for the lowest-income families. As a result, lower-income families have had to increase the share of income they dedicate to caring for their children much more rapidly than higher-income families have had to. In the end, it is the children of the United States who suffer.

America does not ambitiously care for its children. Quite the opposite: We are careless with them and their futures. We minimize and even commodify this carelessness by turning caregiving into a "business case" (an idea further explored in Chapter 8), as even the most well-intentioned policymakers do when they promote the expected economic payoffs from investment in early childhood care and education. Though it may sound banal, every child deserves to be cared for and nurtured to a higher degree than we currently do. Still, we can't focus just on the young adults of tomorrow. We must also remember the older adults of today, those who are often left out of the caregiving equation, many of whom raised us, supported us, and made us who we are as individuals and as a country.

CARELESS TOWARD OLDER ADULTS

Taking care of older adults is also far too low among our social and economic priorities. Consciously or not, because we prioritize caregiving interpersonally—among family, friends, and neighbors—we end up undervaluing and underpaying the "caring professions." The lack of any monetary exchange when many of us help to take care of our own parents or grandparents feeds a misconception that there's not much societal value in having someone help to take care of them. Quite the opposite is the case. And as a result, the caring professions have burgeoned to help fill the void left by too many of us who can't provide the quantity and quality of care we might like to for older family and friends (often because we have to go to work). The caregiving professions are not only underpaid but also horribly structured, with workloads, hours, and emotional demands that leave these workers among the most burnt out.[50] And even after some 60 years of modern feminism, women still do most of the formal and informal (i.e., the paid and unpaid) caregiving for older adults in our society.

America's fragmented system of eldercare delivery is not truly a caring system—certainly not an ambitiously caring one. Older people in institutional care, for example, are deprived of many activities and subjected to unnecessary suffering.[51] Institutions prioritize protecting themselves from litigation and regulatory fines over the quality of life of those they are meant to serve. The regulatory system itself is designed to avoid death—which is, of course, critical—but sadly not to also embrace (and enhance) quality of life.

It's not just older Americans in eldercare facilities who are too often marginalized and mistreated. According to a 2018 report by the US Federal Reserve, nearly a quarter of households with two adults 65 or over can't afford certain necessities.[52] This study found that, under the official poverty measure, 4.7 million adults aged 65 and older in the United States live in poverty (some 9.2%); that number increases to 7.2 million (14.1%) when measured through the federal government's Supplemental Poverty Measure (SPM). (The SPM, released by the Census Bureau, seeks to address many criticisms of the official poverty measure and to provide an improved statistical picture of poverty.)

These poverty rates increase with age and are higher for women, Black people, Latinx people, and people in relatively poor health—and especially for those at the intersections of these groups. Nearly 3 million women aged 65 and above have incomes below poverty under the official poverty measure, a number that rises to more than 4 million under the SPM. Though there have been periods in which these numbers have improved, shocks to the economy have set back such progress. The 2008 financial crisis erased decades of improvements in material well-being for the older US groups, and the COVID-induced recession had a similar impact.[53]

Racial disparities abound. According to a study by the Center for American Progress, aging non-Whites are more likely than aging Whites to be poor. Black people make up only about 9% of the older adult population in the United States, but the study found they account for 21% of the older adult population living below the poverty line.[54] Today, the researchers concluded, nearly one-quarter of all older Black Americans live below the poverty line. As with too many of the sobering statistics on the carelessness of our society, the costs fall disproportionately on ethnic minority communities.

This study also found that more women of all ethnicities, relative to men, are in precarious positions financially in retirement. More than 2.3 million women older than 65 (11.5%) live at or below the poverty line, the researchers found, while slightly over 1 million (6.6%) of men older than 65 live in poverty.[55] Women aged 75 and above, the study found, are over 3 times as likely to be living in poverty as men in this age group.[56] This is partly because Social Security lacks a system of "caregiver credits" (i.e., pension credits) awarded to people who spend time out of the paid workforce engaged in caregiving (for dependent children or sick or elderly relatives). These credits help women, in particular, whose gaps in paid work often lead to fewer years of contributions to Social Security and to lower lifetime average earnings—both of which lead to collecting lower Social Security payments. In striking contrast, caregiving credits are used in virtually all public pension systems in Europe.

America is failing to feed its older adults as well. Millions go hungry as the safety net designed to catch them frays. Nearly 8% of Americans 60 and older—some 5.5 million people—were "food-insecure" in 2017.[57] Food instability among our older adults is expected to grow as the number of older adults as a share of the population overall grows. The Older Americans Act, one of the main federal programs helping seniors— which was passed more than half a century ago as part of the Great Society reforms—is itself starved for money. Its funding has lagged far behind older adult population growth and economic inflation. A 2020 American Association of Retired Persons report found that the biggest chunk of the act's budget—nutrition services—had dropped by 8% in the previous 18 years when adjusted for inflation.[58] Home-delivered and group meals for seniors have decreased by nearly 21 million between 2005 and 2019.[59]

Only a small fraction of those facing food insecurity get any meal services under the act; a US Government Accountability Office report, examining data from 2013, found that 83% got none.[60]

The Support Older Americans Act was reauthorized in 2020 with spending levels far below what advocates for seniors argue is necessary. And according to the Department of Agriculture, adults 60 and older are under-enrolled (meaning there are far fewer enrolled than eligible) in the Supplemental Nutrition Assistance Program, or SNAP, the federal food stamp program for America's poorest citizens. Those who haven't signed up for SNAP are typically unaware they qualify, believe their benefits would be too small to help, or can no longer get to a grocery store to use these benefits.[61] Such neglect is expensive: Many malnourished seniors wind up in hospitals, costing the public far more than free meals would have.

Without financial stability and regular access to food, it's no wonder a portion of older Americans struggle with depression. While estimates of major depression in older people living at home range from less than 1% to about 5%, the figures rise to 11.5% for elderly hospital patients and 13.5% for those who require home healthcare.[62] And that is true even as clinical depression is often believed to be underdiagnosed and undertreated in older adults.[63] Healthcare providers may mistake symptoms of depression for natural reactions to illness or to just getting older. Some older adults share this belief and therefore do not seek help.

The issues facing older adults in the United States don't end there. Elder abuse—defined as including "physical, emotional, or sexual harm inflicted upon an older adult, their financial exploitation, or neglect of their welfare by people who are directly responsible for their care"—is shamefully widespread.[64] Authorities receive more than half a million reports of elder abuse every year. Though that number on its own is alarming, according to the Department of Justice, only 1 in 23 cases of elder abuse are even reported.[65] Meanwhile, 90% of those individuals abused experience this abuse at the hands of their own family or caregivers.[66] In 2016, the Senate approved a resolution to recognize "World Elder Abuse Awareness Day," but this was merely symbolic—a call for more effective prevention strategies and stronger laws and policy.

It probably comes as no surprise that a lot of valuable caregiving for the elderly never takes place due to the failure of work–care policies (discussed in Chapters 2 and 7). But until we truly unlock the workplace—through reduced and/or flexible schedules and through opportunities for people to enter, exit, and re-enter the workforce in ways that aren't career suicide—a great many people just won't have the time or latitude to help care for their older loved ones as they wish to.

Writing in *The Atlantic*, author Jonathan Rauch observed another side of the same problem, namely the failure to help individuals prepare to provide care to older family members: "How can it be that so many people like me are so completely unprepared for what is, after all, one of life's near certainties? What I needed was for the experts to find me and tell me what I needed. We should all be given time off work at age 40 to take a class on elder care."[67]

As the number of seniors in our society continues to climb, all of these issues will only get worse. The nation's health and social services will be forced to handle unprecedented demand as more members of the baby boom generation—roughly 76 million people—settle into retirement, many with eroded savings and underfunded retirement accounts. As they leave the workforce in droves, they're also more likely to experience other pressing mental issues related to caregiving that we often ignore, no matter our age: social isolation and loneliness.

CARELESS TOWARD EACH OTHER: SOCIAL ISOLATION AND LONELINESS

For many, the first wave of coronavirus was a dramatic experience of both social isolation and loneliness, but the trends in both had already been rising across the board before the pandemic hit. One in 5 US millennials reports feeling lonely and feeling like they have "no friends."[68] Teenagers, too, are lonelier than ever, and their absorption in social media and digital entertainment appears to be intensifying the problem. According to a 2018 national survey by the health insurance company Cigna, loneliness levels have reached an all-time high in the United States. Almost "half of the 20,000 adults surveyed report they sometimes or always feel alone and 40 percent sometimes or always feel their relationships are not meaningful."[69]

A 2018 Pew Research Center survey of more than 6,000 US adults linked frequent loneliness to "dissatisfaction with one's family, social, and community life."[70] Loneliness is not the same as social isolation. People can be isolated or alone yet not feel lonely at all. People can also be surrounded by others yet feel profound loneliness. The distinction between isolation and loneliness is sometimes overlooked by researchers and policymakers, though both can cause misery, and the rates of both today reflect a lack of caring in our society. Loneliness is a more subjective feeling about a gap between people's desired level of social contact and their actual level of social contact. Loneliness is, by definition, a dissatisfaction, while it is a matter of individual preference whether a given level of isolation is a problem or not. Social isolation is a more objective measure. These distinctions noted, both reflect a high incidence across our society of not being connected to others in deep ways and not feeling cared for by others. Feeling cared for can be the end product of living in a richly networked community in which one person is connected to many others, or it might be as simple as having at least one meaningful connection to another person.

The increases in loneliness and isolation in our society are particularly alarming because of the associated physical and mental health risks. Lack of social connection raises one's health risks as much as alcoholism or smoking 15 cigarettes a day.[71] Loneliness and social isolation are twice as harmful to physical and mental health as obesity.[72] In addition, perceived social isolation is linked to a wide range of other negative health outcomes: depression, poor sleep quality, impaired executive function, accelerated cognitive decline, poor cardiovascular function, impaired immunity, inflammation, and higher levels of stress hormones.[73] A recent study found that isolation increases the risk of heart disease by 29% and stroke by 32%.[74]

A 2019 study analyzed data from more than 580,000 adults and found that social isolation increases the risk of premature death "from every cause for every race," in particular by 50% for Black people and by 60%–84% for White people.[75] Children who were socially isolated have significantly poorer health 20 years later when compared to children who were not socially isolated, even after statistically controlling for other factors.[76] Meanwhile, a meta-analysis that included 148 studies involving more than 300,000 participants found that greater social connection is associated with a 50% reduced risk of early death. Another study found loneliness to be particularly prevalent—and particularly dangerous—for older populations: Loneliness is associated with a 40% increase in the risk of dementia.[77]

In the United States today, we have loneliness and social isolation across the life span, reflections of a lack of more ambitious caregiving for each other. The most recent census data, from 2010, show that over one-quarter of the population lives alone—the highest rate ever recorded. Rates of volunteerism and religious affiliation— institutional connections that build community—have also decreased. Other countries (Australia, Denmark, and the United Kingdom) have woken up and started to act to combat social isolation and loneliness on a national level; there has been no such national response in the United States.

From the youngest members of our society—our children—to the oldest, and including all ages in between, our society is not ambitious enough in how we care for each other and instead contributes to the frequently too careless status quo.

DEFINING QUESTIONS

- How much care should a country provide to its children? Its older citizens? Its most economically vulnerable? Its sick? Its isolated and lonely?
- Which forms of carelessness have you directly observed in your community? Why is it that so many people go under-cared-for in a country as wealthy as the United States?
- What steps do you think are most important to help create a more caring society?

The Stubborn Caregiving Gaps

Much of the progress that women have made in income parity has
gone to childless women.

—STEPHANIE COONTZ[1]

GLASS CEILING, GLASS CLIFF, OR LABYRINTH?

When Carol Hymowitz and Timothy Schellhardt coined the term "glass
ceiling" in 1986, the metaphor resonated far and wide.[2] Women worked
hard to advance their careers only to eventually hit an invisible barrier,
unable to advance any further. Since then, scholars have modified the
metaphor: Some research suggests a "glass cliff" exists, a phenomenon in
which women are more likely to be appointed to leadership in times of
crisis, meaning their chances of failure are high.[3] Alice Eagly and Linda
Carli, two prominent psychologists who have researched gender and leadership for decades, came up with the notion of the "labyrinth": The path
to leadership is more like a maze with many obstacles on the way, particularly for women.[4] Given the number of obstacles, many women don't
make it to the end. Eagly and Carli explain, "women are not turned away
as they reach the penultimate stage of a distinguished career. They disappear in various numbers at many points leading up to that stage."[5]

Regardless of the analogy used, these gender gaps remain puzzling,
especially given the overall lack of gender differences in leadership

The Caregiving Ambition. Julia B. Bear and Todd L. Pittinsky, Oxford University Press. © Oxford University Press 2022.
DOI: 10.1093/oso/9780197512418.003.0006

performance.[6] Many scholars explain the leadership gender gap in terms of *gender role congruity*, the fit between one's gender role and a given situation. Indeed, gender (as opposed to biological sex) reflects the sociocultural roles that men and women typically play in society: breadwinner and caregiver, respectively.[7] Leadership qualities—assertiveness, for example—are more consistent with men's agentic gender role; women's communal, caring gender role is considered less consistent with such qualities.[8] Given this lack of fit, women in leadership roles often face a double bind, or a catch-22: If they are too assertive, they aren't liked; but if they're warm and likable, they're viewed as not competently performing their roles.[9] In other words, women must prove they are qualified to be leaders, but when they do, they are often perceived as violating gender role expectations, which people often don't like.[10]

Evidence for this phenomenon abounds in social psychology and organizational behavior research. That said, it is important to point out that this work is based predominantly on scenario studies, those in which participants evaluate hypothetical male versus female leaders using vignettes or videos. Still, there is no question that Virginia Schein's "Think manager, think male" stereotype[11] is alive and well. Every semester we teach over a hundred young men and women in undergraduate and graduate courses, many of whom aim to be business leaders in the future. As we discuss organizational cases and business situations, the word *manager* is inevitably followed by the word *he*. Though we quickly correct our students—asking them to use *he or she* or *they*—each semester we begin anew with a batch of students who, more often than not, assume that the generic, hypothetical manager is a *he*.

Although stereotypes play a role in understanding gender gaps in pay and leadership (many of the highest-paying positions are in senior leadership), without addressing issues related to caregiving, these stubborn gaps are here to stay. In fact, the continued emphasis on stereotyping belies the nature of gender gaps' relationship to caregiving, which appears to be the real driver. Notably, wage gaps are small to non-existent among men and women without children.[12] Caregiving, and women's greater propensity to be the primary caregivers in their families, is at the heart of these persistent gaps.

Family leave policies have not solved the problem and understandably so: Not everyone aims to be a chief executive officer (CEO) just because they have caregiving support. Some people aim to engage in caregiving to an even greater extent. In other words, family leave enables caregiving, as it presumably should; but this leads economists to lament the economic costs of these policies in the sense of stifling women's advancement. Yet at certain stages in life, people dive into caregiving because they both need to and want to engage in it deeply.

Whether there's ultimately a ceiling, a cliff, or a labyrinth is somewhat a moot point—they all serve to limit women's professional success while rewarding both men and women who decide to focus solely on their career. Calling the resulting gaps "gender gaps" is not really accurate either—they are best characterized as "caregiving gaps." But before we get into that discussion, let's first consider the basics of what we know about these gaps.

WHAT WE KNOW ABOUT THE GENDER GAPS IN PAY AND LEADERSHIP

Without controlling for any other factors, on average, men earn more than women. Specifically, in the United States, the gap is around 20%, meaning women earn approximately 80% of what men earn. When the statistics are examined by race, the gap is even larger. For example, Black women earn 68% of what White men earn, and Latinx women earn 62% of what White men earn. Internationally, there are some countries with smaller gaps—for example, in Canada, the gap is 11%—and there are also plenty of countries with larger gaps, such as South Korea where the gap is 34%.[13] The gender gaps in leadership positions are even starker: Among S&P 500 companies, 37% of entry- to middle-level managers are women, but the percentage of female managers drops precipitously as people climb the corporate ladder, leaving only 6% at the CEO level.[14] Similarly, only 33 (6.6%) Fortune 500 company CEOs are women—an all-time high.[15]

One way to understand gender gaps is to consider where we don't see them. First, two important and related gaps between men and women have been reversed and narrowed, respectively: education level and years of work experience. Women are now more likely than men to have college and advanced degrees, meaning women now have a greater number of years of education compared to men. The gap in years of work experience, which—not surprisingly—is related to the wage gap, also has narrowed quite a bit, though men still typically report a few more years of work experience compared to women, on average.[16] Furthermore, Janet Shibley Hyde, an eminent psychologist at the University of Wisconsin, has published extensively on what she calls the "gender similarities hypothesis," namely, the idea that men and women are much more similar than they are different and that the differences that do exist between them are quite small and insubstantial.[17] Her work reveals that gender gaps in educational performance and achievement, such as assessments of mathematical and verbal abilities, are now, for the most part, non-existent; and those that still appear are extremely small.

Age and life stage also play important roles. Among young adults in their early 20s, the wage gap is small (4%).[18] As per Stephanie Coontz's quote at the beginning of the chapter, income parity exists but among childless women and childless men. Yet the wage gap balloons around age 35, precisely the time when caregiving for children and aging relatives tends to gear up. Related, women report greater interruptions from employment compared to men.

There is, however, an occupation in which no wage gap appears, even among middle-aged workers: pharmacists. According to economics research, men and women earn equal salaries in this industry, primarily because there is flexibility in terms of scheduling working hours and working extremely long hours is not rewarded, meaning there is no premium for extreme work as in some other industries.[19]

Finally, the pay gap is smaller in some countries, such as Belgium, where the overall wage gap between men and women is only 3.4%. Stronger unions and higher wage floors for low-income earners generally create less variation in wages across the board, what economists call "wage compression." This wage compression translates into lower gaps between men and women.[20]

Even though the wage gap is ameliorated under certain circumstances, it mostly remains steadfast, often linked to specific industries or positions, along with the gap in leadership roles.

Where Do Wage Gaps in Pay and Leadership Appear?

Occupation and industry are now the two main factors that explain the gender pay gap in the United States, as opposed to "human capital" factors, such as years of education, which used to be much more central to the issue. The wage gap is higher and more rigid among high-income earners; compared to other income levels, during the past few decades the gap has changed much less among the highest-paid employees and those in the upper echelons of organizations.[21]

The wage gap is especially prominent in certain industries, such as finance and corporate law, in which jobs demand exceptionally long working hours and offer little flexibility. Claudia Goldin, an economics professor at Harvard and a leading scholar of the gender pay gap, mentioned in Chapter 3, calls these jobs "greedy jobs" for good reason.[22] Positions in these industries involve a great deal of deadline pressure, a commitment to meet clients' needs at all hours, and little ability to substitute employees for one another given the primacy of relationships with clients. Women are less likely than men to work in these jobs, especially over the long term.

For example, consistent with the 4% wage gap among young adults in their early 20s, a study of MBA graduates working in finance found that, initially upon graduation from an elite institution, there was only a small gender gap in salaries. Yet 10 years later, male graduates were earning 82% more than female graduates, an enormous gap that was almost entirely explained by the number of hours worked per week and years of work experience.[23] In other words, most of the women were no longer employed full-time in the finance industry 10 years after completing their MBAs.

Even within industries, there is a great deal of variation in pay and leadership equity, depending in part upon the degree of flexibility and schedule control offered by different positions. For example, women now earn an equal number of medical degrees as men overall, but male doctors still earn more than female doctors both in primary care and across specialties.[24] Women are also less likely than men to advance to leadership positions in medicine.[25] And gender gaps vary depending upon the specialty: In 2019, women made up 83% of obstetrics and gynecology residents but only 15% of orthopedic surgery residents.[26] Still, some jobs within medicine are now considered "stealth family-friendly occupations,"[27] mainly because it has become standard to schedule shifts far in advance, especially in primary care and internal medicine, as more physicians work for large practices rather than managing their own. Control over one's hours and the ability to schedule work far in advance are two factors that parents, especially mothers, value highly. Over the past few decades, both men and women report a markedly decreased interest in specialties that involve less control over one's life, but the effects are stronger for women.[28]

CAREGIVING AND GENDER GAPS IN PAY AND LEADERSHIP

When examining the gender pay gap, the effect of gender on average pay becomes much smaller after controlling for the effects of occupation and industry. In addition, within professional positions—for which the gender gap in participation overall has decreased—women are more likely than men to have interruptions in workforce participation and to work shorter hours. They are also more likely to choose occupations with greater temporal flexibility. Women also confront discrimination and sexism in the workplace.[29] These factors help explain the gender pay gap and the career advancement gap, but there is one factor underlying all of them—the central role of caregiving.

Both men and women, but women in particular, are disadvantaged in organizations that pit working against caring for one's family.

Organizations continue to operate on the assumption, and preference, that employees have no other responsibilities than work, what the researcher Joan Acker famously labeled the "ideal worker."[30] They continue to reward employees—typically men—who can work extraordinarily long hours, ensuring that the wage gap persists. Men are more likely able to stay in industries and occupations that demand these hours and 100% devotion to their jobs, while women are more likely to leave if they want to, or have to, focus their efforts elsewhere, especially during phases in their lives when caregiving responsibility is high.

Therefore, to alleviate the wage gap, it is important not only to accommodate people's often conflicting responsibilities and ambitions at work and at home but also to change organizational cultures that value and incentivize working extremely long hours. The bottom line is that, for today's professional employees, the willingness to work these long hours serves as a competitive advantage that anyone with caregiving responsibilities and ambitions will find it impossible to compete with.

Our cultural insistence on the "ideal worker" is curious when considered in light of the reality of US families. According to the Bureau of Labor Statistics, in 2020, in 64% of married couple families with children under the age of 18, both parents were employed outside the home (and the percentage is even higher in other family structures, such as unmarried domestic partners and single parents).[31] Despite this fact, caregiving among such families is not prioritized by many organizations or by the US government. As first discussed in Chapter 2, the United States significantly trails behind other countries when it comes to policy support for caregiving. In addition to paid time off and other leave support following birth or adoption, many countries, particularly in western and northern Europe, provide a care infrastructure, including day care, preschool, and after-school programs. In this way, parents, and mothers especially, across the socioeconomic spectrum have help in juggling work and family responsibilities and are supported in their caregiving ambitions.

Overall, gender gaps in human capital factors, such as education, are now minimal to non-existent. Instead, caregiving responsibility and caregiving ambition underlie gender gaps typically seen in pay and leadership, particularly in light of the extreme working hours required in many professions. This situation then raises the question of whether greater structural support for caregiving will mitigate gender gaps. In other words, there is no doubt that structural support for caregiving is lacking in the United States, but do family leave policies help eliminate gender gaps? Are these policies a panacea, so to speak, when it comes to gender gaps in pay and leadership? The answer is complicated—It's both yes and no.

Is Family Leave a Panacea for Gender Gaps in Pay and Leadership?

In countries with family leave policies and support for caregiving, women are more likely to be employed outside the home.[32] However, and not inconsistent with the notion of caregiving ambition, women actually advance in their careers at slower rates in countries with stronger work–family polices. For example, when labor economists have compared countries that are economically similar to the United States, they have found that, after these countries introduced family-friendly policies, women's labor force participation increased on average but that women in these countries were less likely to be employed full-time or to have managerial jobs.[33] In fact, in those countries offering the highest number of weeks of paid leave (35 weeks or more)—such as Austria, Germany, and the Czech Republic—the gender pay gap is among the highest in Europe, at 20%–25%.[34]

To counter these trends, some countries have introduced paternity leave policies with a "use it or lose it" incentive, encouraging more men to take paternity leave. It should be noted that women primarily use existing family leave policies, so these new dad-focused policies also allow fathers to follow their caregiving ambitions in a way they may not have been able to in the past. In Sweden, for example, when the government specified that 90 days of the family leave offered could only be taken by fathers, usage by fathers tripled. Other countries that have implemented this type of policy for fathers have seen similar results.[35]

Comparable trends have been found in the United States as well. A study of American companies with varying family leave policies found that the better the maternity leave policy at a company, the fewer women there were in executive positions.[36] The authors of the study—consultants at a private consulting firm—argue that this finding is evidence for bias: Parents, especially mothers, are put on a slower career track and never recover from it. No doubt this explanation has some validity, and it is certainly consistent with what we have found in our research. Specifically, in a study of job offers made to comparable male and female job candidates, female candidates were offered lower salaries and were also more likely than male candidates to be offered a flexible work arrangement characterized as "career dampening."[37] However, the wage discrimination against women disappeared when employers received explicit information showing that the job candidates (both male and female) were their families' primary breadwinners.

Nevertheless, it could also be the case that, if the government and more companies in the United States supported caregiving, not everyone would run out to become a CEO. Based on the findings, it appears that many parents use structural support to engage in what it is intended to support: caregiving. Subsequently, mothers and fathers continue to be actively involved in caregiving, not necessarily focusing on racing up the corporate ladder.

Evidence shows that career advancement is inhibited when women take leave for 6 months or more, leading economists to label the outcomes of these family leave policies "negative effects of extended leaves on women."[38] (A shorter leave is not associated with women's career advancement.) Economically speaking, in terms of career advancement and income, these long-term leave policies may have negative effects, and they do not necessarily lead to more female CEOs or top managers. But such polices help keep women in the workforce, which is important given high rates of poverty, particularly among single mothers with children.[39] It is also vital to point out that most economists do not measure outcomes such as work–family conflict and satisfaction with family when they report the negative effects of these policies. Thus, there are likely additional benefits of these policies in terms of well-being and mental and physical health that are not accounted for when measuring the economic outcomes. Moreover, these policies encourage caregiving, which, ultimately, is what they're meant to do.

What About Men and Fathers?

Often when gender gaps in pay and leadership are discussed, the focus is on women and the ways in which women trail men in terms of pay and leadership. But what about the role of men, and fatherhood specifically? And why do we only consider one side of the coin—gender disparities in economic outcomes? What about the other side of the coin, namely, gender disparities in caregiving?

Extant research has shown that women experience a "motherhood penalty" when they become parents, whereas men experience a "fatherhood bonus." Men's earnings, and managers' and colleagues' views of men, tend to increase after they become fathers—for women, the effects are quite the opposite, hence the terms *bonus* and *penalty*.[40] Nevertheless, even fathers, when they ask for greater flexibility to spend more time with their families, experience what is known as the "flexibility stigma," in which they are viewed negatively and accorded less respect for their desire to give more attention to their families. Specifically, men who request family leave are rated as poorer workers, are more likely to receive penalties, and are less likely to receive workplace rewards compared to men who do not make such a request, even when that request is justified by challenging family circumstances, such as serious illness.[41]

This backlash occurs due to the assumption that these men are not 100% committed to work, which violates their masculine gender role.[42] Just as women experience penalties for violating their gender role—such as the catch-22 women find themselves in, driven by the need to appear simultaneously warm and competent, likable and assertive—men also experience penalties when they don't conform to the expectations of their gender role. Scholars explain these effects in terms of stereotypes and the "precariousness" of masculinity. Essentially, since it is difficult to prove one's manhood, it needs to be proven continually, and even once proven, it is easily lost.[43]

This endless quest of proving one's masculinity plays out in many domains of life, especially at work. In fact, researchers have proposed a model of organizations as masculinity contests, called "masculinity contest cultures" (MCCs).[44] In these MCCs, a key way to prove one's manhood is to put work first and to be a breadwinner, not a caregiver. Indeed, other research has shown that men devise ingenious ways to hide their caregiving roles, especially when they need to leave work early or are engaged in caregiving during non-work hours. In this way, they can still "pass" in the organization as masculine ideal workers.[45] Women, in contrast, are more likely to explicitly seek jobs with temporal flexibility to accommodate caregiving, but this approach often leads to being sidelined and written off as "on the mommy track."[46] For gender equity to occur in organizations, men need to be able to engage in caregiving openly, instead of fearing penalties when they request flexibility or express their interest in actively caring for family in addition to being active earners.

In fact, many men and women report, to an equivalent extent, that parenting is extremely central to their identities.[47] Indeed, new fathers experience hormonal changes similar to those of new mothers—men's prolactin levels increase and testosterone levels decrease immediately following childbirth.[48] Although fathers who are full-time caregivers are still rare (in 2016, 17% of full-time caregivers were men), the percentage has almost doubled in the past few decades (in 1989, only 10% of full-time caregivers were fathers).[49]

However, in terms of time spent on child care, men still trail women substantially, with women engaging in almost double the amount of child care compared men (men report spending 8 hours per week on average, compared to women, who report spending 14 hours per week on average). The statistics for housework are similar: Women report 18 hours a week spent on chores compared to 10 hours a week for men.[50] Indeed, studies abound showing unequal distributions of housework in heterosexual couples even when both partners work outside the home and when women earn more than their male partners.[51] To be sure, the hours that men report spending on child care and housework have increased significantly over the past few decades—their hours spent on both child care and housework have almost tripled since the mid-1960s.[52] Yet very clear disparities in caregiving persist.

There is some evidence that the younger generation of fathers, specifically millennials, has a different attitude toward caregiving and that they spend more time caring for their children. According to the Pew Research Center, "While Millennials may be delaying parenthood, it's not for lack of interest in eventually becoming moms and dads."[53] Members of this generation rated being a good parent as a top priority: Some 52% said it was one of the most important goals in their lives, well ahead of having a successful marriage.[54] Millennial men, in particular, report prioritizing fatherhood more so than previous generations. However, whereas a majority of millennial men believe that caregiving should be divided equally between both partners (66%), a much smaller portion (29%) report actually doing so.[55] Thus, as millennials age and become fathers, their expectations do not always match their lived experiences.[56]

FROM GENDER GAPS TO CAREGIVING GAPS

As mentioned in the opening of this chapter, the term "gender gaps" is not truly comprehensive. Though the phrase is commonly used, such as throughout this chapter, upon examination it is clear that the focus in "gender gaps" is on women, not men. In both academia and the popular press, men are treated as the standard category, while women are compared to that category, such as in "women earn 80% of what men earn." We rarely see the opposite comparison, along the lines of, "men engage in 50 percent of the caregiving that women engage in."[57]

Furthermore, as discussed in Chapter 2, although women now have greater possibilities in the workplace and are encouraged to move into male-dominated industries and positions, the opposite has not occurred for men. For example, despite the increasing need for healthcare professionals, these jobs remain underpaid and primarily filled by women.[58] In the meantime, there is a growing encouragement and promotion of women to move into science, technology, engineering, and mathematics professions; but this effort is not matched by a comparable momentum for men to move into caregiving professions.[59]

Related, Professor Alice Eagly and her colleagues published an investigation of gender role stereotypes across many decades, based on opinion poll data going back to the 1940s. They found that people today view men and women as equally competent and sometimes even report a competence advantage for women.[60] Yet there is still a large gap in how people perceive men and women in terms of communality, the warm and caring traits associated with women's traditional gender role. In fact, people now view women as more communal than they did several decades ago. Thus, communal stereotypes of women have grown, not diminished.

This finding is surprising given the increase in competence for women, as well as women's increased labor force participation. The authors explain the findings, in part, by sex segregation in the labor force and the fact that women tend to work in jobs that emphasize social skills and caring, such as in the education and healthcare industries. Although the authors are optimistic—arguing that many jobs in the future will increasingly require even greater social skills, thereby advantaging women—this communality disparity may only serve to enhance gender gaps by reinforcing the already extensive segregation in caregiving work and the helping professions. And others worry that stereotyping women as preferable for some leadership positions, based on their communal orientations, may, in the end, operate to limit women.[61]

This pattern is further evidence of the fact that, when we dig beneath the surface, the term "gender gaps" is a poor characterization of the societal and economic trends discussed in this chapter. The more useful focus is on "caregiving gaps." Given that caregiving underlies gender gaps, these gaps will only be mitigated when caregiving is valued by society, valued at work, and undertaken by men more than it is currently. Just as women trail men in earnings, men trail women significantly in caregiving, as evidenced by men's participation in caregiving discussed in the previous section. In fact, in absolute terms, the caring gaps are even larger than the earnings gaps: Whereas the aggregate gender pay gap is 20%, the aggregate gender caring gap, based on hours spent on child care per week, is closer to 50%.

We must lessen penalties for engaging in caregiving, such as being sidelined at work, being unable to return to previously pursued careers, and not accruing work credits in Social Security and other benefits, as discussed in Chapter 4. Caregiving jobs must also be better compensated, especially relative to other jobs requiring similar skills. And more men must take on caregiving duties, reducing women's disproportionate load in both child care and eldercare (for example, upward of 75% of all informal, unpaid caregivers in eldercare are women[62]). Of course, as a society we also need to stop negatively stereotyping men who focus on caregiving.

Calling the various disparities in pay and leadership gender gaps, as opposed to caring gaps, is like calling a deep gash a cut rather than a wound. Yes, a wound involves an initial cut, but that is a rather inaccurate portrayal, masking the deeper problem. Moreover, the term "caring gaps" reframes the disparities seen in terms of deficits in caregiving rather than just the knee-jerk deficits in earnings. Why do we tend to focus solely on men's higher salaries relative to women and the other accoutrements of being employed in demanding positions? Instead, why not focus on the concomitant caregiving deficits? As discussed at length in Chapter 4, our society is beset by these caring gaps: between men and women; on an institutional level, for both the young and the old; and in terms of the Social Security system that does not recognize unpaid caregiving. And, as discussed earlier in the section "What we know about gender gaps in pay and leadership," gender gaps in earnings are nominal among young adults and in industries that don't require extreme hours. All of these findings point to the conclusion that caregiving, *not gender*, is the main issue in wage and leadership gaps.

Let's refocus the conversation from solving gender gaps—which often serves as a veiled discussion of how women can become more like men and lean in to their careers—to solving caregiving gaps, which could lead to a new, fruitful discussion of how to enable both men and women to engage in caregiving. Instead of only encouraging young women to become CEOs to "fix" women's earning deficits, let's also encourage men to become nurses and full-time fathers to "fix" their caregiving deficits. Rather than forcing people to choose between careers and caregiving, let's value caregiving and cultivate, instead of squelch, both young men's and women's caregiving ambitions—only then can we start to close these stubborn gaps and support ambition that's not necessarily tied to a paycheck.

DEFINING QUESTIONS

- In what ways does the research discussed in this chapter ring true with your experiences and observations at work and of people you know?
- Do you believe that greater family leave and structural support for caregiving in the United States will ultimately eliminate gender gaps in leadership and pay? Why or why not?
- In what ways is thinking about gender gaps as "caregiving gaps" useful in practical terms?

The Robots Are Coming

> AI is likely to be either the best or worst thing to happen to humanity.
>
> —STEPHEN HAWKING[1]

UNAWARE AND UNPREPARED

Caregiving is surely one of the most characteristically human actions people perform. But as we've seen in so many areas of our lives, we've begun welcoming nonhuman "solutions." Technology and artificial intelligence (AI) have created a world where automation is prioritized, "smart" devices are a cornerstone to nearly all our activities (whether looking up directions or stocking our fridge), and digital is praised over analog. Robots, in one form or another, have become integral to the human experience. AI-driven algorithms recommend what we buy; robots increasingly pack and process the boxes. We increasingly rely on AI for directions and smart cars to get us to the destination. Given how many human activities have become affected by AI and robots, it stands to reason that caregiving is no exception; in fact, it is on the cusp of being transformed by robots as well. And it already is.

We turn, then, to a discussion of these caregiving robots because they will dramatically change the options available for provisioning caregiving,

The Caregiving Ambition. Julia B. Bear and Todd L. Pittinsky, Oxford University Press. © Oxford University Press 2022.
DOI: 10.1093/oso/9780197512418.003.0007

and thus fundamentally change the context in which caregiving ambition is experienced and expressed in the future.

Robot caregivers are here, widely used in Japan and other countries, though still rare in the United States. And that may be a good thing for the time being because Americans aren't remotely ready for them. Most Americans—65%, according to a Pew study—don't realize this technology is already in use or know anything about it.[2] Nor do they even like the idea itself: The Pew study found that roughly half of Americans would not be interested in having their loved ones cared for by a hypothetical robot caregiver. Under such circumstances, there hasn't been much public consideration of what any widespread adoption of caregiving robots will mean in the long run. Such adoption would undoubtedly have major effects on the people being taken care of, the people who are—or would have been—caregivers, and everyone who grows up and lives in a society in which robot caregiving is an accepted societal norm.

Reactions to the idea of robots caring for people—or to the news that it's already happening—range from "Thank goodness" to "Well, why not?" to "Oh my God, that's horrible." All three of these responses have validity. Will robot caregiving become a step forward in our civilization or a step backward? Ideally, the fact of a diversity of opinions will lead to a subsequent approach where extremes temper one another. A thoughtful, productive mix of the appreciation, openness, and skepticism to robot caregivers will have to be sought after and fought for; it will not occur by itself and certainly not through commercial and market forces alone.

On the surface, the advent of caregiving robots is a classic case of supply meeting demand. The most obvious driver of demand in this case is demographics. The care gap in America, and in many other parts of the world, opens up the "caregiving market" for robotic and AI solutions. For example, according to research by the Pew Research Center, 70% of mothers with children under 18 were in the labor force in 2015, compared to only 47% in 1975, and mothers are the primary breadwinners in 4 in 10 US families.[3] When you work, most corporate policies—and the government policies that stand behind them—treat pretty much everything else you do—including raising children—as secondary. With the expense of professional care and so many moms at work, robots could potentially fill these children's caregiving needs.

Then there is the task of taking care of older adults. The United States has 46 million senior citizens.[4] This number is expected to double by 2050, at which time older Americans will be 22% of the US population. And the aging of the baby boom generation could lead to a 75% spike in the number of Americans ages 65 and older who need nursing home care.[5] Again, it is reasonable to ask, could robot caregivers be a solution?

The supply of caregiving in the United States is not rising to meet the demands of caring for our older and younger populations. In fact, the US healthcare system is bracing for a severe shortage of caregivers.[6] The Bureau of Labor Statistics (BLS) estimates that demand for home health aides and personal care aides for the elderly will grow by 36% from 2018 to 2028—an increase of 1,185,800 positions.[7] Paul Osterman, a professor of human resources and management at the Massachusetts Institute of Technology's Sloan School of Management, calls this triple threat—the rate of aging, the increasing need for caregiving, and the coming lack of availability—nothing short of "an absolute train wreck waiting to happen."[8] By 2040, there will be a shortfall of 355,000 paid caregivers. When it comes to informal, nonpaid workers—family and friends—who act as caregivers, the shortfall by 2040 will be much worse: 11 million.

The need for child care workers, according to the BLS, is also expected to grow, coming largely from the turnover rate in child care. The BLS expects employment of child care workers to grow by just 2% from 2018 to 2028, slower than the average for all occupations. The majority of the openings projected each year are expected to come not from new positions but from churn—people deciding the job is just not desirable. These workers who leave the occupation permanently will need to be replaced, if possible.[9] But, as shown in Chapter 4, child care worker positions suffer from low status and low pay, both drivers of a high churn rate.

Can robots help us avert this train wreck? Maybe. Two factors make such a solution plausible: First, technically speaking, it is possible. Originally, the point of robots was to take over simple repetitive tasks, like putting car parts together on assembly lines. But with the advent of AI, which is seriously intelligent, robots can take over more tasks than we may have ever dreamed possible—even caring for babies and older people.

Hold on. Spray-painting car bodies is one thing; taking care of children and the elderly is quite another . . . right? Perhaps, but the rapid adoption of caregiving robots is almost assured due to the profound demand in many countries for reliable, lower-cost care options.

Demand for existing consumer robots—not just Roomba, the robot vacuum cleaner, and its kind but also some caregiving robots, described later in this chapter (see Bots on the Job)—is skyrocketing. According to a report by an industry research firm, the consumer robot market will have a value of $34.1 billion by 2022—up from just $3.8 billion in 2015.[10] By 2035, Japan, a leader in the robotic service sector, expects its domestic industry alone, for caregiving robots for the elderly, to grow to $3.8 billion by 2035, at which point a full third of Japan's population will be 65 or older.[11] The global personal robot market could reach $17.4 billion by 2020, according to a Merrill Lynch report.[12] New technologies tend to sneak up on us like that. (If you don't believe us, go ask Siri.)

The second factor making it plausible for robots to take on a significant role in caregiving is that it is socially plausible, due to the low status and economic value accorded to human caregiving. As discussed, paid caregivers tend to be low-paid, often part-time workers. The social forces discussed throughout the first half of this book that contribute to caregiving's and caregiving ambition's low valuation—failure to recognize caregiving ambition, forces of capitalism, unexpected effects of the feminist movement, low standing of professional caregiving—all come together to make an environment ripe for essentially automating care, taking the human caregiver out of the equation.

The problem that emerges is not so much that robot caregiving will sweep over us but that it will sweep over us with many serious social, emotional, political, and ethical issues left unaddressed. In other words, the wildfire spread and impact of smartphones, social media, and GPS—and that is happening right now with self-driving cars—is about to happen again with caregiving robots. The implications and ramifications may entirely change how we approach caregiving and our caregiving ambition. Keeping that in mind, let's take a look at where we are currently with caregiving robots and where we might be headed.

MEET THE CAREGIVING ROBOTS

In 2019, a consortium of eight organizations collaborated on a research report titled *America, It's Time to Talk About Child Care.*[13] The report identified three types of shortage in child care: access, affordability, and quality. Almost one-third of parents have difficulty finding child care. Even when child care is available, it often involves serious logistical hassles for working parents. Meanwhile, as referenced in Chapter 4, in 33 US states, the average cost of full-time, in-center care for just one child, under the age of 4 (which can, of course, vary in quality), is more than the cost of in-state public college tuition.[14] Quality of care varies as well—only 11% of child care nationwide is accredited. These access, affordability, and quality shortages result in serious economic losses in earnings, productivity, and revenue, totaling an estimated $57 billion per year.[15]

Much the same case can be made with respect to care for the elderly, although the economic losses are due less to lost work by the elderly themselves than to lost work by the middle-aged children caring for their parents and older family members during their own prime working years.

None of these issues are restricted to the United States, and we're not even the most desperate case. Due in part to their cultures' long work hours and their aging societies, China, Korea, and, as mentioned, Japan are on the leading edge of embracing caregiving technologies, with trial deployments of robots well underway. As birth rates in these countries decrease and life spans increase, there are fewer young people to take care of the older people. Eldercare robots are already flourishing in Japan—which has the world's oldest population—because they've made a concerted effort to lead in these bots' development—so much so that an eye-popping "one-third of the Japanese government's budget is allocated to developing carebots."[16]

As robot production has increased, costs of robot labor have gone down, while the cost of human labor has only gone up. According to the McKinsey Global Institute, over the 30 years between 1987 and 2017, the average robot price fell by half in real terms and even further relative to labor costs.[17] The costs are expected to drop more each year as demand grows and technology advances.

Ambivalence

Some caregivers are dead set against the use of caregiving robots in any form. Aiko, a mother of two, for example, is completely opposed: "Absolutely not interested. I think that AI is great for many daily circumstances, but never something that involves caregiving." Ayesha, a mother of three, gave a similarly strong negative response to the use of robot caregivers: "No to robot caregivers for me. . . . I would never be comfortable having a robot caring for my loved ones." Ellen, a mother of two, explained, "Absolutely not, robots are not equipped with the right knowledge and don't have the ability to give the emotional help that children need."

More common was a response involving a great deal of skepticism and worry but not an unequivocal no. Eddie, a father of four, explained his concerns and, simultaneously, his openness to the possibility of robot caregivers, in some specific circumstances: "It depends heavily on the [caregiving] context, the environment, and the specific safety risks." Reuben, a father of three remarked, "It would depend directly on the level of technology available, and my comfort level with it." Indeed, openness to caregiving robots seemed to relate more commonly to individual caregivers' estimation of the abilities of caregiving robots and less commonly to any existential line between humans and robots. As Javier, a father of one, explained, "I know what my iPhone can do, I would need to see what this robot was capable of doing."

Several specific concerns about how robots would specifically lag behind human caregivers were raised:

- *Lack of human fragility.* As Albert, a father of one, explains, "A robot is intended to be 100% correct. But if caregivers don't show any human fragility, then you are depriving the child of some human characteristics that will need to be learned later in life."
- *Ability to truly decode emotions.* Andre, a father of two, puts it thusly: "Vulnerable family members need someone human who can truly understand their emotions." Emily, a mother of one, echoed his worries: "I worry that they'll just never get the really communicated emotions, the jumble and mixed emotions, young children so often display and parents slowly come to recognize."
- *Ability to give love.* Angelica, a mother of two, explains, "I feel that they [robot caregivers] wouldn't give the love and care they deserve."
- *Ability to respond appropriately to complex emotions.* Lei, a mother of three, explained, "I wouldn't trust them [robot caregivers] to know why a child is crying, yes . . . but more so I wouldn't trust them to properly hold a [crying] child." Responding to humans with empathy (and robots' current inability to feel empathy) was a particular concern, well captured by Eleanor, a mother of one, who explains, "Robots don't have human innate emotions like empathy, and that's critical to truly nurturing."
- *Care recipients' feelings and reactions.* Sandy, a father of two, explains, "No . . . because I don't even think they [my children] would ever be comfortable with something like that."
- *Wide array of caregiving skills and tasks.* The wide array of skills and tasks involved in caregiving, Christina, a mother of two, explains, gives her pause about caregiving robots: "I don't think they could do the full range, everything a child needs, when it comes to things like changing pampers or preparing/making food for my child that they will like, then becoming an entertainer, and then a warm body to be near."

Bots on the Job

It's important to get a clear sense of just how many robots are already out there and on the job. Though Japan is leading the "carebot" charge, many countries all over the world are not far behind. These robots may range in size, appearance, function, and purpose; but they all act as a way to fill caregiving gaps. Examples abound.

BeanQ, from Roobo in China, has been called "childcare for the masses."[18] Designed to be "an early educator, sharing some of the parental burden," BeanQ is reportedly already used in millions of middle-class Chinese households. The robot responds with simple words and phrases and an array of emoji facial expressions displayed on a large screen that serves as its face. It also has a "remote babysitting" mode, automatically taking snapshots of the kids and uploading them for their parents to see online.

iPal, from Avatar Mind in China, has wide eyes, working fingers, pastel trimming, and a touchscreen tablet on its chest.[19] This robot can sing, dance, and play rock/paper/scissors. It can also talk with children, answering questions like "Why is the sun hot?," while providing surveillance and video chat for absent parents.

The Care-o-bot, from Fraunhofer IPA in Germany, is at work in a number of German assisted living facilities.[20] Like the social directors, aides, and volunteers typically employed in such facilities, Care-o-bot doesn't just bring food and drinks to the residents but also plays memory games with them to help keep their minds sharp.

The Dinsow eldercare robot, from CT Asia Robotics in Thailand, helps seniors remember to take their pills, tracks their health, and serves as a videophone for calls with family and doctors.[21] It entertains, too—doubling as a karaoke machine.

The Asimo robot, from Honda, in Japan, can climb stairs, jump, and even use sign language, serving as a gofer for the many people with limited mobility. Asimo is especially useful for older adults who live in houses that have become harder or more dangerous for them to navigate as they've aged.[22]

ElliQ, from Intiriont Robotics in the United States, is a smart, social robot companion that engages its owner throughout the day, providing appointment reminders and assisting with video calls to friends and family. It can suggest a walk when its human is overdue for some exercise. ElliQ can also share a spontaneous fact or humorous video with its users.[23]

Jennie, from Tombot in the United States, is a robot puppy designed to meet the needs of seniors with dementia in nursing care. Jennie understands voice commands and its behaviors are programmed to create a sense of novelty and discovery. Jennie doesn't walk, however, as designers feared mobility would make the robot too easy to trip over.

GenieConnect, from Service Robotics Limited in the United Kingdom, is a companion robot for older adults.[24] This robot can perform a variety of functions, including reminding its companion to take medication and go to appointments, contacting a doctor or therapist, and helping companions make video calls to their family and friends. Its owner can also just chat with GenieConnect itself.

Buddy the Robot, from Blue Frog Robotics in the United States, is a companion robot designed to establish empathy and create an emotional bond between itself and the user.[25] Buddy has oversized anime eyes and exaggerated, childlike facial expressions. The robot can move around, make video calls, send messages, monitor its user's home, serve as a calendar and alarm clock, and help older adults with day-to-day activities. When connected to WIFI or a user's smartphone, Buddy can even detect fires and burglaries and send alerts if it senses something is wrong.

There are many, many more on the way or already on the market. Pricewise, they range from a few hundred dollars for more simple models, aimed at the lower-end consumer market, to hundreds of thousands of models with advanced features, aimed at caregiving institutions (nursing homes, child care centers). And as with every other high-tech product— from smartphones to televisions—each new version or iteration will likely be more alluring, more dazzling, and even cheaper than the last.

When thinking about robotics and AI in caregiving, keep in mind it's not just physical robots with human-like features being employed— there are many other forms of caregiving technology. For example, senior citizens may increasingly rely on the likes of AI from household devices, like Alexa, which are heavily advertised to the elderly. These ads are often designed to show the many ways these "digital assistants" can be helpful to the elderly, for example, by reminding forgetful seniors to eat.

All of these examples show that robot caregivers are on the rise, and there are good reasons for it. A growing and global demand for care that can't be met the "old-fashioned" way is being met in a new way. Isn't that how it's supposed to work? And aren't all of the aforementioned benefits positive? Why not just say, "robots for everyone!" and move on? Well, before we make any such sweeping statement, we of course need to take into account all sides of the story; and once we do, a robotic caregiving future may not seem quite like the utopia many of us would hope for.

TROUBLES ON THE HORIZON

There's nothing wrong with taking a new approach when new technologies offer innovative options. All around us, we see disruptive technologies dramatically change how we live as individuals and how industries, businesses, and governments operate. It could be argued that this is one way we progress as a society. But there are always missteps that could have certainly been avoided if we just took the time to consider the results of our actions. Sometimes we find that maybe it's best to roll out an idea or an approach slowly, methodically, and in due time. Sometimes it's essential we think of the greater good, and not let economic concerns, only, drive the course of development and the rollout of new technologies.[26] Doing something extremely important in an extremely new way without giving it the necessary thought or testing before implementation tends to be a one-way road to disaster[27] (for example, the unforeseen role of social media in political manipulation). And the caregiving robot revolution might end up falling under this category if we don't take precautions.

There are a number of threats in automating caregiving, but the underlying threat comes from modern society's widespread failure to acknowledge how much it means to people to care for others and to be cared for by others. Think of it this way: We will soon have the technology to keep the human race procreating at whatever level we want without people necessarily being intimately involved (e.g., new reproductive technologies including artificial wombs). But do we really want that "convenience"? In the same vein, if caregiving ambition is left out of the discussion and we swiftly move forward into AI care, the empathy that is crucial to caregiving could be entirely lost. Beyond the threat to caregivers' ambition—or to those who might have been caregivers—there are risks to the people being taken care of. Some of these risks are direct, while others are indirect and long-term.

First, in regard to child care, we have no right to experiment on a couple generations of children so that the developers of caregiving technology can "perfect" their offerings. These technologies are simply too new to be proven. While each company will produce a pile of data to support its offerings, the science will be necessarily provisional; there are obviously no long-term studies. The United States already has a rich history of rolling out not-ready-for-prime-time technologies on vulnerable populations, including children. Perhaps the most classic case is that of flame retardants, which were heralded as lifesavers. In the 1950s and 1960s, for example, flame-resistant chemicals were added to children's pajamas, car seats, and other items to protect them from fire. Unfortunately, by the late 1970s researchers discovered that two commonly used fire-retardant technologies—brominated and chlorinated flame retardants—were very dangerous, to the point of mutating DNA.[28] Substitute chemicals brought online to replace them were themselves linked to increased hyperactivity and lowered IQ. Regulatory agencies do an imperfect job, sometimes missing real physical risk. Other times these agencies more subtly, but potentially equally dangerously, fail to look beyond physical safety and assess the total picture.

Second, we have to keep in mind that caregiving robots are being developed largely by for-profit interests or by educational institutions with an eye toward commercializing them. Their primary motives are growth and profits—period. When it comes to presenting data on the robots' efficacy and side effects, they will cherry-pick the best outcomes and suppress any ominous results as long as they can. From cigarettes to seat belts, from vaping to addictive iPhone apps targeted to children, there are innumerable examples of this type of corporate behavior. We would be short-sighted not to anticipate the financial priorities of these companies; thus, we must be vigilant about the potential benefits, and costs, of new technologies.

Third, there can be incredible risks when technologies are used in unanticipated ways. Television wasn't invented to keep kids quiet. Facebook wasn't created as a news source, let alone a potential electoral power broker. But we've all witnessed their migration toward these uses. Similar possibilities for caregiving technology are endless, ranging from the benign if misguided—too much screen time—to the downright evil—direct marketing and political or social indoctrination.

Finally, one overall advantage of human care is that the mere fact that someone else cares about you can itself have healing powers.[29] Removing humans and replacing them with robot caregivers likely removes this intrinsic benefit as well. Can the fact that some*thing* else takes care of you have these same kinds of effects? We certainly don't know and would be wise to assume not until proven otherwise.

Robot caregiving needs to be approached with a humility and patience that have so far been lacking in the introduction of other similarly far-reaching technologies. Online social networking was introduced entirely on the basis of its creators' dreams. Some of those dreams were quite high-minded, but none was buttressed with any large-scale testing or accumulation of experience. The result: Social media has already taken over our lives, with enormous social, emotional, political, and ethical issues barely addressed. For example, we have grown comfortable with dramatic increases in rates of mental health ailments and social isolation among vulnerable populations in our society.[30] Though not solely a product of social media, they are an interrelated product of our contemporary society and, in some ways, its tech obsession.[31] In several studies, teenage and young adult users who spend the greatest amount of time on social media platforms (Instagram, Facebook, and others) reported a substantially higher rate of depression than those who spent the least time (66% versus

13%). The most recent systematic review at the time of writing found that across many different measures of social media use all domains correlated with "depression, anxiety and psychological distress."[32] Correlation is not causation. But it is a reason to look critically at their interplay to see how causal of a role social media use, and technology use more generally, plays. Whatever they find to be the root cause, today, with iPhones and hybrid cars, we are churning out people prone to a range of mental illnesses who live their lives with feelings of isolation. The US Centers for Disease Control reports that slightly over a quarter of Americans aged 18 and above, 26%, will suffer from a diagnosable mental disorder in a given year.[33] And 46% of Americans aged 18 and older will have a mental health disorder over their lifetime.[34]

Given that robot caregiving touches on matters every bit as fundamental to human life as social networking does, we can expect it to present us with equally fundamental issues. What say this time around, we address them before it's too late?

Business priorities will not ensure a holistic development and rollout of caregiving robots. For businesses, growth and profit reign supreme. If society doesn't make its own decisions about robot caregiving intentionally—and mighty quickly—the tech industry will have made them for us without our even realizing it. We are already starting to get anxious about what new AI technologies have "given" us without asking if we really wanted it. If AI-driven caregiving falls short of human caregiving, we may simply get used to it, just as we have so quickly adjusted our expectations and morals when it comes to enormous infringements of privacy and enormous loss of social life.

Supply, Demand, and a Robo-Care Future

Beyond threats to the caregivers and the cared for, there are threats to society as a whole. What will become of caregiving ambition if technology is always there as the first, easiest, and cheapest "solution"? Do we really want to outsource this cornerstone of our humanity?

Consider again the "demand" that seems to be driving the supply of robot caregiving. How real is this imbalance? Yes, the global demographics are real enough, but is the supply of caregiving really as inadequate as it seems? To some extent, it is actually artificially low: There could be a lot more human caregiving than there is, even if that still left a shortfall to be filled by robots, if we only treated caregiving as of high value and, in a professional setting, compensated it accordingly. Nothing gets supply off the couch like paying more for what you want.

The low supply of caregivers comes in part from the low status and resultant low pay accorded to those who do it for a living. But truly good caregiving is a skill—or a gift, however you see it—and it's one of great value. Spend some time in a nursing home or day care facility. Watch the best nurses, therapists, aides, and teachers. Pay attention to how loving they are to people they don't know or have only known a short time. Try to understand how they figure out what someone who can't speak comprehensibly needs. Imagine how they keep their good nature even when someone is being belligerent. Then ask yourself: Could I do all that?

If our government provided greater support and our places of employment weren't so greedy with our time, it would be easier to see that there is not a true caregiving shortage. Society—including our social "safety net" programs—is too disdainful to pay market rates for quality, human caregiving by family members or caring professionals, maintaining instead a regime of low wages and overly long working hours with inadequate social support for hired caregivers.

This misunderstanding of the supply and demand of caregiving speaks to how the caregiving problem is socially created. And it may be dangerous to accept a technological solution to a social problem. If we hand caregiving over to robots without any change in the way society values caregiving, is there any reason to think companies will have higher standards for the care robots provide to our friends, family, and loved ones than they do now?

As a society, we've accepted many changes that have come with negative consequences: the speed of modern life and the demands of work; the toll of constant connectedness, with tech companies telling us it's necessary and our peers and families encouraging us to join the trend; highly processed foods pushed on us and our children, even though science now proves the virtues of eating simply. We feel compelled to accept these changes by the demands of the moment and by the enticing features of some new technology. We are likely to make the same compromises in accepting robot caregiving because it will solve so many immediate problems for so many people but fix none of our long-running societal ones.

WHERE ROBOTS SHOULD FIT IN

Though we must keep the risks, threats, and potential downsides in mind, if approached properly, robots can play a helpful and healthy role in caregiving and its future. They can, and should, wash the dirty diapers; but they should not give the baby the hug before plopping her on the changing table, nor should they be the ones to kiss her little belly button when she's all clean once again. In short, robots should support human caregivers, not supplant them.

Robots cannot make a caring connection, especially the type that comes from a strong caregiving ambition. Though they may be able to perform all sorts of duties as well as, or better than, humans, caregiving ambition is now, and always will be, uniquely human. Still, people are prone to empathize with humanoid robots, in ways similar to how we empathize with other people.[35] We can even come to feel that robots love us. Though this idea may be comforting to some of us, it leaves us vulnerable to the robots' programmers and creators.

Humans truly need other humans, particularly when it comes to caregiving. As a society, we all seem to agree with this notion more or less. And it is central to deciding where robots should fit in. A 70-year-old male respondent from that study cut right to the heart of whether human caregivers and robot caregivers are true substitutes for each other: "There is a difference between care and caring!"[36] An IV drip takes care of you; the nurses who change it can't do what the IV does, but they care about you, which the IV drip cannot. When someone cares about you, they partake in the act of caring.

The respondents in the Pew study are not alone—even many AI proponents agree. For example, Dr. Lee Kai-Fu, AI expert and former head of Google China, thinks humans in relationship with an individual needing care should first and foremost provide care, with paid caregivers the next best thing to close family and friends and robots a distant third: "People really want to connect with other people and I think giving them primitive, fake, inanimate and non-emotional robots to interact with is a cruel thing that we should not do."[37] But when it comes to certain aspects of caregiving, robots may have particular strengths and may even beat human caregivers.

First, fellow humans are more susceptible to sentimentality. This, of course, can be an aspect of caregiving, for many perhaps a central part. But human sentimentality has two downsides. First, it can override other concerns. Including, sometimes, the wishes of the individual being care for. When, for example, people create a living will, they believe their wishes for the end of their life will be honored—but a growing body of research finds the instructions are often ignored[38]—sometimes to avoid liability but many other times due to the sentimentality of caregivers who do not wish to part with their loved one and may even hide from hospital staff the existence of a living will. Another related benefit of caregiving robots' potential lack of sentimentality relates to negative sentiment. Sentiment can be love, yes; but it can also be negative sentiment. Robot caregivers will not, for example, take a dislike to any particular person and treat them unfairly. They will not feel insulted or put upon, all sentimental responses human caregivers at times can understandably manifest. Robot caregivers will evolve and likely will one day embody emotional responses, but this kind of sentimentality over rationality is unlikely to be part of their repertoire, unless it is programmed.

Of course, to view robots' lack of sentiment relative to human caregivers as a virtue is a complicated call and not without many caveats and nuance. Human caregivers make many tricky calls; parents, for example, often follow and yet often violate their own "parenting protocols" as they weigh other considerations. Humans exercise great discretion in their caregiving, for example, allowing an older adult in their care occasional splurges outside their prescribed diet or allowing a child to stay up far later than routine for a particular experience. There is no form of AI yet with that mix of discretion. And even the display of negative sentiment may, in some caregiving situations, be a valuable aspect, helping those cared for to learn the limits of what they can (and should) expect from others. Yet there are situations, for example, late-stage Alzheimer's disease, where human sentiment can be so stretched that some support from a less sentimental robot caregiver might be a valuable aid to the caregivers and care recipient.

A second potential strength of caregiving robots relative to human ones is the fact that robots are no more liable to error than humans and are less liable in many cases. Human caregivers can certainly make mistakes or nod off, particularly when they are juggling caregiving with other activities. Human error due to fatigue or emotion, for example, is not an issue for robots. They do not get tired. Nor do they get cranky or bored. They also lack circadian rhythms or family and social lives, so they can work through the night. Humans simply have limitations that robots do not have.

Given a sufficient supply of robots in a given facility, the same robot could attend a particular patient indefinitely, which could never be the case for, say, a hospital nurse or nursing home aide. They could have access to all medical records all the time and, in fact, to more or less infinite medical data. Properly programmed, robots will not forget one task due to a sudden rush of other tasks—unlike most of us, a robot could be suddenly diverted to assist in an 8-hour surgery and then remember to go back to a patient's room and pick up a Kleenex off the floor. They can also "move in" to someone's home much more easily than a human caregiver can, which may make it easier for more older adults to stay out of the nursing homes they often dread.

Robots can also assist human caregivers with heavy physical tasks, such as rolling someone over in bed or even just picking up a baby. They are much less prone than humans to mechanical strain, and in any case, they can easily be repaired or replaced should they break or malfunction. They also can't catch any diseases from humans or from medical equipment such as needles. Depending on their outer materials, robot caregivers would still be capable of carrying and passing on at least some communicable diseases, so even robots might need to wear gloves; but they would never find them annoying or forget to change them or try to hoard them.

These tasks and advantages are mostly technical, which is where it seems the caregiving robot industry is most focused. Companies in this industry appear to be working on what they consider the most important issues: how to develop more sophisticated technology (hardware and software), how to keep the price low enough to serve a potentially enormous global market, and how to offer the software and algorithms in a package—a physical presence—that doesn't creep people out.

Meanwhile, as a society—not only those who will actually use such robots but all of us who will live in a world in which such robots exist—we need to consider some less technical but more profound issues: What are the ways in which robots can replace human caregivers, and what are the ways in which they can't—or shouldn't? Looked at another way, the issue is, how do we safeguard a human's role in a world of caregiving robots?

THE WISE ROLE FOR ROBOTS: ROBOT-ASSISTED CAREGIVING MODEL

The best approach to 21st-century care is not to ditch the humans or the carebots but to create a more holistic *robot-assisted caregiving model* (RACM). The idea is that all tools—up to and including the most sophisticated robots—should augment human caregivers, not replace them. This augmentation could include helping out with physical tasks, as mentioned, thereby freeing up more of human caregivers' time and energy for interacting with the people they are looking after. Or these reinforcements could come in the form of supporting the mental health needs of caregivers, who may, for example, be struggling to cope with a loved one who has dementia or who is in great pain or very near death.

Robot caregivers might do this by providing coverage for human caregivers to take much needed short breaks at points of weariness or by lightening the load of domestic household chores the caregivers often need to do concurrently, like laundry.

With RACM in mind, a number of guidelines with respect to the design and use of the robots themselves should be followed.

Design and Use

The best applications of technology empower individuals, not bypass them. To that end, the best caregiving does not infantilize care recipients. Robots should be designed to react to the humans receiving care, not to intrude on them or act in too overbearing of a manner. Imagine, for example, a robot that could give older people a list of tasks to do in the morning—this would be a mistake. Instead, the robot should shadow its users, prompting them if it senses that a critical daily routine, such as taking prescribed medication, was skipped. In this way, the people receiving assistance from the robot remain independent, aided by the robot but not subject to it. The risk of overbearing care by robots is the same as overbearing care by a human: a cycle of dependency, in which a care recipient (young or old) constantly needs to be told what to do and how to do it by the caregiver.

Robots should be designed, and deployed, with great consideration for another kind of dependency: emotional dependency. It will be very natural, and even unavoidable in some cases, for people to become emotionally attached to robots; and this impulse to form a connection could be further magnified and exploited by design. With wide, childlike eyes or soft fur, many ultra-cute caregiving robots are purposefully designed to elicit attachment, such as some of those mentioned earlier in the chapter (see *Bots on the Job*). Such emotional dependence raises deep ethical considerations (e.g., is feeling loved by a robot meaningful?) as well as legal considerations (e.g., can an elderly person, for example, leave their estate to a robot who cared for them?).[39] When children are the care recipients, other ethical and legal considerations arise.[40] For example, robots caring for children raises ethical considerations such as when (if at all) a child should know their caregiver is a robot (and not a living creature in the traditional sense, depending of course on your definition of "alive"). Legal considerations include the question of whether a child has a "right" to contact a former caregiving robot it bonded to, after the caregiving robot may have "moved on" to a new child.

Caregiving robots should be customizable. For example, a clear benefit of robots is that they are tireless. But is this trait always desirable? If the person receiving the care is supposed to "graduate" at some point to needing less or no care, the robot itself has to change what it does and doesn't do—as human caregivers would.

With no long-term studies of the effect of robot caregiving on children or the elderly, robot caregiving should be introduced carefully, a little at a time, and studied all along the way. These studies must be performed by qualified researchers (not necessarily academic) who are not connected in any way with these robots' manufacturers or the institutions that may have motivations to justify the investments of their top managements and boards.

As we start to go down a long path of burgeoning AI technologies, privacy must be taken seriously this time. One of the major selling points of many caregiving robots is their ability to monitor and record, 24/7. Is that caregiving or jail? Do we want every moment of our earliest years captured, recorded, and potentially analyzed? We may want our doctors to know about what we eat, our exercise regime, and our compliance with prescriptions; but do we want them knowing about all the intimate details of our lives?

Whenever robots are used, let's make sure they are part of a larger plan for socialization for the care recipient, a plan that should be routinely re-evaluated. Robot caregivers should be part of a broader commitment to ensure that people interact with other humans as much as possible. Many research studies show that human-to-human, face-to-face contact plays a critical role in people's health—boosting mood and life span[41]—something we likely can't get from a robot.

Caregiving robots, when caring alongside human caregivers, should have boundaries; and there should be a clear hierarchy in place. The human caregiver, not the robot, should be in the driver's seat. Making a human caregiver second to a robot caregiver not only raises a host of ethical concerns; it puts their respective strengths precisely backward. Robots are very good at repetitive and mundane tasks and should be given them. Humans need to be engaged in activities that demand attention and preferably are interesting—those aspects of caregiving should, for the foreseeable future, be left to human caregivers. The more mundane aspects, and some of the more physically demanding ones, might be more beneficially outsourced to a robot. In this way, human caregivers play a central role, and the robot plays a supporting role. A human caregiver should be charged with making sure caregiving robots are being used wisely, as a tool or medium for support. Robots, even "smart" ones, should not be left to decide what's in the best interest of their charges.

Last, remember that, just like humans, robots are not infallible. We need to have a tolerance for robot malfunctions and to expect and plan for such malfunctions. Humans are trusted with other humans' lives despite being demonstrably imperfect. So are all sorts of medical devices today, and caregiving robots will be tomorrow.

Social Context

We have a new opportunity to use AI to help reduce disparities and improve care overall. Will a given robot be able to make people of various genders, races, sexual orientations, and other backgrounds equally comfortable? Or will it be designed by a homogenous group of engineers for a dangerously narrow group within our society? Human caregivers are prone to some racial bias in recognizing (and, as a result, fully treating) patients' pain.[42] Will this bias be carried over into caregiving AI? We already know, unfortunately, that facial-recognition systems are more likely to misidentify people of color more often than White people.[43] This failure becomes extraordinarily troubling in the case of caregiving robots.

Technologies, to be inclusive, must be designed for diverse constituencies that, together, make up our society.[44]

Finally, class dynamics need to be considered. The digital revolution was heralded by many as a great equalizing force. Yet we've seen one digital divide after another emerge, with the wealthier strata of society having significantly greater access to everything from high-speed internet to the highest–fuel efficiency vehicles. Is it possible that those of us who can afford human care will receive it while those of us who cannot will be stuck with robots? Or will working-class children grow up raised by low-end, $100 caregiving robots, while wealthy children are raised by elite models, featuring more functionality that directly impacts the quality of care delivered?

No matter the social impacts or considerations, when trying to put in place wise guidelines for robot caregivers, we must remember that human caregivers are far from perfect—they, too, do not always have the appropriate oversight, have their own biases, and provide different levels and quality of care. Any given human caregiver probably can't make everyone equally comfortable either. The standard here would be to avoid whatever potential problems can be avoided, knowing what we do about caregiving today.

It is likely to be a rocky road. Have you tried to pick out a television lately? Or to decide on the right phone? Imagine what it's going to be like picking out a caregiving robot to take care of your loved ones. We're right to take precaution now as technological advancements are occurring rapidly.

DEFINING QUESTIONS

- Which aspects of caregiving can we comfortably give to robots, and which should we retain for human caregivers in order to retain our humanity?
- How similar should we expect robot caregivers to be in comparison to human caregivers?
- Should the use of robot caregivers be different for different groups—such as children, older adults, hospital patients, and people with Alzheimer's and other forms of dementia?

PART III

Taking Care

A "Freedom-to"
Work–Care Agenda

Freedom is the opportunity to make decisions.

—Ken Blanchard (and colleagues)[1]

"FREEDOM-FROM" AND "FREEDOM-TO"

In Chapter 2, we saw how the work–care agenda primarily aligns with corporate interests, leading, in part, to persistent work–care conflict. But the story doesn't end there. The way in which those interests play out in how work–care programs are designed is, at best, to support provisioning care, not providing care. Though the work–life movement may be well intentioned, it undermines ambitious caregiving by embracing only one form—provisioning ambition—and too often treating the other—providing ambition—as if it didn't exist.

The programs and policies that support provisioning care are "freedom-from" accommodations—they grant freedom from the demands of caregiving. Those that help an employee manage work and life responsibilities by creating space for direct caregiving are "freedom-to" accommodations—they grant freedom to provide care directly. On-site child care, for example, is a "freedom-from" accommodation—it frees you from child care so that you can get more work done. Family leave

The Caregiving Ambition. Julia B. Bear and Todd L. Pittinsky, Oxford University Press. © Oxford University Press 2022.
DOI: 10.1093/oso/9780197512418.003.0008

is a "freedom-to" accommodation—it frees you from work—presumably without sabotaging your career—to provide care, like tending to an ill child. Other forms of "freedom-from" accommodations and benefits include child care vouchers and free or heavily subsidized tutoring for employees' children.[2]

"Freedom-from" accommodations are likely to fulfill the needs of people with high provisioning ambition, whereas "freedom-to" accommodations are likely to fulfill the needs of people with high providing ambition. "Freedom-to" allows the flexibility to care for your loved ones directly—not just to provision it from others. "Freedom-to" accommodations honor provisioning ambitions.

As explored in Chapter 3, this distinction between providing and provisioning care—and providing and provisioning ambitions—lies at the very core of the work–care challenge, the gap in women's advancement, and the "mommy wars." Most work–life programs are designed from the employer's point of view, making it easier to ensure that someone is taken care of while employees are at work advancing their own careers—and the company's success.

"Freedom-to" work–life policies challenge the "work devotion schema" common across many industrialized societies—the notion of workers as entirely focused on careers.[3] This view has roots in the Protestant work ethic, which views work as a responsibility to the divine.[4] Today, this ethic serves a different deity—the corporate bottom line—and is central to capitalist cultures. The ideal worker is conceptualized as someone always available for, and committed to, work. Workers who reveal their caregiving ambitions run the risk of being penalized.[5]

A company's interest is in providing women with every chance to advance their careers by proving themselves valuable to their employers. As a result, the majority of work–life policies are of the same flavor, favoring "freedom-from" over "freedom-to." This basic recognition helps to explain research findings on how employers' work–life policies affect employees. On the one hand, researchers find ample evidence that the use of work–life policies is beneficial for the employees who use them.[6] On the other hand, evidence shows a mix of positive and negative outcomes of usage of work–life policies. As discussed, those who use work–life policies may be penalized with lower wages, fewer promotions, and reduced career mobility.[7] Despite the variety of work–life policies and outcomes, researchers and practitioners have not yet conceptually "debundled" the broad set of policies to understand which sorts have which effects (positive, negative, or neutral) on employee careers, employee well-being, and outcomes for their families.[8]

Many of the creative perks offered by some workplaces—often in an attempt to seem progressive—are designed to keep an employee at work longer while someone else does any caregiving. Google does have a policy limiting the amount of time, continuously, that employees can stay on its campus: *72 hours at a time*.[9] Matthew Weaver, a former Google employee described literally living where he worked: "They had three meals a day at the cafeteria and there were showers at the gym. There was a free laundromat on campus, so I could wash my clothes. There were all sorts of rooms with pianos and foosball tables. . . . I had plenty to do when I was taking a break from work. And we had places in the parking structure where I could work on and maintain my bicycle."[10]

Silicon Valley and Wall Street may raise the bar for the work–life benefits of the future, but their offerings are largely "freedom-from" accommodations.[11] For example, subsidized egg freezing, offered by many Silicon Valley companies, is a poignant, if complex, example of such an accommodation.[12] And yes, these accommodations are fantastic for people who are high on career ambition and low on caregiving ambition in general, and low on providing ambition in particular. Such workers are very comfortable and well served by "freedom-from" accommodations, which help them to provision care.

And, of course and most critically, it is a small sliver of employees—particularly those employees in the most successful technology and finance companies—who have access to the aforementioned smorgasbord of "freedom-from" work–life policies. If we look at all workers (particularly those in the retail industry and in small businesses), they have access to far too few work–life programs of any kind.

As we hope for more work-life programs for most employees and as we look at the small sliver of highly sought-after workers in a few select industries, we must do so recognizing that "freedom-from" accommodations are more aligned with employer interests. But freedom from caregiving is not what employees want all the time. And the overwhelming focus on "freedom-from" accommodations is potentially ruinous for people who are high on both career ambition and providing ambition.

"Freedom-to" accommodations are much more aligned with the reality of caregiving ambition, especially providing ambition: Caregiving takes considerable time, as well as mental and physical energy; and the demands can be unpredictable. Truly recognizing caregiving ambition alongside career ambition underscores the calls for significant "freedom-to" accommodations and innovative solutions that will allow employees not just to provision their caregiving but to provide it. Before we consider some of these solutions, it's important to remind ourselves how we got here and to further recognize how "freedom-from" and "freedom-to" options, or the lack thereof, affect our caregiving ambitions.

FREEDOM-TO CARE

In the 1960s, White women in the United States marched into the workforce in droves, upending both the traditional division of labor in many families and caregiving in society more broadly. Other groups of women, most notably Black women, always had higher rates of participation in the paid labor market. This was true regardless of age, regardless of marital status, and regardless of the presence of children at home. In 1880, more than a third of Black women who were married were in the paid labor force compared to just 7.3% of White women.[13] But even Black women's labor force participation increased in the 1960s. Today, 66% of White, Asian American, and Latinx mothers with young children are in the workforce, compared to 78% of Black mothers with young children.[14]

To address the challenges that women's greater participation in the paid workforce has surfaced, a work–family movement, later rebranded "work–life," replete with consultants, conferences, certifications, and nonprofits, dedicates itself to improving employees' ability to balance their work and careers with their caregiving ambitions and personal lives. Today there is even an industry lobbying group dedicated to these issues—the Alliance for Work–Life Progress. Not to be outdone, academic institutions have opened research centers to study the dynamics of work and family, perhaps most prominently Boston College's Center for Work & Family and the Center on Working Families at the University of California, Berkeley. And, of course, book after book provides research and commentary on how to work and live while pursing our career and caring goals.

What do we have to show for all this investment by industry, universities, government, and individuals?

Very, very little.

In fact, "freedom-to" provide care, and those who are ambitious about providing care, may be losing ground—that is, people are less able, not more, to be ambitious in their careers and caregiving. As shown in Chapter 2, despite all the investments, work–care conflict is not being effectively reduced—it is even growing. Would we stay invested in a stock for 40 years if its value kept decreasing? Doesn't it behoove us to take stock and ask ourselves whether this investment in work–care balance is paying off and, if not, why? And more important still: What might we do differently?

If those with providing ambition are to log a win for true work–care balance, "freedom-to" accommodations are the battle for the workplace of tomorrow. Rather than pouring money into solutions that don't meet most people's ambitions and institutionalizing policies that don't actually work, organizations would be well served to develop solutions that recognize and honor people's caregiving ambition and allow them to fulfill it. Bringing creativity to the task, organizations can develop new and innovative ways to help empower workers. Instead of just generally managing employees' career and caregiving ambitions, organizations can develop new ways to help them be ambitious in their careers while also being able to provide care—themselves and directly—not outsource it to others. There are a number of "freedom-to" accommodations or policies already in use that should be considered for widespread adoption.

Three Common Examples of "Freedom-to" Accommodations

One example of a "freedom-to" care policy is job-sharing, in which meaningful jobs are carved into two and split between two individuals, both the time spent at the job and the workload. For an ambitious caregiver, the part-time schedule of a shared job can make all the difference between staying in a career or abandoning it; but job-sharing is only really a solution for the career ambitious if it involves career-track jobs. Therefore, the position must be on a career path with potential for advancement, covering a wide range of roles, including senior ones.

Job-sharers work together; they create a schedule that accommodates both of them, and they may or may not work at the same time. Though they communicate regularly, some job-sharers may never see each other, while others may work a couple of hours together each week. Shared jobs are different from typical part-time jobs, which tend to be more piecemeal in nature and are not always available for highly trained, highly skilled, and leadership positions. Part-time options mismatched to people's career trajectories often force them to choose between career and caregiving ambitions. Job-sharing, on the other hand, embraces a far broader swath of jobs than the standard part-time work options, allowing for career progression.

One of the reasons job-sharing is such a valuable "freedom-to" policy is that it provides caregivers with the ability to be ambitious about both their caregiving and their careers. They also can cover each other's shifts seamlessly if, as often happens in life, "something comes up." There is a flexibility and comfort in knowing someone "has your back" at work. Job-sharing also makes it easier to plan for days off. The salary is, of course, cut in half, which is a major consideration; but for many workers, this accommodation is a viable option for defined or extended periods of time. While many companies are experimenting with job-sharing, like Raytheon, Agnes Uhereczky observes, writing in *Forbes*, job-sharing remains largely "untapped potential."[15]

Paid caregiving leave, touched upon throughout the book, is another critical "freedom-to" accommodation. At some point, almost everyone must take some time away from work to care for someone, often a new-born child or a sick family member. Nearly a quarter, 24%, of US civilian workers (33.6 million Americans) do not have access to paid sick leave for themselves, let alone those they may care for, according to the federal Bureau of Labor Statistics (BLS).[16] ("Civilian labor force" is a term the BLS uses, which refers to US workers excluding military personnel, federal government employees, retirees, and several other groups.) This lack of support affects all workers, but it places working families in a particular bind as it becomes economically difficult, and in some cases impossible, to take unpaid time off to care for a child or other family member. Though paid leave gradually is being offered by private companies, and through local and state legislation, it is still a rare benefit: According to the BLS, as of 2018, 17% of all civilian workers had access to paid family leave.[17] (As mentioned, in 2020, President Donald J. Trump approved paid parental leave for federal workers, increasing access.) Since only a minority of Americans have access to paid family leave, the majority must make difficult choices between their financial and caregiving responsibilities. Unpaid or even half-paid leave goes underused because it isn't financially feasible; paid leave, however, is feasible and supports caregivers and caregiving.

A third example of a "freedom-to" accommodation would apply to society as a whole: changing how Social Security treats leaves for caregiving. At the time of writing, leaving the workforce for more than 5 years triggers a significant penalty in subsequent benefits. When you leave the workforce for caregiving for more than 5 years—no matter how long you've paid into the system—your Social Security Disability eligibility ends.[18] If you, as an unpaid caregiver, become disabled, Social Security would not provide you with any disability support on your own merits, and at retirement you would receive no credit for your earlier work. Unpaid caregivers who are married can receive benefits based on their spouse's past work history, but they must be still married when applying or must be divorced from an at least 10-year marriage to an eligible spouse.[19]

In essence, Social Security currently rewards us for pursuing career ambition and punishes us for pursuing caregiving ambition. At minimum, the government could create a freedom-to policy by removing the penalty for full-time caregiving. Better yet, Social Security could treat caregiving as honorable and worthy of recognition, providing credit toward future Social Security benefits based on the caregiving individuals perform that removes them from, or keeps them out of, the workforce.[20]

"Freedom-to" accommodations are expensive. But so is continued investment in work–life policies that aren't moving the dial on stress and well-being (let alone all of the people they are unable to fully care for). Can we do better? Of course. Consider: It wasn't until late into the 20th century that pants were deemed appropriate clothing for women outside the home.[21] Or consider credit cards: As late as the 1960s, a bank could, and often did, legally refuse to issue a credit card to a woman who was not married. Married women who wanted credit cards were required to have their husband cosign for the card but not vice versa.[22]

These advances may seem commonplace now, but they were hard-won. So, why do we continue to accept the status quo—or less—when it comes to caregiving? Women can finally act on their career ambitions; isn't it time to advocate for policies that empower women to act on all their ambitions as well? Developing more "freedom-to" accommodations is the frontier for progress for all employees and employers who care. To that end, let's consider some more "freedom-to" examples that might help us find a true work–care balance.

Three Emerging Examples of "Freedom-to" Accommodations

Employers lose talented workers who, when confronted with provisioning care as their only option, leave the workforce to follow their providing caregiving ambitions. As a result, some forward-looking employers have begun experimenting with three specific "freedom-to" policies: returnships, un-limited paid vacation, and a 4-day workweek.

RETURNSHIPS

Returnships are essentially internships for people who are coming back to a career rather than just starting out in it. They are a tool for expanding opportunity for, and tapping into a pool of, ambitious, experienced workers who have been focused on caregiving for years or even decades. In the 2013 comedy *The Internship*, two salespeople whose careers have been decimated by the tech age find themselves in coveted internships at Google, where they must compete with young, tech-savvy hotshots for an actual job. With actors Vince Vaughn and Owen Wilson, hijinks ensue, of course; but the premise is certainly based in reality. For one reason or another, many of us must remove ourselves—or are removed—from the workforce at some time. With the rapid rate of technology and speed of everyday life, workplaces change quickly, even within a few years; and it's easy to feel left behind. The prospects of coming back are daunting.

Returnships facilitate https://www.mercer.us/our-thinking/healthcare/new-survey-finds-employers-adding-fertility-benefits-to-promote-dei.html the transition back into the workplace for people who have left the workforce for a few years, often when a child was young or when someone in the family was ill. They usually last "a few weeks to a few months, [and] typically [offer] payment that's commensurate with an individual's level of experience."[23] The goal is to provide extra training and mentorship, helping people reacclimate to the culture and pace of a former job and refresh their skills and introducing them to new technologies. Returnships also provide caregivers with a current position they can list on their résumés, fighting the stigma that can come from looking for a job without current employ-ment, while elevating their application's status in some employers' minds.

Companies worldwide have very different returnship programs. All of them recognize that not everyone has a traditional career path and that many people—women in particular—go off that path to focus heavily on caregiving. Deloitte LLP's Encore Program is an example. The program typically lasts 3–4 months, during which time participants not only are assigned to a paid consulting project but further have access to leadership development resources and mentors. The combination of recent experience, training, and coaching is powerful and helps previously full-time caregivers to successfully rejoin the paid workforce into positions, within the company or outside. Deloitte talent director Diane Borhani explains, "There's actually a very large population of people out there who are interested in returning to the workforce but don't know how to go about it."[24] For employers, it's just smart business, providing a means to recruit from a talented pool of qualified, diverse people who can—with the right opportunities—enhance their workforce.

Hewlett Packard's Path Forward returnship program describes itself as a "career reboot" that "allows for a smoother, more confident transition back to work."[25] The program targets those people who banked 5 or more years of experience in the paid workforce earlier in their careers and left the workforce for at least 12 months to provide care. This returnship includes "a temporary assignment lasting up to 16 weeks; online training to refresh your technical knowledge and skills; mentorship, buddy programs, and other networking support; [and] the opportunity to apply for full-time employment at the end of your assignment."[26] Similar programs are offered by Cloudflare, Goldman Sachs, Credit Suisse, and the advertising firm GTB.[27]

Returnships are still rare. And slots in the ones that exist are very, very competitive to get, with "reported acceptance rates varying from .025% at General Motors to .019% at Goldman Sachs."[28] To be accessible, and make a difference for caregivers more broadly, the availability of returnships must be greatly expanded, while taking care not to exploit the skills and challenges that confront women returning to the workforce, in particular.[29]

Unlimited Paid Vacation Benefits

Unlimited paid time off (PTO)—increasingly adopted by a range of firms—has the potential to be truly empowering for caregiving. These programs and policies give employees permission to take the odd day off to deal with life or take a break from work without triggering fear about using up the fixed amount of PTO normally allotted to them. Their vacation days are, at least in theory, "unlimited." Companies offering this work–life policy ask employees to get approval for long stretches of vacation or for an abundance of days, and they can, of course, deny requests that are deemed unfeasible.

These policies are a fixture in Silicon Valley tech companies and start-ups and are now being adopted across the United States by more established companies and employers in more traditional industries. According to the 2019 MetLife U.S. Employee Benefit Trends Study, employees respond positively to these policies, with 72% of the 2,675 full-time employees studied expressing interest in receiving unlimited PTO.[30]

In practice, "unlimited paid vacation" policies do not result in employees taking unlimited amounts of time off.[31] Overwhelmingly employees do not abuse, overuse, or exploit the policy—typically employees just want or need the flexibility that comes with unlimited paid vacation. Emma Brudner, director of People Operations at Lola.com—a travel management app with 115 employees—noted that for most employees the company's unlimited vacation policy is "less about spending weeks at the beach and more about managing their lives more effectively" and about "a parent taking an afternoon off to see her child in a school play, or someone with a chronic illness not having to carefully allocate vacation time so they can go to regular doctor's checkups."[32]

These policies, however, can have unintended consequences. Companies that implement them, with the intention of helping employees make space to care for others (or themselves), sometimes find that employees take less time off than they had before. In the absence of clear rules and assurances that they won't be evaluated unfavorably for exercising the benefit, employees may take fewer days off than they would under a standard plan.[33] An unlimited vacation policy also won't gain traction if the managers who enforce it do not themselves take time off, giving permission and creating norms by example. Ideally, there would be some "minimum time away" expected to set the norm and encourage employees to use these benefits.

A 4-Day Workweek

"Freedom-to" give care ambitiously increases when one has open periods to do so—for most traditional workweeks, that available time is on the weekend. So what if weekends were 3 days and thus included 1 day—either Friday or Monday—when everything is open and one can arrange doctors' visits, attend school functions, and be home to meet the school bus?

The idea of a 4-day workweek has been around for about 100 years. In 1928, John Maynard Keynes, the famous economist, predicted a 15-hour workweek would arrive within a century.[34] Experiments with it have produced mixed results, and so far, the idea has not taken off. But workers and labor advocates are once again promoting it as a more realistic way to provide "freedom-to" for caregivers.

In December 2020, Unilever New Zealand implemented a 4-day work-week trial for many employees, letting people work "80% of the time, while retaining 100% of their salaries and deliver[ing] 100% of their . . . output."[35] Whether that and other such experiments will succeed depends on several factors. One is simply the norm that a workweek is 5 days and that anything else isn't a real workweek. That norm has been eroding but—unfortunately—in the "wrong" direction as new technologies allow and encourage the day's work to carry on at night and on weekends, holidays, and even vacations.

A second factor is whether working intensely for 4 days is as productive as working the traditional 5 days. Again, the data are mixed: Some studies find the same, or even better, productivity in 4 days, and some find less.[36] Supporters point out that 4-day workweeks are characterized by more focus and less schmoozing with co-workers. Others suggest that the amount of work expected in most jobs can be done in 4 days anyway and that the 5-day workweek leaves employees looking around for something to do—say online shopping or checking social media—just to pass the time. London School of Economics professor David Graeber highlighted how working more hours than the work actually requires can, in some cases, have detrimental effects on productivity and mental health.[37]

A third factor is the need to prioritize caregiving ambition, according it equal credibility with career ambition. This recognition of caregiving ambition has not typically been part of the discussion of 4-day workweeks. Unilever, for example, has been clear that it is only experimenting with the 4-day workweek; and a top executive said, "For this to be deemed successful, we need great business results, our people telling us they have the mental and physical energy to bring the best version of themselves to work and our customers continuing to receive the same level of excellent service we pride ourselves on."[38] That is, there was no suggestion that making room for caregiving ambition, and caregiving, was itself worth achieving. The equation will only balance—that is, the full benefits of the 4-day workweek will only materialize—if one does a full accounting of work and life outcomes.

Two More Curious Examples of "Freedom-to" Accommodations

Egg freezing and flexibility are two examples of accommodations that may seem somewhat curious, both of which warrant further investigation. Not widely available, though increasingly common, egg freezing can be seen as alternatively a "freedom-to" or a "freedom-from" accommodation. Either way, it's likely to become increasingly common as the procedure costs come down. Flexibility, the most lauded of all work–life benefits, is perhaps well described as a "dangerous darling" of the work–life movement because, as can be said for many things in life including egg freezing, "it's complicated."

EGG FREEZING: FREEDOM-TO OR FREEDOM-FROM?
Elective oocyte cryopreservation, commonly called "egg freezing," is perhaps the newest form of "freedom-from" accommodation, though it should be more accurately categorized as "freedom-from for now; freedom-to tomorrow." Egg freezing allows women to delay childrearing.

In some cases, it is done to allow one to focus intensely on one's career ambitions. In other cases, it is more about one's life stage and relationship status. For others, it is a way to buy time in deciding whether or not one wishes to have children. Egg freezing does not, of course, guarantee that one can become pregnant in the future. It does increase the odds of having a child once the woman decides to do so. Egg freezing is very nuanced—attractive to some, and worrisome for others. Simply put, it's complicated.

From the company's point of view, egg freezing is a recruiting tool for top talent. Companies offering elective oocyte cryopreservation include Apple, Microsoft, Alphabet (Google), Netflix, Uber, Citigroup, and JP Morgan Chase, along with some large, elite law firms such as Cleary Gottlieb and Kirkland & Ellis. According to a Mercer National Survey of Employer-Sponsored Health Plans, the number of large employers offering egg freezing almost tripled from 6% in 2015 to 19% in 2020.[39] This jump suggests that many women are open to forgoing motherhood and caregiving to develop a high-powered career. Egg freezing still prioritizes careers but recognizes that the desire to start a family and be a caregiver is a real impulse for many of the company's valued employees. Claire, a mother of one, explains her personal support for egg freezing programs: "It gets more difficult for a woman to get pregnant naturally as they age, employers should offer benefits for reproductive technology like freezing one's eggs. Offering egg freezing employee benefits to women essentially means that companies are meeting women where they are."

But companies that promote egg freezing for career-focused women may be subtly encouraging a riskier choice than is often appreciated. First, not all the frozen eggs will prove viable; just like in ordinary attempts to become pregnant, a woman's age when she has them frozen can be a factor in viability. Second, the procedure is intense and somewhat painful. Third, there can be side effects, such as ovarian hyperstimulation syndrome, a reaction to the fertility drugs that promote ovulation. And fourth, more longitudinal data is needed to uncover any long-term effects of the egg freezing process. So, anyone to whom this benefit appeals should know going in that it's not a matter of "freezing and forgetting." It's also important to remember that companies are in this game to "empower" employees to focus on career ambition.

Take the case of Jasmin Rosenberg, who describes her decision to freeze her eggs: "Sometimes I wish I'd never frozen my eggs—wish I hadn't been so quick to tamper with my body, without asking any questions, researching the dangers or rates of success (the chance of one of my 36-year-old frozen eggs resulting in a baby could be anywhere from 29.7 to 60%)."[40] She concludes, however, that she wouldn't change her decision.

Egg freezing is a highly individual choice. Indeed, it can be beneficial for women who want children eventually but not at the particular point in time when they freeze their eggs. The process also illustrates one of the frontiers in addressing the needs and wants of employees with multiple ambitions. In the long term, egg freezing becomes a "freedom-to" accommodation since it opens up the possibility of future childrearing—perhaps at a later age than would otherwise have been possible. In the short term, however, this benefit is "freedom-from" because it allows women to pursue their career ambitions without competition from their caregiving ambitions.

FLEXIBILITY: THE DOUBLE-EDGED DARLING

Flexibility, whether of schedule ("flextime") or location ("flexplace"), is undoubtedly the most hyped work–life and work–care policy. But it's also the most double-edged. In principle, flexibility allows you to exert greater control over your work schedule by customizing the timing and the location of more of your work hours, thereby leaving you more time to work around (and engage in) key activities in the rest of your life, including to care for your family and others. Flexibility does have some risks. Your work can end up spilling over into the rest of your life, and ambitious people, in particular, are at risk of this. With flexibility, they can end up burning both ends of the candle, causing their employer to benefit much more than they themselves do. Moreover, taking advantage of workplace flexibility tends to be stigmatized; as a result, employees who utilize flexible work policies typically overcompensate by working additional hours to prove that they are "truly" devoted to their jobs.[41]

Sociologist Heejung Chung found that employees in Germany worked more hours, in total, when given greater flexibility in scheduling the "when" of their workday, a result that held true even when Chung accounted for a range of factors that influence an individual's likelihood of working longer hours, such as level of authority and type of job.[42] In fact, many different studies have come to a similar conclusion: If you want your people to work more, give them flexibility.

We saw this impulse—to appreciate flexibility but to work harder to compensate for it—in the caregivers we researched. Gabby, a mother of one, explains, "My dad was very sick at the hospital and had to undergo a surgery. My employer is very flexible and I used my paid-time off days to stay at the hospital with him. I worked so hard all day, so I could feel I could leave early." According to Lily, a mother of one, the flexibility afforded to her by her employer (about 2 months of workdays spread out flexibly over a year) to support her mother and her husband who were both ill, and both passed away in the same year, is the single most important reason she "values working there."

This mutual benefit, for both employee and employer, may be one reason flexible work arrangements have surged in popularity since 2000, and continue to evolve.[43] In the United States, even prior to the COVID-19 pandemic, 94% of employers provided at least some employees with some form of flexible work arrangement, according to a survey conducted by the International Foundation of Employee Benefit Plans.[44] The COVID-19 pandemic was, among other things, a tremendous trial in telecommuting on a grand scale and a massive experiment in flexibility of location: At the time of writing, spring 2020, the Brookings Institution reports that "half of American workers are currently working from home, more than double the fraction who worked from home, 'at least occasionally,' in 2017–18."[45]

Of course, telecommuting is not an available option for all forms of work—many jobs, such as in retail and hospitality, cannot be done from home. And these jobs are not distributed evenly across all social groups. Asian American workers appear to have the highest rates of being able to telecommute for work (37%), followed by White workers (30%), while only 20% of African American workers and 16% of Latinx workers are able to work from home.[46] In addition, some companies tout flexible scheduling, but in reality they simply cut pay and hours. This was the case for Ayesha, a mother of three, who found, "when my son was sick and I couldn't get anyone else to take care of my son I asked to leave early and make up the hours—it was granted but I found out later why he [the manager] was so quick to say yes—my paycheck was simply cut short for the hours [and the missed hours were never rescheduled]."

To celebrate flextime and flexplace, like so many experts do, without calling into question the real and very worrisome associated costs is short-sighted. Yes, flexible work arrangements can, for example, help employees cut down commute times. And they can help an employee to get to the parent–teacher conference on time or take an aging parent to a cardiologist appointment. But when people are ambitious about their caregiving, they can flex themselves into an unhealthy state. Setting one's schedule takes mental energy—self-scheduling moves a burden from the employer to the employee.[47]

Flexibility sometimes involves choosing from among different possible shifts—some employers break the 24-hour day into two or three shifts, and employees can choose from them. This can allow employers to better capitalize on their facilities and to deliver services around the clock. In theory, flexible work shifts like this can also empower caregiving. But flextime in the form of choosing shifts to work, just like flextime in the location one works, can both support and undermine caregiving.

Let's say a working couple manages to flex their schedules so that one works a day shift and the other a night shift. In some sense, it's great that this situation allows at least one parent to always be with the children.[48] They also manage to avoid the tremendous cost of quality child care (discussed in Chapter 4). But what kind of hit does family life take? Ambitious caregivers will deal with this new schedule by sleeping less so that they can have some family time that includes both parents.

Consider the story of Jennifer and David. Jennifer, a steel cutter, sets off at 4:40 a.m. for her shift at the American Axle and Manufacturing Plant in Detroit, while her husband, David, remains at home and cares for the children until the afternoon, when he heads to work at the same steel plant and Jennifer returns home.[49] In between their shifts they have a brief (half-hour) overlap when they "hand off" their four children to each other. The hardest part of this schedule, David explains, is not seeing his wife and the toll it has taken on their marriage. They aren't alone—studies show that when one partner in a couple works a night shift, a divorce or separation is up to 6 times more likely.[50] The flexibility has resulted in David and Jennifer being on a seemingly "never-ending cycle of chores and work."

There are at least 5 million so-called split-shift couples in this country.[51] They are often parents struggling to make ends meet. They want (and need) to save on child care and spend quality time with their children. For millions of working families, child care is simply unaffordable and even exceeds the average annual cost of in-state college tuition.

There is a useful physical parallel to the dangers inherent in flexible work arrangements. Physical flexibility—or limberness—is important, which is part of the reason so many people stretch and practice yoga and t'ai chi. But there is actually a medical condition—generalized joint hypermobility—that comes from being too limber. The body's connective tissue becomes more elastic than it should be, placing a person at risk of injury. Constantly pushing your body further than a normal range can occur when there's too much flexibility in your joints and muscles—and jobs. You can force yourself further in fulfilling your ambitions for both caregiving and breadwinning than is actually safe or healthy, all enabled by a well-intentioned but double-edged flexibility accommodation.

Freedom-to Accommodations: More to Be Envisioned

There is so much more to be discovered about how companies can enable "freedom-to" cultures and work–care programs and policies—how they can support employees in ambitiously providing care, not just provisioning it. It's time to think innovatively about how to support caregiving ambition. The coronavirus pandemic already pushed the bounds in terms of what is possible by creating an international experiment in virtual work. Here, we propose some additional ideas that are not necessarily the most pragmatic but are intended to catalyze brainstorming.

First, companies can truly encourage vacations—and the space they provide for people to connect with and care for their loved ones. Specifically, managers can transform vacations from a mere policy, often underused, to a powerful form of "freedom to care."

Another possibility is to find creative ways to mitigate the individual effects of the unavoidable spikes in an individual's workload. Dealing with these tends to come at the expense of caregiving, but employers could encourage more workgroup sharing of spikes and peak loads. This would have the double benefit of conferring "freedom-to" both in individuals' private caregiving and in co-workers' caregiving for each other, itself an underrated but powerful force with both personal and business advantages.

Another way to develop a work culture of "freedom-to" is to tone down the company-sponsored fun at the workplace and put some of that energy into building camaraderie and mutual understanding and respect—in fun ways—around caregiving roles. For one thing, work parties and company outings often come at the expense of caregiving time. People may come to the company events so as not to be party-poopers, while wishing they were at home engaged in caregiving. So why not encourage people to share something truly meaningful to them from outside of work, related to caring for others and for the community? Hold a company photo contest in which people can submit cherished funny, fun, beautiful photos of their loved ones. Hold a company storytelling contest—"story slam" style—with a caregiving theme. Such events would allow people to connect on the things that define who they are and on a key but typically unacknowledged part of why they work at all—that is, their caring relationships. Despite all the gush about following your passion and loving what you do, many more people work hard because they love their families. And that's a beautiful thing—why not celebrate it?

LOOKING FORWARD

Though "freedom-from" and "freedom-to" accommodations have their own pitfalls, work–life and work–care policies and arrangements have been associated overall with positive outcomes both for employees, such as higher job performance[52,53] and higher salaries,[54] and for employers, in terms of the attraction and retention of top talent.[55] Despite these positive outcomes, research finds that, as mentioned, only a fraction of the employees who could benefit from these policies actually use them. In the United States, for instance, fewer than 50% of employees use available work–life policies and arrangements.[56]

Why? Some employees avoid using these policies and arrangements because they fear career penalties if they were to use them. They fear wage penalties, fewer promotion opportunities, and reduced career mobility within and across organizations. These concerns are rational as negative career consequences have indeed been reported in these areas.[57] Research also finds that supervisors attribute certain motives to the use of work–life policies.[58] Specifically, they see their use as prioritizing personal life over workplace productivity. "Freedom-from" accommodations minimize this challenge because their use can be interpreted as showing that, while employees have obligations outside the workplace, they are most supremely ambitious about their careers.

As discussed, employers often treat work–life policies and programs as though they were all created equal—with equal stigmas, penalties, and rewards. Most research and public discussion also tend to either study just one policy in isolation or bundle different work–life and work–care policies together by using counts of available policies. This approach limits our understanding of the variation in career consequences.[59]

"Freedom-to" programs and policies must be more widely adopted and supported. Will they lead to greater stigma and to more negative career consequences than "freedom-from" accommodations? Possibly. That's why seriously well-intentioned employers "leaning in" to "freedom-to" policies must take extra steps to explain them. They must inform employees as to why these accommodations are being offered and educate them on what it does and does not—or should and should not—mean when colleagues avail themselves of such polices. Of course, they must also first educate themselves and their top management. Companies have to show that their culture does not stigmatize employees who wish to not only provision care but also to provide it while ambitiously pursing their career goals. They need to raise awareness about the programs and policies, encourage senior leaders to demonstrate their commitment to "freedom-to" policies, and work to make these policies accessible to all employees.

The freedom from something and the freedom to do something have battled throughout history in philosophical, political, and economic thought as basic categories of human experience. They are palpably different matters when it comes to balancing caregiving ambition and work ambition. Broadly speaking, work–life and, specifically, work–care accommodations have focused on freedom from engaging in other life domains, as opposed to freedom to engage in other parts of life, most profoundly, caring for others.[60] All parties to the work–life discussion— the various shapers, providers, administrators, and users of work–life policies—need to take the "freedom-to" and "freedom-from" distinction more seriously. Without doing so, issues will remain muddled that could in fact be much more satisfactorily resolved, allowing "freedom-to" accommodations to honor caregiving not just as a duty or obligation but as the ambition so many of us believe it to be.

DEFINING QUESTIONS

- Which type of work–life policy is most attractive to you? Do you think this has changed, or will change, at different ages and life stages?
- What would be gained socially and economically if we reallocated our social emphasis on "freedom-from" accommodations to "freedom-to" accommodations?
- What currently holds employers back from "freedom-to" accommodations, relative to the more comfortable "freedom-from" accommodations?

The Case Against
the Business Case

Caring companies will pioneer innovative solutions for the needs
of their workforce and create a badly needed set of new best
practices. In turn, they will inspire other companies to follow in
their path.

—Joseph B. Fuller and Manjari Raman[1]

THE BUSINESS CASE FOR WORK–LIFE PROGRAMS

Chief executive officers (CEOs), human resources (HR) managers, and
academics across a variety of industries often tout the business case
for work–life programs. The argument typically goes something like
this: When employees' work lives and personal lives are balanced, they experience less conflict and less mental and physical strain. They are happier
and healthier employees, which makes them more engaged and productive at work. Ultimately, promoting and supporting work–life balance is
good for the bottom line.[2] Or so the mantra goes. A closer look at the
evidence reveals that, yes, employees are happier and healthier, but the
connection to the bottom line is tenuous.

Another popular argument is that work–life and work–care programs
are good for firms' reputations and an effective way to attract talent,

The Caregiving Ambition. Julia B. Bear and Todd L. Pittinsky, Oxford University Press. © Oxford University Press 2022.
DOI: 10.1093/oso/9780197512418.003.0009

which, in turn, benefits the bottom line. There is some evidence that share prices indeed go up after public companies announce family-friendly HR programs—particularly those involving working mothers—indicating a boon for the firms' reputations. However, some studies report minimal effects.[3]

Cause and effect are also difficult to parse—offering benefits for reputation and talent management may be a result of success, not a precursor to success. In 2015, for example, Netflix famously announced unlimited paid leave for its salaried employees during the first year after birth or adoption, citing talent management as the primary reason for the new policy. Was Netflix able to offer this benefit because it's such a profitable company, or did it offer it to make the company more profitable? It's hard to know, though Netflix certainly garnered a great deal of positive publicity at the time.[4]

But let's take a step back and consider, what is a business case, really? One generally accepted definition is, "A justification for a proposed project or undertaking on the basis of its expected commercial benefit."[5] According to this definition, work–life programs should lead to increased profits for the companies that sponsor them. Yet if the business case is so compelling, then why don't companies truly buy into it? To put it another way, if the business case is so powerful, why do some of today's most profitable companies—Amazon, for example—operate in a way that is completely counter to the business case for work–life, even though they have great policies on the books? Why do the top law and finance firms in the country grind through talented young men and women with extreme working hours and demands yet continue to be highly successful?[6]

Based on the two main business case arguments, companies that don't support work–life balance and work–care policies should be losing talented employees either due to attrition—they're unhappy and unhealthy and move on to another organization—or reputation costs—they don't want to work in these companies in the first place. Such organizations should ultimately succumb to other companies that offer greater support for work–life. But this doesn't seem to be the case at all.

On a more philosophical level, why do we even need a business case to justify enabling employees to live healthy, happy lives and to care for their families and communities? Why isn't this simply a moral imperative for our society? Why does parental leave require a justification in terms of commercial benefit as opposed to the well-being of infants and their parents? Still, academics and HR specialists alike are strong purveyors and proponents of the business case when it comes to work–life issues and caregiving.

You may be thinking to yourself that, regardless of whether the business case is entirely persuasive, without it, companies wouldn't implement work–care policies at all. So even if it's a little strange to make a commercial justification for supporting newborns and their parents, the ends might justify the means. The problem with that utilitarian argument is that, first, the business case is less persuasive than is often portrayed. And, second, even when the business justification is apparent, ultimately relying on the business case only helps employees who will provide the commercial benefit. This second point has important implications.

Perhaps Netflix's generous paid family leave policy did help the company attract employees in a highly competitive industry in which employers vie for talent. But the policy only benefited the company's salaried, professional employees, so the benefit remained part of a two-tiered system.[7] Warehouse employees and hourly workers have children too, whose well-being is also as important; yet competition is less fierce when it comes to attracting and retaining those employees. So the business case for the new policy only extended to professionals—Netflix followed the business case and no more. After extensive criticism—the public, it seems, wanted more than just what the business case dictated the company should do for its professional workers, Netflix extended its policy, though not identically so, to all employees.[8] Work–life as a business case means, not surprisingly, that companies support work–life and work–care programs only when it's potentially good for business.

In reality, the business case for work–life is weak, and understanding this weakness helps explain why so many organizations focus on "freedom-from," rather than "freedom-to," accommodations (as discussed in Chapter 7). More importantly, the business case, by definition, is flat out absurd in its connection with ambitious caregiving—as a society, we should not be justifying support for caregiving by its commercial benefit. A case for humanity is much more logical, not to mention compassionate. By freeing ourselves from the business case, we can develop a more humane approach to supporting all workers and their caregiving ambitions. Though we'll dig further into these topics, let's first discuss some historical context around the business case and what led to its prevalence today.

THE COMPANY TOWN

Prior to industrialization in the United States, for some, work and family were intertwined in an essentially agrarian society. In fact, there was no need for a business case for combining the two—they were inextricable as is. That's not to say conflicts didn't exist, but work and family were co-located and, for all intents and purposes, one and the same. Family life involved work as much as, if not more than, it involved care; families were business ventures in addition to sources of caring and sentimentality.[9]

With industrialization, the spheres of work and family were separated. A particularly interesting phenomenon, the company town, sprang up next to manufacturing locations throughout the country. Companies opened factories and, in the same areas, built housing and provided basic services for workers and their families. The company town enabled management to control employees by managing their work, their personal lives, and the local economies. Some company towns, such as Hershey, Pennsylvania, were idyllic, albeit paternalistic, featuring libraries, green spaces, and decent housing. Though iron fists in velvet gloves, some of them were relatively comfortable places. Other company towns were neglected and dirty, barely providing even the most basic services.[10] These highly exploitative towns, such as the infamous coal camps of West Virginia, held little regard for employees' well-being, or even lives.[11]

These towns exemplify the original "business case" for work–life. Companies closely monitored workers' home and family life for the "good" of their business. For example, Ford's company representatives from the Ford Sociological Department—first called "investigators" and later called "advisors"—regularly conducted home visits, asking employees personal questions about their children's school attendance, their marriages, and their family life in general.[12] There was a business case for this interest in marriage and family life: Employees in stable marriages with children were more likely to be reliable employees.

Though these employees faced grueling working conditions, invasions of privacy, and unwilling indebtedness to their employers, there was some positive progress on the work–life front during the Industrial Revolution period. The basic idea that there should be limits on the amount of time a person spends at work dates back to late-1800s manufacturing laws, which limited women's work hours and restricted child labor. By 1938, after decades of strife between labor and management, the Fair Labor Standards Act established a 44-hour workweek, although certain sectors of the economy—such as service industries and caregiving jobs—were excluded from the original legislation.

Still, compare these company towns with contemporary company "campuses"—the similarities are striking. Silicon Valley giants like Facebook are famous for offering every possible service under one roof: healthcare (both medical and dental), dry cleaning, meals, sleep pods. Sound familiar? There are fewer interruptions from work. No need to leave the campus for a pesky errand. The distractions of daily life are removed, so there is more time to take care of business—ostensibly benevolent but ultimately facilitating total devotion to the company.

FEMALE WORKERS DURING WORLD WAR II

During World War II, there was a precipitous uptick in women's employment, as well as the concomitant creation of government child care. With the male workforce occupied at war and the war effort requiring increasing levels of manufacturing and production, women's employment increased by 50% between 1940 and 1945. Approximately 75% of these new entrants to the workforce were married with children. The government responded by subsidizing child care centers, which, at one point, cared for as many as 1.5 million children.[13] For the government, the business case was to invest quickly in child care so that its female workers could come to work. Yet immediately following the war, when men returned home and resumed working, women's employment was no longer needed, so they were laid off or relegated to more menial jobs. The idealization of the breadwinner father and housewife mother that characterized the 1950s had begun. Government-subsidized child care centers were closed, and employer-provided child care, driven by the particular business case of World War II, generally disappeared, not to resurface again until 1971, when StrideRite famously opened the first on-site child care program by an employer.[14]

Women's employment during World War II highlights the precarious-ness of the business case for work–care programs: The business case is only as good as the commercial benefit. When the commercial benefit is no longer present—such as when men returned from war and women were not needed in the factories anymore—the structural support for caregiving disappears. Compare that case to the humanistic one, which is based on supporting children and families and a societal commitment to high-quality child care. This case is not ephemeral but rather grounded in valuing caregiving and empowering individuals who are ambitious in their caregiving, while being less subject to financial concerns only.

THE WORK–LIFE MOVEMENT GOES CORPORATE

Although governmental and societal support for caregiving were dormant following the end of World War II, these issues played a central role in the second-wave feminist movement, as discussed in Chapter 3. However, the feminist platform lost a great deal of momentum after the Equal Rights Amendment legislation was felled in the late 1970s by conservatives. In its wake, Reagan's administration cut social programs. Nevertheless, given the increased number of women in the workforce and the concomitant demands of work and family, corporate America stepped in and offered new work–family initiatives, mostly fringe benefits and child care as opposed to any radical work redesign that would have made an impact on work-care conflict.[15] Thus, a more milquetoast, corporate movement was born in the early 1980s, primarily focused on issues faced by White, female, salaried, professional employees.[16]

At the same time, the primacy of shareholder value came to dominate corporate America. Famously argued by University of Chicago economist Milton Friedman, the shareholder value philosophy states that companies exist solely to enrich shareholders, with no other responsibilities to any other stakeholders. This audacious idea—that the only social responsibility of business is to make money—provided a justification for almost anything that would increase profits: hostile acquisitions and takeovers, aggressive buyouts and financial machinations by financiers, and outsourced production to take advantage of cheaper labor.[17] By the early 1980s, it seemed that the only legitimate justification for anything business-related became short-term, shareholder value.

In this way, the corporate business case turned into the dominant paradigm for the work–care movement, with various family-friendly benefits at organizations' discretion, solely dependent upon the latest financial calculations. Still, by the late 20th century, in a range of settings—corporate, government, and nonprofit—employees began to call for more capacity to manage, or to balance, their professional and personal lives. Corporations took notice. However, this paradigm creates a conundrum: If the business case for work–care must take into account enriching shareholders in the short term, then the link between work–life benefits and the bottom line should be strong. In fact, the modern business case is weak from both sides of the equation.

THE (NOT SO) ALMIGHTY BOTTOM LINE

Research shows that lower work–family conflict indeed makes employees healthier and happier. But the final link—from employee health and happiness to profits—is not well supported,[18] and business leaders seem to recognize this tenuous association between job satisfaction and profitability. For example, depending upon the measures, the correlation between job satisfaction and job performance specifically is around .30, which is considered a moderate correlation.[19] Job satisfaction has stronger relationships with other outcomes more directly related to profitability, including turnover (leaving a job).[20] Job satisfaction is also closely related to what organizational psychologists call "organizational citizenship behaviors," meaning the willingness to help colleagues and generally behave in positive ways for the organization, above and beyond just the expectations of one's position.[21] But, again, the direct link with the bottom line is not well supported. Also, as mentioned in the beginning of the chapter, studies have investigated whether announcing work–family benefits really impacts firm reputation by examining whether stock prices change immediately following such announcements. A few studies have found positive effects, though very small, while many studies have found no effects at all.[22]

To be sure, not all business thinkers promote such a narrow focus on the bottom line, and new models have emerged that recognize multiple stakeholders, not just shareholders. For example, the Balanced Scorecard, developed by Robert Kaplan and David Norton in the mid-1990s, operationalizes strategy using a more holistic approach to a company's success. The scorecard consists of four components, both financial and non-financial: customer, internal (employees), learning and growth, and financial.[23] Considered a breakthrough when it premiered, and still useful for executives in many ways, the scorecard does not necessarily buttress the business case for work–life and work–care. Though it addresses the importance of focusing on employees' learning and growth, the authors also explain that ultimately all scorecard parameters should be tied to financial objectives. Although the scorecard has been cited as a way to support the business case for work–life, the link, yet again, is tenuous.

From the life and, in particular, the care side of the equation, benefits such as on-site child care and other services that facilitate working more may engender greater work commitment but not necessarily better caregiving. These benefits provide "freedom-from" caregiving accommodations as opposed to "freedom-to" caregiving accommodations (detailed in Chapter 7), and more often than not, as discussed, they remain on the books but go unused. This experience is widespread. Just ask all the parents who find ways to work from home or attend school events surreptitiously, hiding where they are and what they're doing from their bosses, since they fear that being up front about it may lead to negative consequences.

Men, in particular, report engaging in this behavior to help take care of their families while maintaining their reputations as "ideal workers" (as shown in Chapter 5).[24] In fact, Harvard Business School explicitly recommends this type of behavior. In their guide to work–life, one prescription is as follows: "Be as physically visible in the office as possible—taking the long way to the coffee machine—so colleagues consider you around and available, even when you're at the pediatrician's office again."[25] If the business case for work–care were so strong, would a manual by the country's premier business school be advising people to strategize just so they can take their kids to the doctor?

Putting aside the argument that work–care should be justified on its own terms and not as a "business case," if we simply take the business case at face value, it is problematic—the link to the bottom line itself is poor. And the reputation effects, when they occur, are likely fleeting. These facts may help explain why recent attempts at work redesign, which have wonderful effects on employee well-being, ultimately lack support from top management.

THE LACK OF A CORPORATE INCENTIVE

In their book *Overload*, sociologists Erin Kelly and Phyllis Moen describe their extensive research and intervention program with a work redesign initiative called STAR, an acronym for "Support. Transform. Achieve. Results." A subset of employees in the information technology division of a Fortune 500 company (pseudonym TOMO) was randomly assigned to either participate in the STAR program or to a matched control group, in which participants continued conducting business as usual.[26]

According to the authors, STAR had three main goals: "(1) increase employees' control over where and when they do their work; (2) promote social support for personal and family lives (including recognizing the need for time off from work); and (3) manage high work demands by focusing on results rather than time spent in the office or online and by reducing low-value work whenever possible."[27] These goals were accomplished in multiple ways, but primarily by training both supervisors and employees in how to identify new work practices that would increase employee control, reduce time spent on low-value work, and recognize and support employees' family and personal lives. Like the Results Oriented Work Environment (ROWE)—the work redesign program at Best Buy discussed in Chapter 2—STAR was subsequently retracted after TOMO was acquired by another company. New management nixed the program.

According to the data collected while the program was still in use, the benefits of STAR included reductions in burnout, stress, work–life conflict, and turnover and increases in amount of sleep, personal and family time, and job satisfaction. The results were extremely impressive, and STAR was clearly beneficial to employees' lives. *Notably, however, there was no effect on productivity or on performance*:

> The company and . . . the research team worked hard to fairly assess whether STAR positively or negatively affected productivity and performance. In the end, all we could say was that the company metrics showed no dramatic improvements or declines over time and no clear differences by condition. STAR *neither helped nor hurt productivity or performance* as measured by company data. Given the benefits we do see on other measures . . . we take this finding of no negative effects on productivity or performance as good news. (italics are ours)[28]

The benefits speak for themselves, yet this example illustrates exactly the problem with the business case: *It's not a business case at all.*

Amazon is another powerful illustration. One of the most successful companies of the last few decades, Amazon is notorious when it comes to its treatment of its employees—both blue collar and white collar alike. Similar to the company towns of the past, Amazon often opens up warehouses in areas of the United States (and abroad) where they become one of the only substantial employers in town, exerting tremendous leverage over their employees. Stories abound of horrendous working conditions in the warehouses, including employees fainting from lack of air conditioning and being denied bathroom breaks.[29]

Among Amazon's white-collar workers, an infamous, front-page story in the *New York Times* revealed how employees experience tremendous mental strain as they try to cope with stressful life events while maintaining an intense devotion to the company, involving long working hours and nonstop travel. Employees described giving birth, miscarrying, undergoing cancer treatments—you name it—and then going back into the office or getting on a plane to fly to a meeting immediately afterward for fear of losing their jobs.[30]

The overall impression is one of heartless workplaces, a far cry from the work–life mantra of how happy and healthy employees are better employees. Amazon has never appeared on the *Working Mother 100 Best Companies* list, nor is it likely to.

Jeff Bezos, the CEO of Amazon, has fought back against these accounts. He argues that journalists cherry-pick their stories, only reporting the most extreme examples and discounting all of his satisfied employees. That critique likely has merit. However, it is also true that if the business case for work–life were as strong as its proponents claim, then Amazon should have burned out years ago, given its failure to adhere to the work–life paradigm. Instead, Amazon, founded in 1994, grew astronomically in just a few decades. The company reported $5.2 billion in net income for the second quarter of 2020.[31] Bezos, its CEO and founder, is officially the world's richest person, with a net worth of an estimated $202 billion.[32]

Then there's Google. The tech giant's employees enjoy a variety of substantial benefits, including paid family leave for both mothers and fathers for the first year of their child's life. However, far less reported is that 54%

of Google's employees are contractors, temporary workers who receive much less generous benefits than those of permanent employees, especially work–life benefits.[33] Again, if the business case were so sound, then why create what is, for all intents and purposes, a second-tier workforce that works in the shadow of the permanent one in terms of security, work–care benefits, and a host of other employee investments? Wouldn't these contractors also be motivated by, and benefit from, all of the perks that the permanent employees receive, leading to even greater profit? Of course. Yet, as discussed, work–life and work–care policies haven't been proven to increase profits, which is why top management in major corporations typically doesn't support them.

But if the business case for work–life and work–care is so weak, now what? If we put aside the business case, what's left? What case can we make for supporting people's work lives and their caregiving ambitions?

AFTER THE BUSINESS CASE? THE HUMANISTIC CASE FOR CAREGIVING

Let's abandon the business case altogether. Not the case for work–life and work–care but rather its Achilles heel—the commercial justification. Discarding the business case would free us up to acknowledge that the humanistic case lies at the heart of why we cooperate as a larger society. Though competition and self-interest are perhaps sexier and more exciting than cooperation and caregiving—and therefore get more attention—cooperation and shared humanity are at the core of our evolutionary development and what makes us human.[34] Moreover, as a society we've made the humanistic case for mutual support about a variety of other issues, such as Social Security, Medicare, and Medicaid—what makes support for work–care policies and caregiving ambition any different?

As the COVID-19 pandemic made clear, caregiving and health are mutual, communal, societal issues, not individual, commercial ones. The business case for work–care, however, has always rested on a larger, invisible pillar of beliefs about individuals versus societies, namely that individuals should more exclusively care about themselves and their families and that caregiving is solely an individual responsibility. Based on this core belief, businesses must then pick up the slack for the lack of societal support but only inasmuch as it contributes to their financial success and helps their individual set of employees (so they can continue to improve that financial success). In contrast, if we view work–care issues from a humanistic perspective, then not only do we acknowledge the need for mutual aid but this shaky bulwark for the business case becomes moot. In other words, part and parcel of moving to the humanistic case is reframing work–care challenges from the individual level—an issue to be worked out with one's family or one's individual employer—to the societal level—an issue to be addressed together as a society.

As the pandemic swept over countries from Asia to the United States and beyond, the fatal logic of these pillars of individualism was revealed. For example, many companies, especially retail and food service, offer no paid sick leave for hourly workers. These workers are therefore incentivized to come to work, healthy or not. In the face of a highly contagious virus, this individualist approach fell flat, and the links among people became clear: If we don't take care of our employees, we will all, literally, become ill. And, suddenly, at the start of the pandemic, companies began offering paid sick leave to hourly and contract employees, a practice which was practically unheard of prior to the pandemic.[35] Temporary legislation— the Families First Coronavirus Response Act (FFCRA)—was passed on March 18, 2020, creating paid sick leave both for individuals who fell ill themselves and for individuals caring for sick family members, including children.[36] It could be argued that FFCRA was simply another example of the business case: It was in the companies' and the country's best interest to offer paid sick leave at the height of the first wave of the pandemic.

Moreover, abandoning the business case will also allow us to have an honest discussion about how to support work–care from a financial perspective; it will be crucial to examine the role of businesses versus the role of governments in supporting caregiving responsibilities. Paid caregiving leaves obviously cost money, so the people of the United States must consider the most efficient way to fund these costs.

The European model of a strong safety net funded via higher tax rates is often touted as an ideal approach, but it would likely need to be seriously modified to work in the decentralized, US system, in which both business lobbying groups and individuals bristle against any type of centralized system for paid leave.[37] President Joe Biden, while running for office during the 2020 presidential election, unveiled a plan for child care and eldercare—"21st Century Caregiving and Education Workforce"—that included expanding child care, including universal preschool; expanding eldercare options, especially in-home care; and improving working conditions and pay for those employed in caregiving. His proposal would primarily be funded through new tax policies and some tax credits.[38] As discussed in Chapter 2, as president, Biden also promoted programmatic proposals covering paid family leave, subsidized child care for families at or below certain income levels, and universal pre-kindergarten. Republicans have also proposed paid leave plans. They tend to advocate for the use of tax credits and/or tax incentives for businesses that offer paid leave[39] (Senator Marco Rubio also proposed such a plan in his 2016 campaign for president[40]). Although the devil is truly in the details, by freeing ourselves from the myth that companies will support work–care because there is a business case to do so, we can begin to come up with realistic and workable solutions.

These solutions likely will involve a mix of private and public funds, but they will also hopefully, and finally, treat caregiving as the communal issue that it truly is. With this approach, businesses might actually pursue "freedom-to," not only "freedom-from," accommodations, particularly if they were buttressed financially by some type of private–public partnership or tax incentive program. This model is becoming more prevalent for infrastructural investments, such as major investments in roads, highways, and transportation infrastructure[41]; and it could be a way to support "freedom-to" accommodations that would be financially feasible for organizations.

In the meantime, the myth of the business case will continue to be a distraction, a way to avoid these difficult discussions. And make no mistake: This myth is being rehashed constantly. In a report published by

Harvard Business School in January 2019, called *The Caring Company*, the authors write,

> businesses must avoid the temptation to delegate solutions to the federal or state governments. The stakes are too high for employers to await the type of broad-based mandates federal legislation is likely to yield. Smart employers will seize the opportunity to gain an advantage in the increasingly ferocious war to recruit and retain talent through a deliberate strategy to become a corporate care leader. *Caring companies will pioneer innovative solutions for the needs of their workforce and create a badly needed set of new best practices. In turn, they will inspire other companies to follow in their path.*[42] (italics are ours)

Yet again, the myth that companies will create a series of best practices, and others will be inspired to follow the same path, persists. We've seen this movie before. ROWE and STAR—both innovative solutions following best practices—were created and then retracted before they had a chance to inspire others to follow the same path—not because they didn't do good but because they didn't deliver the profits from the "good."

Perpetuating this myth also promulgates elitism. The lucky employees, mostly white-collar and highly educated, who work for companies such as Netflix or those that make the top 100 list for working mothers, enjoy work–family flexibility and support. However, non-professional and non-unionized workers' caregiving ambitions and responsibilities remain at the whim of their employers. Apparently, these employees should keep waiting until the companies they work for are "inspired" to follow in the path of others that pursue best practices.

Myths can be difficult to give up on. What child doesn't want to continue to believe in the tooth fairy? Sometimes we continue to buy into them even though in our heart of hearts we know they're false. But myths also come at a cost because they often facilitate avoiding, rather than addressing, hard truths. The hard truth here is that the business case for supporting work–life is weak. There isn't a strong commercial justification to support work–life. And even when there is commercial benefit for work–life support, typically only a lucky few reap the rewards.

Some CEOs and leaders provide organizational supports because they feel that it's the right thing to do, the humane thing to do. But we need more than just reliance on the goodness of people's hearts. We need a societal commitment to support birth, adoption, child care, and eldercare based on our shared humanity. In other words, we need fundamentally to change our mindset about caregiving and how we support caregiving ambitions. Rather than thinking about how caregiving relates to dollar signs, we need to think of it as a shared goal that we support together for humanistic reasons, a way to contribute to the success and well-being of our present and future society.

DEFINING QUESTIONS

- If you work outside the home for pay, are there policies for managing work–life at your organization? Do employees use them liberally? Why or why not?
- Why do you think corporate managers, academics, HR executives, and others continue to argue for the business case despite the lack of strong evidence for it?
- What do you believe it will take for our society to embrace a humanistic case for supporting work–life programs and policies, specifically work–care ones?

Lessons for Living Ambitiously

Big results require big ambitions.
——Michael Hammer and James Champy[1]

THERE'S NO WAY TO MAKE THIS EASY

Throughout the book, we've made a case for large-scale societal changes, including a more humanistic approach and greater valuing of caregiving. More locally, we hope that employers will embrace greater "freedom-to," as well as "freedom-from," workplace accommodations. And across the board, we call for caregiving ambition to be recognized and respected as seriously as career ambition. In that process, society will lean toward caring more—for children, for older adults, and for each other.

But, in the meantime, every individual has their own choices to make as breadwinners, as caregivers, and, so often, as both. Most people want to do well no matter which they take on, and when they tackle both at the same time, they want to do well at both. Therefore, we turn to a discussion of how you, as an individual, likely an ambitious one, can turn those ambitions into results—in your caregiving and your career.

We've written a great deal about what various institutions and systems might do, and even should do, to make this a viable path for you and the legions like you. In the meantime, we as a country are where we are. And you are who you are. There's a good chance you're ambitious to provide the

The Caregiving Ambition. Julia B. Bear and Todd L. Pittinsky, Oxford University Press. © Oxford University Press 2022.
DOI: 10.1093/oso/9780197512418.003.0010

best care you can rather than just so-so care. It's also likely that you want to take an active part in providing that great care, not just exclusively provision it. And all the while, you're probably wondering and worrying about career ambition, not to mention financial concerns, which inevitably play a major role in decisions around work and care. You can't just wait for the systems and institutions to evolve—unfortunately, there's no guarantee they ever will, and if they do, it will likely be slow.

Even if they do evolve, the policies and practices offered might not get you to where you want to go. That's one of the less encouraging lessons of the Scandinavian and European work–care policy experience, a phenomenon described in Chapter 5. Yes, official support starts at birth, with mandated maternity leave that protects a woman's job while she stays home from work for the first few weeks, months, or even years of her baby's life. Yes, this maternity leave can be fully paid, replacing her salary, as it is in France and Germany, or partially paid, as it is in Austria. It's also true that many European countries provide fathers with fully or partially paid paternity leave; others offer an extended leave to one or both parents, though usually at a lower pay rate. And yes, after maternity or paternity leave, some European government programs provide comprehensive child care.

Yet, as shown in Chapter 5, women with caregiving ambitions in those countries don't necessarily climb to the apex of their careers much more, if any more, than they do in the United States. In fact, in the Nordic and European models, women are less likely to advance in their careers compared to women in the United States. Although this disparity may be due to the valid choice to take advantage of these policies and focus on caregiving, as discussed, it also means that these policies are not automatically a panacea for someone with both caregiving and career ambitions.

So, for better or for worse, much depends on how you conduct your own work–care balancing act. You are the only one who can decide how to proceed with your dual ambitions as you're confronted with the various interrelated choices that you'll inevitably have to make. If anyone had really figured out a sure-fire way to manage work–care, it would be well established by now. The fact is, the process remains a puzzle because there are too many conflicting impulses and influences for work–care ever to be manageable by a formula or "three easy steps."

And in the short term, creating work–care balance is likely only going to get more difficult. Career challenges will become even more demanding as technology continues to revolutionize work, particularly as it enables work to colonize our homes and what used to be truly "private life." This is the case for the many professionals whose health, relationships, and other activities increasingly are overshadowed by long hours and un-relieved stress as technology continues to make their work flows more "24/7."[2] Caregiving robots, discussed in Chapter 6, could assume greater caregiving responsibilities, but as we showed in that chapter, it's not a solution most people relish—in particular, people high on caregiving ambition.

While society figures all this out—assuming it ever does—what can the individual reading this book do?

We offer four principles to guide you and then discuss three options currently available to help you pursue ambition in care and at work. While we feel this counsel is the best there is, nothing we suggest can make this pursuit easy—because there is no easy way to do it. Moreover, decisions concerning caregiving and careers are personal and often depend upon a constellation of factors, including not just yourself but also your partner (if relevant) and the people you're taking care of, plus a variety of situa-tional circumstances, such as your occupation and the job market.

FOUR PRINCIPLES

These four principles are the distillation of the lessons from the legions of books and research we have reviewed, as well as the empirical research we have conducted with thousands of diverse caregivers. We've shared many of the results from our surveys and interviews throughout the book, so you'll likely see connections between these findings and these principles. These are meant to be straightforward and customizable for your per-sonal, unique situation.

You Do You

Own the ambitions you have—caregiving, career, or both—and, for that matter, the ambitions you don't have. Recognize, too, that they can evolve over time. As the world continues to change, so do you, as do relationships, children, priorities. Take some time every few years—or when any big change or crisis occurs in your life—to remind yourself of which ambitions are, are not, or are no longer the most important to you. Expect that they may, or may not, evolve with time.

This principle sounds simple, but it can be quite challenging in practice. We all have a natural tendency to engage in social comparison processes, evaluating ourselves in comparison to others.[3] In doing so, we assess ourselves in relative rather than absolute terms. For example, our satisfaction with our salaries depends not only on the amount we earn but also on how it stacks up (or how we think it stacks up) to those of our peers. If we earn less than those around us—regardless of whether the amount is high or low—we will likely remain unsatisfied. This tendency is even greater when an objective measurement is unavailable; it's the exact same case when it comes to ambition, which is also subjective. Lacking an objective yardstick, we typically resort to social comparison.

These comparisons are magnified and distorted via social media[4]: Family activities, such as baking, playing games, and eating dinner, were once simply what people engaged in during their private lives. Now they have become fodder for elaborate, curated material to be posted on social media. The same is true for travel and other leisure activities that have morphed into competitive sport rather than pleasurable activities engaged in occasionally when people have the time and money to do so. When we are bombarded by information about what other people do, and how effortlessly and glamorously they seem to do it, it is easy to get caught in the social comparison trap, feeling that we fall short in some aspect of our lives or that we should be more ambitious in one way or another, even if that's not where our personal ambitions lie.

A great antidote to this feeling is to remind yourself that the comparison is irrelevant. Not everyone can or should aspire to everything; honestly identify and focus on your ambitions, the ones you have and the ones you don't. An honest reckoning allows you to do you, while supporting and celebrating others who may have different ambitions than you or who may make different life choices than you.

Honor Role Models, Don't Seek Heroes

Throughout your life, plenty of people will try to influence you and sell you on their "secrets to success," but don't be drawn off course by someone else's brand or algorithm for work and care. We are relentlessly marketed to, recommended to, and suggested to; filtered information is forced upon us before our own whole possible selves are even on the table. Don't assume that Instagram moms are the benchmark for your ambitious parenting any more than Jeff Bezos is your role model for your career ambitions. You may be able to learn something from them, but they are not you.

Work–care balance means something different to all of us, and people who may be role models for caregiving are not necessarily good role models for career and vice versa. That is not to say that role models aren't useful, but choose them wisely. Remember that, in the end, they, too, are just people with a certain set of ambitions, often great success but in a particular domain, and not people with all the answers.

The Grass Is Rarely Greener

The Greek and Roman teachers of Stoic philosophy taught that the one surest path to happiness is actually straightforward: First, differentiate between the aspects of your life that you control and those aspects that you cannot control; subsequently, concentrate on those that you control, and accept with equanimity what you cannot control.[5] This idea could be misinterpreted as a recipe for complacency, which likely won't sit well with an ambitious reader. But there is some truth to the observation for even the most ambitious among us: Too often, people fall prey to the myth that the grass is greener on an "other side" of the fence as opposed to focusing on (and nurturing) their own grass. Those who choose to primarily provision care focus on those who chose providing; those who choose to primarily provide care focus on those who chose provisioning. And those who balance multiple ambitions for caregiving and career focus too much on how other people are doing the same.

Avoid over-romanticizing either type of ambition or the combination. Both caregiving and careers are demanding, with a mix of rewards, costs, and regrets. You can't avoid the costs and regrets; you can only decide if the rewards outweigh them. Tend to your grass—don't ruminate about the grass on the "other side of the fence." Focusing on your neighbor's lawn, so to speak, is not helpful. In fact, an anxious sense that the "grass is greener" has been linked to lower self-confidence and even feelings of depression.[6]

We can become defined by always wanting more—and when that happens, what we have, by definition, will never be enough. As Yaacov, whom we first met in Chapter 1, shared with us, he learned early on—from a bumper sticker of all places!—that the grass isn't greener on the "other side"; it is greener where he chooses to water it.

Plan for a Journey, Not a Linear Path

Ambitious people tend to desire a linear path from point A to point Z, and everywhere in between. But any ambition, or combination of ambitions, requires an openness to changing course as needed. From high school counselors on, we are advised to think of our careers, and accompanying career ambitions, as paths. This common framing is true in one sense: Real paths in the world are typically bumpy, curvy, and even forked. Likewise, our careers are bumpy, curvy, and forked. But the path metaphor is misleading.

Paths go forward from a starting point to a destination—life seldom does. Your life so far probably hasn't been perfectly linear, nor will it be so in the future. You may, for example, train for years as an engineer or a marketing exec, then discover that, as much as you love it, you love parenthood or teaching or a religious vocation even more. That's not a betrayal to yourself or your accomplishments; it's personal evolution. As Aimee, a mother of one, reported, "I went to school to be a teacher 12 years ago and ended up becoming an artist once I became a mother. Being an artist helped me be able to spend lots of quality time with my son and teach him to unleash his artistic abilities." Silvia, a mother of three, described how she and her husband made numerous changes at work after having children: "I've had to take breaks in my career to have children, and my husband had to rearrange his career entirely."

Caregiving ambition, like career ambition, is not necessarily fulfilled in a linear way either. The desire to have children may be derailed by relationship or fertility issues. The adoption process can be bumpy and demanding, influenced by capricious laws and rules. Illness and poor health may come unexpectedly, leading to unanticipated needs for providing and provisioning care.

In general, caregiving may turn out to be much more exhausting or exhilarating than previously anticipated. Your ambitions may decrease or increase along the journey, too. Many new parents report being taken aback by their passion and immersion into caregiving when their first child is born, leading them to rethink their work arrangements, as well as the caregiving arrangements they had planned for prior to the birth, as we discussed in Chapter 3.

THREE WAYS TO PURSUE TWO AMBITIONS

In addition to the four principles, we have identified three options, among those caregivers we researched and the scores of research papers and mountains of advice books, for those with both caregiving and career ambitions. These options are especially relevant for people whose caregiving ambition is primarily of the providing, rather than provisioning, approach. We'd love to offer you 10 or 12 such options, but these three are the most authentic we've found. We've seen these options in action, and they are how real people manage their multiple ambitions, specifically caregiving and career.

Option One: Sequence Smartly

Claire, whom we first met in Chapter 7, grew up in a household that embodied caregiving: She is the oldest of five children, and her mother also regularly fostered babies who were born addicted to alcohol and drugs. Claire not only grew up surrounded by caregiving; she later became a professional social worker, building a successful career in which she helps victims of domestic violence navigate the legal system and rebuild their lives.

Claire had never intended to have children of her own, but she became a new mother at age 40. Thrilled at the prospect of motherhood, her ambition was to stay home with her daughter until she went to kindergarten and then go back to work. (Both she and her husband agreed that their daughter would be their only child.) Professionally, Claire had started a doctorate in social work, so she decided that, while staying home with her daughter, she would continue to work on her thesis.

This decision was not simple. Her husband, a captain in the New York City Fire Department, earns a nice living and has job security as a civil servant; but with her temporarily leaving the workforce, they had to sacrifice her income in the short term. Even with a middle-class salary, New York City is an expensive place for families. In the long term, Claire planned to finish her doctorate part-time, start a private practice, and rejoin her husband in breadwinning after their daughter went to school. She had clearly thought out an approach to her caregiving and career ambitions, with a specific plan to put her career ambitions on hold (though she continued to work on her thesis and teach on a part-time basis) for approximately 5 years to focus on her caregiving ambitions and then return to pursuing both. And, indeed, thus far she has relished the time spent caring for her daughter and is very satisfied with her plan.

Claire's plan exemplifies the *sequencing* approach, which involves making deliberate decisions about when to enter and exit the professional workforce. Sequencers "opt out" of the workforce temporarily but then lean back in as soon as they're ready.

The term "sequencing" was introduced in 1986 by Arlene Rossen Cardozo, a journalist who wrote about work and family issues, in her aptly titled book *Sequencing*.[7] Cardozo argued that engaging in caregiving and careers in various sequences enables women to "have it all"—just not at the same time. The concept has since then entered the work–care lexicon. Economist Sylvia Ann Hewlett made similar arguments about intentionally sequencing careers and caregiving in her book *On Ramps and Off Ramps*.[8] This option is a good fit for people who want to make a major commitment to caregiving—particularly in providing rather than provisioning care—for a defined period of time and, importantly, who have a partner who can support them financially during that time. Sequencing involves a deliberate decision not to try to maximize both ambitions at once. Desiree, a mother of three, endorsed this approach: "I believe that the best approach to take when caregiving and working is the sequencing approach. I think that it's best to make sure that you make time for both the person(s) you are caring for and your work. It's not impossible to do both, but it does require much time, patience and care."

This approach requires a long-term perspective, and it comes with the risk (or perhaps the unintended benefit) that your ambitions may evolve, a point too frequently unacknowledged in the work–life advice literature. Sometimes when people "opt out" of their careers temporarily, motivated by their caregiving ambitions, with perspective, they come to view those same careers as part of the "rat race" and less of a noble calling than they might have once believed them to be.[9] Stepping out allows them a perspective on their work that they might otherwise not have seen when caught up in the day-to-day grind. This perspective may inform a new direction when subsequently returning to the workforce, often involving a desire for more personally meaningful work.

The other, more serious risk in sequencing comes when people try to re-enter the workforce. Even those who had been successful in their careers prior to their caregiving stage may find returning to work exceptionally difficult, especially in a fast-paced field. In fact, some counsel against sequencing for exactly this reason: Re-entry after an extended leave is difficult, at least at the level that one left the workforce.[10] Thus, sequencing is financially risky and next to impossible without a stable partner who is employed outside the home and/or some other source of income.

Returnships, described in Chapter 7, are designed to address the challenges of sequencing. Furthermore, although programs such as returnships make sequencing much more possible, as noted, they are rare, highly sought after, and competitive. And in this chapter we are not describing the world as it might be; we are analyzing choices and possibilities confronting individuals in the world as it is, a world where programs like returnships are far too rare.

There are two other specific ways that ambitious individuals who choose to sequence can reduce the formidable challenges of re-entry into paid work and their careers—active networking and skill rejuvenation. First, keeping your network alive while you're out of the workforce is imperative as networks are a critical aspect of most job searches. They can even be more valuable for ambitious caregivers who are ready to sequence into an ambitious career stage. Keeping your network alive can range from staying in touch with former colleagues socially to doing occasional free-lance projects with them to volunteering together. When you're ready to go back, tell your family, friends, acquaintances, and former colleagues that you're completing a stage as a full-time caregiver and planning to return to work. Most likely, if you reach out to your network when you're ready to, colleagues and friends will be more than happy to help.

Second, individuals who have sequenced into caregiving for an extended period might consider taking classes toward a new degree or certificate prior to, or during, re-entry into the workforce, such as Claire's plan to complete her doctorate. Technology is always changing, and it's essential for job-seekers to keep up to date on the latest industry best practices. Also, degrees and certificates provide recent professional accomplishments to add to your resume. Classes are also an opportunity to meet others who are investing in their careers and who can help to enrich your network. And by connecting with an institution such as a university, even just for a class or two or more formally a certificate program, not necessarily a full-fledged degree, you can tap into resources available through career centers and alumni networks.

Nina, a speech therapist and mother of four whom we first met in Chapter 3, recounted a challenging, often rocky, re-entry to full-time employment, involving retraining and reaching out to an experienced mentor for guidance. However, her efforts paid off and ultimately ended well when she landed a stable, permanent position in a school district:

> My return to full time work was not until my youngest was in 7th grade. At that point, I had worked part time as a speech therapist in so many different settings that I felt that I had a basic knowledge of many disciplines within my field, but expertise in none. As my confidence waned, I considered and dabbled in other lines of work and even let my license lapse. When my ex was laid off from yet another job, I made a decision that I would reclaim my career and set out to take the courses I would need to reinstate my license. I also enlisted a friend who has worked as a speech therapist in the schools for over 20 years to mentor me through the process. I was lucky to find a secure job in a school district within a year of making the decision to reclaim my career. Someone remarked to me that that was like winning the lottery. I think if it had not been for the fact that I speak Spanish proficiently, it would have taken me far longer to work my way into a school district, through a combination of subbing and leave replacements. It was a steep learning curve.

Nina's experience also reflects the psychological challenges of re-entry, in addition to the professional ones, both of which can be daunting.

Finally, when you are ready to return to work, especially full time, prepare yourself, and everyone else involved, for a major transition. Cindy, a mother of two, told us how when she started a demanding full-time job after many years of working fewer hours, and mostly during the school day, her younger son was surprised and exasperated. At one point, he said to her, "Mom, what's going on? Now you're working as many hours as Dad does!" His comment was difficult for her to hear because it made her feel guilty, but it was an accurate observation—the rhythm of her and her family's life was very different from how it had been. Her response was that they could still spend plenty of time together, just on the weekends rather than on the weekdays as they had been able to before her new job. Like many parents who return to work after an absence, this mother found that the transitions inherent to sequencing involve not only you but your whole family, and they will undoubtedly entail an adjustment period.

Option Two: Choose One Ambition over the Other

Jim, a father of two whom we met in Chapter 2, exemplifies someone who chose to exclusively fulfill his caregiving ambition. Together with his husband, Jim made an intentional decision to be a stay-at-home father, devoting himself to raising their daughter and son. When their daughter was born, both aspired to provide rather than provision care. Given that Jim's husband was the higher earner and had a more stable job, they decided together that Jim would be the stay-at-home caregiver— and he hasn't looked back since. He enjoys taking care of their children and does so with gusto, relishing the joys and challenges of stay-at-home parenthood.

Among his many caregiving activities, Jim organizes a play group for families in his neighborhood with similarly aged children. His family's home and backyard are full of carefully selected toys and organized with play spaces in mind. He is active in his children's school parent–teacher association. He frequently takes his children to library programs and other enrichment activities. And he invests a great deal of time and effort into holiday celebrations in their home, with a strong emphasis on making the celebrations child-friendly so that their children, as well as the children of friends and relatives, can engage in and enjoy the events.

Yet we live in a time when we are told that, instead of making choices, we should do everything. Since the late 1970s, marketers have cultivated this notion of "having it all," an idea that was, and continues to be, aimed particularly at women.[11] But just because we've been sold this concept doesn't make it true—and it never was. Jack Welch, the formidable and controversial chief executive officer (CEO) of General Electric for 20 years, from 1981 to 2001, announced at the Society for Human Resource Management's annual conference in 2009, "There's no such thing as work–life balance . . . . Instead, there are work–life choices, and you make them, and they have consequences."[12] These blunt words—which were rightly criticized by both journalists and conference attendees for being aimed too narrowly and derisively at women—speak to the seemingly inescapable conflict between career and caregiving ambition in the 21st century. You may have strong ambitions in both areas but find it simply impossible—or at least too stressful—to give them both their full due. So you pick the one that's more important to you. You may live with regret, and perhaps at times even anger, of having lost out on the other; but you will be able to fully pursue your chosen ambition.

In this option, you either curtail work completely or become a dedicated "career man" or "career woman." The most important aspect of this option, though, is that you make the decision with intention. Don't be surprised if your choice is not respected, especially if you've followed your caregiving ambition or if you have mixed feelings about your decision. There are stay-at-home parents who report feelings of self-doubt and even shame, especially when asked the perennial question "What do you do?" because they have refused to prioritize a career above all else. Imagine if, instead of answering this perennial question with the typical (often apologetic or defensive) response "I used to work in public relations" or "I'm home with my kids now," the response was "Who do you care for?"

This second option is difficult for ambitious people because they are not inclined to accept consequences that aren't what they most want, especially if they had envisioned pursuing both ambitions. Modern psychology, however, offers a practical adaptation for this option: Justify your decision to yourself. Justifying your choices, once made, often comes naturally—it is an adaptive mechanism for coping with regret.[13] Nietzsche called this "amor fati"—learning to love one's fate.[14] Simply put, how we rationalize our choices can help us become satisfied with them. Nicole, a mother of two whom we introduced in Chapter 3, exemplifies this approach. She described justifying her decision to care for her children at home full-time while they are young and, in the process, coming to peace with the profound complexity and ambivalence of her decision:

> Prior to having children, I established and managed two hospitality businesses. The long hours and demanding pace did not allow me to be present when I needed to be. I made the decision to leave my leadership role and stay home with our children. The daily challenges, respect from peers and financial independence are some of the things I mourn. At home my children supply a new set of challenges and minimal respect. There are days I want to shout, "Do you know who your mother was!?" . . . Even though I have given up parts of who I was to create two new beings, I am confident that I will find all my parts again.

To be sure, choosing caregiving over career unfortunately can be a very risky choice financially, as noted in Chapter 4, due to the lack of Social Security safety for informal caregivers in the United States and because one's family and financial circumstances that enable providing care directly can change. However, prioritizing your career at the expense of caregiving has other psychological and relational ramifications. Either way, these choices should be respected and not cast in an overly reductionist or simplistic light. And there is no question that going "all in" on caregiving or career can be a great investment and a deeply meaningful experience, enabling you to fully engage in your chosen ambition. As Keisha, who was employed previously as a lawyer, told us, "I am completely focused on caregiving. I left my career to be a caregiver, and I am completely satisfied with my choice."

Option Three: Pursue Both Ambitions with Focus

Imagine you have one foot on one moving treadmill and the other foot on another moving treadmill. It would be nerve-wracking: It's a lot more difficult than just running on one, and you could easily get hurt. But it's also probably a bit exhilarating. Indeed, this experience is akin to what people often feel as they simultaneously pursue both their caregiving and career ambitions, accepting a swirl of emotions. The tension, fear, risk, and excitement are all part of the experience, not something to be managed or balanced away.

Mary illustrates well the challenges and potential of pursuing both ambitions simultaneously. A divorced mother of four children, who has shared custody since her children were very young, she concurrently maintains an active career as a lawyer, running her own successful practice, with active and ambitious caregiving.

She starts her workday extremely early so that she can end early and be home for the after-school time, through to bedtime. When she finishes work in the afternoon, she goes immediately and fully into providing mode for her children—preparing snacks, monitoring homework, hearing about their days at school. She also provisions ambitiously—a network of babysitters, dog walkers, religious school, sports teams, and music camps. When the kids are asleep, she does house chores and everything else that she needs to catch up on (from work to paying bills to planning family trips). And she has pursued her career ambitions passionately all the while. Though many might move "in house" to a larger law practice, she has built and continues to run her own, highly successful practice, a career passion since her days in law school, even with all of the added work of running a business.

She is as ambitious about both—caregiving and career—at the same time. Her ambitions compel her to work hard on all fronts, and her stamina, educational opportunities, and health have allowed her to pull it off. Yet "balance" would not be the first word to come to mind in describing her life: focused, energetic, busy—but not necessarily balanced.

In fact, though "balance" is often used in describing our work–care approach, it's misleading. "Balance" implies that the amount of time and effort we spend working and caregiving are somehow perfectly calibrated and equal. Yet this notion is unrealistic, and the word itself has come under fire in recent years. Proposed alternatives include "integration," "harmony," and "blend."[15] As psychotherapist and award-winning author Adam Phillips writes in his book *On Balance*, many important things in life, including how we manage our close relationships and raise our children, are born of excess as opposed to balance. Strong feelings and experiences, as opposed to moderate ones, often guide us the most. Rather than quieting these excess desires, Phillips maintains that we should listen to them.[16]

Another reason this option is attractive is that it enables both men and women to live full lives in multiple domains simultaneously. As discussed in Chapter 1, according to extensive research, people are motivated to attain both competence and relatedness, work and love.[17] This option provides that opportunity. In addition, this option does not require relying on a breadwinning partner or some other source of income.

Some parents who have chosen this option, such as Jamie, a father of two, described a fairly strict delineation between paid work and caregiving: "I have a job where I work away from home for 12 hours at a time. I can focus on work while I'm at work and focus on my family when I get home. . . . I really feel that I can bond with my children and provide what they need to grow while I am with them. [But] I miss some important time with them by working my shifts." Others, such as Heather, a mother of two whom we discussed in Chapter 3, laid out more of a constant juggling act: "I've been focusing on both working and caregiving simultaneously since I returned from my first maternity leave. I love being able to have both of these roles in my life, and in general I'm very satisfied with how this has worked for me, but I do always feel like I'm falling short in both areas. . . . I often say that my life is in balance, it's just that both sides of the scale are too heavy and sometimes I feel like it could break. But I'd prefer this feeling of being overburdened to feeling like my life is out of balance."

Of course, there are potential downsides to simultaneously pursuing both career and caregiving ambitiously, such as spreading yourself too thin, as Heather described. Gayle, a mother of three, reported similar feelings: "I am able to do both. The only downside is when I am not able to give 100% to both." To alleviate this issue, try thinking in terms of focus rather than balance. On a concrete level, your attention to work and care will never balance out neatly; focus may be a much more helpful way to think about pursuing dual ambitions. During the times of the day when you are caregiving, be as focused as you can on caregiving. When you're making your children breakfast and talking about plans for the day, stay present—try not to check your email or prep for a meeting. During the times of the day when you're at work, try to be completely focused on work. When you're working, try not to obsess over your kids' after-school plans. Forget about balancing in the sense of a math equation as well— sometimes you will be much more focused on work as opposed to care-giving and vice versa.

Easier said than done: Focus is not simple, particularly given all the distractions vying for our time. Our jobs spill over into our personal lives, aided and abetted by devices that raise the expectation that we should be working all the time. And caregiving, too, does not follow particular boundaries. You can try to solely focus on your job while you're at work, but the reality is that calls from our children's child care provider or school are inevitable and appropriately distracting, as is worrying about our children. Nonetheless, focus can be critical for getting a lot done, which, let's face it, you're going to have to do if you simultaneously pursue both ambitions.

Being intentional about your focus will also help you avoid the constant nagging feeling that while you're at work you should be with your family or while you're with your family you should be working. With intentional focus, you gain the security of knowing that in this moment you have a particular focus, but at a different moment you will have another partic-ular focus.

Also recognize that every transition will bring with it a new normal. Transitions—such as another child, a child's move to a new grade, a promotion at work, a new co-worker, an ill parent, or a new job—are assured as you pursue your caregiving and career ambitions. This dynamic situation cannot be easily "fixed" or "balanced." Instead, embrace these experiences to the extent you can. As research shows, people absolutely need to feel that they have control over their lives,[18] but be realistic about the intensity and busy-ness that pursuing both ambitions really entails. To that end, it also helps to apply the focus approach to your downtime as well so that you can carve out time to take a break from it all and rest— you'll need it. As Tyra, a mother of three, commented, "Sometimes I get tired and I feel as if I should be able to handle everything all the time."

If they partner, people who pursue option three often seek lifelong partners, or negotiate with their lifelong partners, to make choices that complement their decisions and enable the pursuit of both ambitions. In her book *Unfinished Business*, Anne-Marie Slaughter, the CEO of the New America think tank and emerita professor at Princeton, discusses the logic behind one parent being the "lead parent" and one parent being the "lead breadwinner." Her husband, Andrew Moravcsik, himself an accomplished academic, explained it simply: He put his wife's career first and became the "lead" and "primary" parent for their two children, to allow her to focus more on her career ambitions.[19] Still, as a tenured professor at Princeton, Moravcsik clearly has engaged in, and fulfilled, both his career and caregiving ambitions.

Finally, if you choose this option, do not buy into the latest, greatest work–care solutions and fads. Case in point: In 2013, Sheryl Sandberg advised us to *Lean In*; subsequently, in 2019, Marissa Orr advised us to *Lean Out*.[20] Avoid seeking "the secret" or "the recipe" for work–care balance. Acknowledge that, for you, a life well and fully lived involves two feet on two different treadmills.

Coda: Two Caveats for the Three Options

The options of sequencing, choosing one ambition, or pursuing both with focus can all be helpful for decision-making in the short term; but life situations also evolve and change. These options must therefore be evaluated with both short-term and long-term goals in mind, which can be difficult. For example, the physical and emotional demands of parenting are dynamic. Particularly for those with high providing caregiving ambition, it can be easy to lose perspective in the daze of feedings and sleep deprivation, immediately followed by the demands of toilet-training an oppositional toddler. Although it's easy to forget how exhausting, and wonderfully absorbing, having babies and small children can be, parents with older or grown children often remind us sagely that the years go by fast. It can therefore be helpful to think long-term when immediate stresses weigh on us. Moreover, caregiving usually only lasts for certain periods of time. Careers are long—in fact, people are working much longer than in previous decades.[21] Remembering this fact can help us get through the difficult periods when the combined demands of work and caregiving seem insurmountable.

The second caveat is that plans are just that—plans. It is easy to forget how illusory our control over our lives often is, as the COVID-19 pandemic so painfully reminded us. Plans for having children may be upended by fertility challenges; plans for our careers may be upended by economic downturns or capricious bosses; and plans for a lifelong partnership may be upended by divorce, poor health, or death. As you think about these options, keep in mind that being open to change and the possibility of different plans can be very useful.

Serendipity plays a large role in life as well. Being in the right place at the right time, choosing a career that turns out to be in a burgeoning field (or not), your child or children's temperament and health—all of these factors influence our futures in countless ways that we cannot necessarily plan for. Decisions are made at one point in time and may or may not hold depending upon what the future brings. So, by all means, cultivate ambitions and make plans and decisions, but also remember that life is dynamic and things are guaranteed to change at some point in time.

Our hope is that these principles and options will be helpful as you seek to achieve your caregiving and career ambitions. As we stated at the beginning of the chapter, there is no easy way to do this. But we firmly believe that you can find the right way for you and your loved ones, with some circuitous detours and serendipitous encounters along the way.

DEFINING QUESTIONS

- Which of the four principles will be most helpful for you?
- Do you feel pressure (from friends, family, or extended family) to choose one of the three options even if it doesn't feel right to you? Which one, and why?
- Which of the three options do you actually feel is most right for you? Why?

Conclusion

Caregiving as the Passion Project

> Your work is to discover your work and then with all your heart
> to give yourself to it.
>
> —BUDDHA[1]

As observed throughout the book, working, not caring for others, gets
most of the limelight in our modern culture. That is true in general and in
terms of what is typically rewarded, and it is also true in the popular con-
ception of ambition and being ambitious. Career ambition, not caregiving
ambition, gets the lion's share of glorification. Of course, the impulse to
care for others is profoundly deep—the desire to form close attachments
with others is ingrained within us.[2] As a result, the notion that careers
should be primary and the people in our lives secondary requires rein-
forcement, whether by the companies we work for, the institutions we
trust in, or the politicians we put in office. Still, many of us have a sense of
unease at just how central work has become in our lives, as we push other
important aspects of living off to the sidelines.

What happens when we start to wonder if there is more to life than
work? What happens if our "work," per the quote from the Buddha, is
through caring for others, leading us to question the focus on careers? We

The Caregiving Ambition. Julia B. Bear and Todd L. Pittinsky, Oxford University Press. © Oxford University Press 2022.
DOI: 10.1093/oso/9780197512418.003.0011

are told these questions indicate a lack of passion for work, which is seen as a problem. The message is to find happiness in work and our careers, especially if we just "follow our passions." For some of us, there is a career, and a specific job within that career, that allows us to follow our interests, our "passions." But for many of us, likely not. In the meantime, many such pursuits are not economically viable, and passion in and of itself does not guarantee successful career outcomes.[3]

But right in front of many of us is a second, quite different source of passion: the people we most care about and, in particular, the ones who we help to care for. Simply put, instead of work and careers, what if caring more, individually and collectively, was celebrated as an equally important passion project? Imagine if caring—not work—were the value around which we organize society.

What would this society look like? On a concrete level, honoring and valuing individual caregiving ambition translates into making sequencing and caregiving leaves standard rather than something to be frowned upon. From a work perspective, companies would support "freedom-to," not only "freedom-from," accommodations (Chapter 7). From a societal perspective, we would make a humanistic case for caregiving, rather than relying on the illogical and ineffectual business case (Chapter 8). And we could finally rethink the gender gaps in pay and career advancement, which really boil down to caring gaps (Chapter 5). A new approach is sorely needed, based on the state of caring for children, older adults, and each other (Chapter 4), and before we all end up being cared for by robots (Chapter 6). The upshot—we would support caregiving structurally through policies that enable people to care for others, based on the deeper value that caregiving in and of itself is valuable to society and doesn't need to be justified by some tenuous connection to a financial bottom line.

From an individual perspective, we would honor and value people's caregiving roles and relationships. We would recognize caregiving ambition as a legitimate part of life, as important as, if not more so, than career ambition (Chapter 1). Work–life, and work–care programs, in particular, would actually prioritize the life and care part of the equation, not just the work part (Chapter 2). Rather than treating caregiving ambition as a problem that needs to be solved somehow, a distraction from work, we would embrace it as one of the most meaningful parts of life, with a particular eye toward the distinction between and the differential demands of providing and provisioning care (Chapter 3). Of course, life involves trade-offs and choices, as we made explicit in the four principles and three options for fulfilling caregiving and career ambitions (Chapter 9). And every individual views these trade-offs differently. But with people working through their 70s, why should a caregiving leave taken for several years in one's 30s, say, derail a five-decade career? Why not embrace the notion of lives well lived, brimming with close relationships and communities, as well as work?

Advocating for structural change is important, but we also must deal with the world as it is right now. So what can we do as individuals to help recognize and honor caregiving ambition in the meantime? A good place is to start celebrating caregiving ambition rather than being distracted by judging others' choices. Whether it's the "mommy wars," which serve only to create a feeling of damned if you do, damned if you don't among mothers, or looking askance at men who focus on caregiving rather than breadwinning, this type of judgment and shaming only serves to sidetrack people from the real issue: honoring caregiving both emotionally and concretely. As writer Kim Brooks observes, "Rather than questioning the system and the culture and the lack of support that makes it so hard for all of us, we turn against one another . . . flaunting and justifying whatever path we've chosen."[4]

While we're at it, let's also stop hiding our caregiving and pretending at work that we don't have other ambitions, especially among men. It may be good for one's career, but norms will never change this way. Let's also allow ourselves greater ambition in terms of caregiving than perhaps we thought was possible. For example, a Microsoft manager who had recently become a mother commented on the use of the company's family leave policies as follows: "I feel really fortunate to have this time at home . . . she [the manager's new baby] knows who I am."[5] Setting the bar for caregiving at the level of having one's baby recognize its mother: a realistic goal in corporate America but awfully unambitious in an existential sense.

We tend to celebrate too narrow a definition of the life well lived. Why, for example, does Sheryl Sandberg have so powerful a voice in setting the women-and-work agenda? There are never going to be many of her, male or female—the top of a pyramid is always small and narrow. The solutions we need must therefore work for everyone, the telemarketer and the dialysis tech and the barista, not just the one in a billion talented and lucky few who make it to top management.

But consider this: When it comes to caregiving ambition, the telemarketer and the dialysis tech and the barista and Sheryl Sandberg are probably all pretty similar. Why not put that ambition in the spotlight, making sure that it is respected and empowered?

We each don't need millions of dollars to live well. But at some point in time, we all need to care for others and need to be cared for. Doing so ambitiously is not just a worthy cause in general but indeed an animating aspiration for many of us. It's high time we start to live up to it.

APPENDIX

The Caregivers

Name	Age	Sex	Race/Ethnicity	Current Employment	Occupation	Education	Current Marital Status	Number of Children
Aaliyah	56	F	European American/White	Full-time	Not specified	Some college	Widowed	1
Aiko	38	F	Asian American	Full-time	Administrative assistant	College	Married	2
Aimee	39	F	Native American/American Indian/Alaskan Native	Not employed outside the home	Artist	Some college	Married	1
Albert	38	M	Asian American	Full-time	Financial analyst	College	Married	1
Alicia	30	F	African American/Black	Full-time	Security officer	Some college	Married	1
Alora	41	F	European American/White	Full-time	Social worker	Master's	Divorced	2
Andre	32	M	African American/Black	Full-time	IT officer	College	Married	2
Angelica	21	F	Asian American	Not employed outside the home	Homemaker	Some college	Never married	2
Asia	42	F	African American/Black	Not employed outside the home	Space planner	Master's	Married	4
Ayesha	54	F	Multiracial (African American/Black/not specified)	Not employed outside the home	Clerical associate	High school	Married	3

Name	Age	Gender	Race/Ethnicity	Employment	Occupation	Education	Marital status	Number
Christina	23	F	Multiracial (African American/Black, Latinx/Hispanic, Asian American)	Part-time	Self-employed entrepreneur and freelancer	High school	Married	2
Cindy	42	F	European American/White	Full-time	Development officer	Master's	Divorced	2
Claire	45	F	European American/White	Part-time	Social worker	Master's	Married	1
Crystal	33	F	Multiracial (African American/Black, European American/White)	Full-time	Higher education admissions officer	College	Never married	1
David	41	M	European American/White	Part-time	Not specified	College	Widowed	2
Desiree	30	F	African American/Black	Not employed outside the home	Homemaker	Some college	Never married	3
Diana	31	F	Latinx/Hispanic	Part-time	Not specified	Some college	Married	5
Eleanor	31	F	African American/Black	Part-time	Not specified	College	Never married	1
Elena	26	F	European American/White	Not employed outside the home	Not specified	High school	Never married	2
Emily	47	F	Asian American	Full-time	Professor	Postgraduate	Married	1

Name	Age	Sex	Race/Ethnicity	Current Employment	Occupation	Education	Current Marital Status	Number of Children
Gabby	41	F	Asian American	Not employed outside the home	Homemaker	College	Divorced	1
Gayle	52	F	African American/Black	Full-time	Educator	Master's	Widowed	3
Gwen	49	M	European American/White	Part-time	Professor and administrator	Postgraduate	Married	4
Heather	46	F	European American/White	Full-time	Public health coordinator	Master's	Married	2
Jamal	35	M	African American/Black	Full-time	Nurse	College	Married	1
Jamie	37	M	European American/White	Full-time	Water treatment plant operator	College	Married	2
Jared	34	M	African American/Black	Not specified	Not specified	College	Married	0
Javier	36	M	Latinx/Hispanic	Full-time	Sheet metal apprentice	Some college	Married	1
Jessica	34	F	Latinx/Hispanic	Full-time	Not specified	College	Married	4
Jim	42	M	European American/White	Not employed outside the home	Music therapist	Master's	Married	2
John	23	M	European American/White	Full-time	Not specified	College	Married	1

Name	Age	Gender	Race/Ethnicity	Employment	Occupation	Education	Marital status	
Jonelle	44	F	African American/Black	Full-time	Teaching assistant	College	Married	2
Jorge	29	M	Latinx/Hispanic	Full-time	Analyst	College	Married	2
Keisha	30	F	Multiracial (African American/Black, Caribbean)	Not employed outside the home	Lawyer	Postgraduate	Married	1
Lauren	57	F	European American/White	Full-time	Not specified	Some college	Widowed	2
Lei	33	P	Asian American	Part-time	Data analyst contractor	Master's	Married	3
Lily	50	F	European American/White	Full-time	Fashion/retail buyer	College	Widowed	1
Lydia	36	F	European American/White	Part-time	Not specified	Some college	Married	4
Mary	57	F	European American/White	Full-time	Attorney	Postgraduate	Divorced	4
Michael	43	M	European American/White	Full-time	Not specified	Some college	Married	1
Michelle	50	F	European American/White	Not employed outside the home	Not specified	Some college	Married	2
Nicole	39	F	European American/White	Not employed outside the home	Restaurateur	Some college	Married	2
Nina	49	F	European American/White	Full-time	Speech therapist	Master's	Divorced	4

Name	Age	Sex	Race/Ethnicity	Current Employment	Occupation	Education	Current Marital Status	Number of Children
Priya	43	F	Asian American	Full-time	Software engineer	College	Married	2
Reuben	44	M	European American/White	Full-time	Engineer	College	Married	3
Rodney	44	M	African American/Black	Full-time	Insurance manager	College	Married	2
Sandy	38	M	Latinx/Hispanic	Full-time	Delivery driver	High school	Separated	2
Sarah	44	F	European American/White	Part-time	Not specified	Some college	Divorced	4
Silvia	38	F	Latinx/Hispanic, European American/White	Part-time	Navy sailor	Master's	Married	3
Susan	46	F	European American/White	Full-time	Not specified	High school	Married	3
Tom	60	M	European American/White	Retired/not employed outside the home	Not specified	College	Never married	2
Tracy	49	F	European American/White	Full-time	Analytic consultant	Postgraduate	Married	2

Tyra	42	F	African American/Black	Full-time	Office supervisor	Postgraduate	Married	3
Vince	50	M	European American/ White	Full-time	Employee relations Manager	College	Married	2
Yaacov	49	M	European American/ White	Full time	Professor	Postgraduate	Married	1

Note. Names (listed in alphabetical order) are either real names or pseudonyms. For sex, F = female, M = male, and P = prefer to self-describe. Not all respondents reported sexual orientation. Among those who reported, there was a mix of sexual orientations and gender identities. In some cases individuals reported more than one racial or ethnic category and/or chose multiracial. The table reflects participants' self-reported race and ethnicity. IT = information technology.

NOTES

INTRODUCTION

1. Fraser, K. (2019). Ambition is a fabulous word. *Professional Case Management*, *24*(6), 317–318.
2. Ko, A., Pick, C. M., Kwon, J. Y., Barlev, M., Krems, J. A., Varnum, M. E. W., Neel, R., Peysha, M., Boonyasiriwat, W., Brandstätter, E., Crispim, A. C., Cruz, J. E., David, D., David, O. A., de Felipe, R. P., Fetvadjiev, V. H., Fischer, R., Galdi, S., Galindo, O., . . . Kenrick, D. T. (2020). Family matters: Rethinking the psychology of human social motivation. *Perspectives on Psychological Science*, *15*(1), 173–201.
3. Association for Psychological Science. (n.d.). Caring for loved ones the top priority for people worldwide. https://www.psychologicalscience.org/publications/obser ver/obsonline/caring-for-loved-ones-the-top-priority-for-people-worldwide.html. Ko et al., Family matters.
4. Association for Psychological Science, Caring for loved ones. Ko et al., Family matters.
5. Inagaki, T. K., & Orehek, E. (2017). On the benefits of giving social support: When, why, and how support providers gain by caring for others. *Current Directions in Psychological Science*, *26*(2), 109–113.
6. National Opinion Research Center. (2014, May). *National survey on long-term care: Expectations and reality.* https://www.norc.org/NewsEventsPublications/ PressReleases/pages/national-survey-on-long-term-care-expectations-and-reality. aspx
7. Weber, L. (2019, August 29). Younger workers report biggest gains in happiness with pay. *The Wall Street Journal.* https://www.wsj.com/articles/younger-workers-report-biggest-gains-in-happiness-with-pay-11567071000
8. Anderson, J. (2012, July 24). The sandwich generation: 21st century super-caregivers. *Senior Living Blog, A Place for Mom.* https://www.aplaceformom.com/ blog/sandwich-generation-super-caregivers/
9. Rosalynn Carter Institute for Caregiving, Georgia Southwestern State University. (2011, May 26). *Written testimony of former first lady Rosalynn Carter before the Senate Special Committee on Aging.* https://www.cartercenter.org/news/editorials_ speeches/rosalynn-carter-committee-on-aging-testimony.html

10. Fraser, Ambition is a fabulous word.
11. Bear, J. B. (2019). The caregiving ambition framework. *Academy of Management Review*, *44*(1), 99–125.
12. Bowlby, J. (1982). *Attachment* (2nd ed.). Basic Books. Mikulincer, M., & Shaver, P. R. (2007). *Attachment in adulthood: Structure, dynamics, and change*. Guilford Press.
13. Baumeister, R. F., & Leary, M. R. (1995). The need to belong: Desire for interpersonal attachments as a fundamental human motivation. *Psychological Bulletin*, *117*(3), 497.
14. Inagaki & Orehek, On the benefits of giving social support.
15. Ibid.
16. Park, S. Q., Kahnt, T., Dogan, A., Strang, S., Fehr, E., & Tobler, P. N. (2017). A neural link between generosity and happiness. *Nature Communications*, *8*(1), 1–10.
17. Leary, M. R., Kowalski, R. M., Smith, L., & Phillips, S. (2003). Teasing, rejection, and violence: Case studies of the school shootings. *Aggressive Behavior*, *29*(3), 202–214.
18. Graham, J. (2020, March 30). *How to decide whether to bring your elderly parent home from assisted living during the pandemic*. CNN. https://www.cnn.com/2020/03/30/health/parents-assisted-living-nursing-homes-coronavirus-wellness/index.html. North Country Public Radio. (2020, May 5). *As COVID-19 ravages care facilities families wonder: "Should we bring them home?"* https://www.northcountrypublicradio.org/news/npr/850901609/as-covid-19-ravages-care-facilities-families-wonder-should-we-bring-them-home
19. Acker, J. (1990). Hierarchies, jobs, bodies: A theory of gendered organizations. *Gender and Society*, *4*(2), 139–158.
20. Vitaliano, P. P., Strachan, E., Dansie, E., Goldberg, J., & Buchwald, D. (2014). Does caregiving cause psychological distress? The case for familial and genetic vulnerabilities in female twins. *Annals of Behavioral Medicine*, *47*(2), 198–207.
21. Delmore, T. (n.d.). It's time to bring these 5 white-collar perks to the wider workforce. *SFGATE*. https://www.sfgate.com/business/article/It-s-Time-to-Bring-These-5-White-Collar-Perks-to-15135181.php (dated March 23, 2020).

CHAPTER 1

1. King, W. C. (2013). Introduction. In *Ambition, a history: From vice to virtue* (p. 4). Yale University Press.
2. Merriam-Webster. (n.d.). Ambition. In *Merriam-Webster.com dictionary*. https://www.merriam-webster.com/dictionary/ambition
3. Jones, A. B., Sherman, R. A., & Hogan, R. T. (2017). Where is ambition in factor models of personality? *Personality and Individual Differences*, *106*(1), 26–31. Judge, T. A., & Kammeyer-Mueller, J. D. (2012). On the value of aiming high: The causes and consequences of ambition. *Journal of Applied Psychology*, *97*(4), 758–775.
4. Hogan, J., & Holland, B. (2003). Using theory to evaluate personality and job-performance relations: A socioanalytic perspective. *Journal of Applied Psychology*, *88*(1), 100. Hogan, R., & Chamorro-Premuzic, T. (2015). Personality and career success. In M. L. Cooper & R. J. Larsen (Eds.), *Handbook of personality and social*

psychology (Vol. 4, pp. 619–638). American Psychological Association. Judge & Kammeyer-Mueller, On the value of aiming high.

5. Judge & Kammeyer-Mueller, On the value of aiming high. Kern, M. L., Friedman, H. S., Martin, L. R., Reynolds, C. A., & Luong, G. (2009). Conscientiousness, career success, and longevity: A lifespan analysis. *Annals of Behavioral Medicine*, 37(2), 154–163. Van der Heijde, C. M., & Van der Heijden, B. I. J. M. (2006). A competence-based and multidimensional operationalization and measurement of employability. *Human Resource Management*, 45(3), 449–476.

6. Freud, S. 1930. *Civilization and its discontents* (J. Riviere, Trans.). Hogarth.

7. Erikson, E. H. (1968). *Identity: Youth and crisis*. Norton.

8. Maslow, A. H. (1943). A theory of human motivation. *Psychological Review*, 50(4), 370–396.

9. Kenrick, D. T., Griskevicius, V., Neuberg, S. L., & Schaller, M. (2010). Renovating the pyramid of needs: Contemporary extensions built upon ancient foundations. *Perspectives on Psychological Science*, 5(3), 292–314.

10. Baumeister, R. F., & Leary, M. R. (1995). The need to belong: Desire for interpersonal attachments as a fundamental human motivation. *Psychological Bulletin*, 117(3), 497–529. Bowlby, J. (1982). *Attachment and loss: Vol. 1. Attachment* (2nd ed.). Basic Books. Mikulincer, M., & Shaver, P. R. (2007). *Attachment in adulthood: Structure, dynamics, and change*. Guilford Press.

11. Brim, G. (1992). Our drive for growth and mastery. In *Ambition: How we manage success and failure throughout our lives* (p. 17). HarperCollins.

12. King, Epilogue. In *Ambition, a history*.

13. Ko, A., Pick, C. M., Kwon, J. Y., Barlev, M., Krems, J. A., Varnum, M. E., Neel, R., Peysha, M., Boonyasiriwat, W., Brandstätter, E., Crispim, A. C., Cruz, J. E., David, D., David, O. A., Pereira de Felipe, R., Fetvadjiev, V. H., Fischer, R., Galdi, S., Galindo, O., . . . Kenrick, D. T. (2020). Family matters: Rethinking the psychology of human social motivation. *Perspectives on Psychological Science*, 15(1), 173–201.

14. Roberts, B. W., O'Donnell, M., & Robins, R. W. (2004). Goal and personality trait development in emerging adulthood. *Journal of Personality and Social Psychology*, 87(4), 541–550.

15. Senior, J. (2015). *All joy and no fun: The paradox of modern parenthood*. Virago.

16. Bear, J. B., & Pittinsky, T. L. (2019). *Caregiving ambition* [Unpublished raw data].

17. For a discussion of the role of dependency in caregiving, see Kittay, E. F. (1999). *Love's labor: Essays on women, equality, and dependency*. Routledge.

18. Fonda, S. J., Wallace, R. B., & Herzog, A. R. (2001). Changes in driving patterns and worsening depressive symptoms among older adults. *The Journals of Gerontology Series B: Psychological Sciences and Social Sciences*, 56(6), 343–351.

19. Schein, V. E., & Davidson, M. J. (1993). Think manager, think male. *Management Development Review*, 6(3), 24–28.

20. Coontz, S. (2016). My mother was a saint (p. 68). *The way we never were: American families and the nostalgia trip*. New York, NY: Basic Books.

21. Ashby, J. S., & Schoon, I. (2010). Career success: The role of teenage career aspirations, ambition value and gender in predicting adult social status and earnings. *Journal of Vocational Behavior*, 77(3), 350–360. Cassirer, N., & Reskin, B. (2000). High

hopes: Organizational position, employment experiences, and women's and men's promotion aspirations. *Work and Occupations, 27*(4), 438–463. Litzky, B. E., & Greenhaus, J. H. (2007). The relationship between gender and aspirations to senior management. *Career Development International, 12*(7), 637–659. Powell, G. N., & Butterfield, D. A. (2003). Gender, gender identity, and aspirations to top management. *Women in Management Review, 18*, 88–96. Reis, S. M. (1991). The need for clarification in research designed to examine gender differences in achievement and accomplishment. *Roeper Review, 13*, 193–198.

22. Powell, G. N., & Butterfield, D. A. (2013). Sex, gender, and aspirations to top management: Who's opting out? Who's opting in? *Journal of Vocational Behavior, 82*(1), 30–36.

23. Ashby & Schoon, Career success.

24. Cassirer & Reskin, High hopes.

25. Fels, A. (2005). *Necessary dreams: Ambition in women's changing lives.* Anchor Books.

26. Fels, A. (2004, April). Do women lack ambition? *Harvard Business Review.* https://hbr.org/2004/04/do-women-lack-ambition

27. Bursztyn, L., Fujiwara, T., & Pallais, A. (2017). "Acting wife": Marriage market incentives and labor market investments. *American Economic Review, 107*(11), 3288–3319. Bursztyn, L., Fujiwara, T., & Pallais, A. (2017, May 8). The ambition–marriage trade-off too many single women face. *Harvard Business Review.* https://hbr.org/2017/05/the-ambition-marriage-trade-off-too-many-single-women-face

28. Croft, A., Schmader, T., Block, K., & Baron, A. S. (2014). The second shift reflected in the second generation: Do parents' gender roles at home predict children's aspirations? *Psychological Science, 25*(7), 1418–1428.

29. Croft, A., Schmader, T., Beall, A., & Schaller, M. (2019). Breadwinner seeks bottle warmer: How women's future aspirations and expectations predict their current mate preferences. *Sex Roles, 82*, 633–643.

30. Croft, A., Schmader, T., & Block, K. (2019). Life in the balance: Are women's possible selves constrained by men's domestic involvement? *Personality and Social Psychology Bulletin, 45*(5), 808–823.

31. Gadiesh, O., & Coffman, J. (2015, May 18). Companies drain women's ambition after only 2 years. *Harvard Business Review.* https://hbr.org/2015/05/companies-drain-womens-ambition-after-only-2-years

32. Eddleston, K. A., Veiga, J. F., & Powell, G. N. (2006). Explaining sex differences in managerial career satisfier preferences: The role of gender self-schema. *Journal of Applied Psychology, 91*(2), 437–445. Gino, F., Wilmuth, C. A., & Brooks, A. W. (2015). Compared to men, women view professional advancement as equally attainable, but less desirable. *Proceedings of the National Academy of Sciences of the United States of America, 112*(40), 12354–12359. Litzky, B. E., & Greenhaus, J. H. (2007). The relationship between gender and aspirations to senior management. *Career Development International, 12*(7), 637–659.

33. Croft, A., Schmader, T., & Block, K. (2015). An underexamined inequality: Cultural and psychological barriers to men's engagement with communal roles. *Personality and Social Psychology Review, 19*(4), 343–370.

34. Bear, J. B. (2021). Forget the "mommy track": Temporal flexibility increases promotion aspirations for women and reduces gender gaps. *Psychology of Women Quarterly, 45*(3), 294–307. Brown, E. R., & Diekman, A. B. (2010). What will I be? Exploring gender differences in near and distant possible selves. *Sex Roles, 63*(7–8), 568–579. Cinamon, R. G. (2006). Anticipated work–family conflict: Effects of gender, self-efficacy, and family background. *The Career Development Quarterly, 54*(3), 202–215. Fetterolf, J. C., & Eagly, A. H. (2011). Do young women expect gender equality in their future lives? An answer from a possible selves experiment. *Sex Roles, 65*(1–2), 83.

35. Sandberg, S. (2013). *Lean in: Women, work, and the will to lead.* Random House.

36. Eccles, J. S. (1994). Understanding women's educational and occupational choices: Applying the Eccles et al. model of achievement-related choices. *Psychology of Women Quarterly, 18*(4), 586.

37. Hays, S. (1998). *The cultural contradictions of motherhood.* Yale University Press.

38. Lareau, A. (2011). *Unequal childhoods: Class, race, and family life.* University of California Press.

39. Stone, P., & Lovejoy, M. (2019). *Opting back in: What really happens when mothers go back to work.* University of California Press.

CHAPTER 2

1. Senior, J. (2015). *All joy and no fun: The paradox of modern parenthood.* Virago.

2. Greenhaus, J. H., & Beutell, N. J. (1985). Sources of conflict between work and family roles. *Academy of Management Review, 10*(1), 76–88. Nohe, C., Meier, L. L., Sonntag, K., & Michel, A. (2015). The chicken or the egg? A meta-analysis of panel studies of the relationship between work–family conflict and strain. *Journal of Applied Psychology, 100*(2), 522–536. Wattis, L., Standing, K., & Yerkes, M. A. (2013). Mothers and work–life balance: Exploring the contradictions and complexities involved in work–family negotiation. *Community, Work & Family, 16*(1), 1–19.

3. Beard, A. (2019, January–February). Ideal worker or perfect mom? *Harvard Business Review.* https://hbr.org/2019/01/ideal-worker-or-perfect-mom. Geiger, A. W., Livingston, G., & Bialik, K. (2019, May 8). *6 Facts about U.S. moms.* Pew Research Center. https://www.pewresearch.org/fact-tank/2019/05/08/facts-about-u-s-mothers/

4. Livingston, G., & Parker, K. (2019, June 12). *8 Facts about American dads.* Pew Research Center. https://www.pewresearch.org/fact-tank/2019/06/12/fathers-day-facts/

5. Aumann, K., Galinsky, E., & Matos, K. (2011). *The new male mystique.* Families and Work Institute. https://cdn.sanity.io/files/ow8usu72/production/251245fa4de08d1cb6ff22475edb45e017d60bdd.pdf

6. Allen, T. D., Herst, D. E., Bruck, C. S., & Sutton, M. (2000). Consequences associated with work-to-family conflict: A review and agenda for future research. *Journal of Occupational Health Psychology, 5*(2), 278–308. Ford, M. T., Heinen, B. A., & Langkamer, K. L. (2007). Work and family satisfaction and conflict: A meta-analysis of cross-domain relations. *Journal of Applied Psychology, 92*(1), 57–80.

Grandey, A. A., & Cropanzano, R. (1999). The conservation of resources model applied to work–family conflict and strain. *Journal of Vocational Behavior, 54*(2), 350–370. Parasuraman, S., Purohit, Y. S., Godshalk, V. M., & Beutell, N. J. (1996). Work and family variables, entrepreneurial career success, and psychological well-being. *Journal of Vocational Behavior, 48*(3), 275–300. Williams, K. J., & Alliger, G. M. (1994). Role stressors, mood spillover, and perceptions of work–family conflict in employed parents. *Academy of Management Journal, 37*(4), 837–868.

7. Demerouti, E., Geurts, S. A., Bakker, A. B., & Euwema, M. (2004). The impact of shiftwork on work–home conflict, job attitudes and health. *Ergonomics, 47*(9), 987–1002. Fenwick, R., & Tausig, M. (2001). Scheduling stress: Family and health outcomes of shift work and schedule control. *American Behavioral Scientist, 44*(7), 1179–1198.

8. Wagner, D. L., Lottes, J., & Neal., M. (2006). *The Metlife caregiving cost study: Productivity losses to U.S. business.* Washington, D.C.: Metlife Mature Market Institute and National Alliance for Caregiving. Retrieved from https://www.care-giving.org/wp-content/uploads/2020/05/Caregiver-Cost-Study.pdf

9. Friedman, S. D. (2013). *Baby bust: New choices for men and women in work and family.* Wharton Digital Press.

10. The data reported here are from the 2018 data set. However, the means reported for 2018 are consistent with past years as well. In 2016, people reported having an average of 1.85 children, while reporting 3.38 as the ideal number of children. In 2014, people reported having an average of 1.82 children, while reporting 3.36 as the ideal number of children. Reviewing the GSS data since 2000, there is a consistent trend such that the mean for the ideal number of children reported is higher than the mean for the actual number of children reported. Smith, T. W., Davern, M., Freese, J., & Hout, M. (2018). *General social surveys, 1972–2016.* NORC. NORC at the University of Chicago [producer and distributor]. Data accessed from the GSS Data Explorer website at gssdataexplorer.norc.org

11. Cinamon, R. G. (2006). Anticipated work–family conflict: Effects of gender, self-efficacy, and family background. *The Career Development Quarterly, 54*(3), 202–215. Westring, A. F., & Ryan, A. M. (2011). Anticipated work–family conflict: A construct investigation. *Journal of Vocational Behavior, 79*(2), 596–610.

12. Catalyst. (n.d.). *Women's earnings—The pay gap (Quick take).* Retrieved on March 2, 2020 from https://www.catalyst.org/research/womens-earnings-the-pay-gap/

13. Livingston, G., & Thomas, D. (2019, December 16). *Among 41 countries, only U.S. lacks paid leave.* Pew Research Center. https://www.pewresearch.org/fact-tank/2019/12/16/u-s-lacks-mandated-paid-parental-leave/

14. Working Mother. (2019). *2019 Working mother 100 best companies.* https://www.workingmother.com/working-mother-100-best-companies-2019

15. Society for Human Resource Management. (2017, June 19). *2017 Employee benefits.* https://www.shrm.org/hr-today/trends-and-forecasting/research-and-surveys/pages/2017-employee-benefits.aspx

16. Davidson, J. (2019, December 20). Federal workers will get 12 weeks of paid family leave. Should everyone? *The Washington Post.* Retrieved from https://www.washingtonpost.com/politics/federal-workers-will-get-12-weeks-of-paid-family-leave-sho

uld-everyone/2019/12/19/b9e9c502-228b-11ea-9c2b-060477c13959_story.html.
Nagele-Piazza, L. (2019, December 20). *Trump approves paid parental leave for federal workers.* Society for Human Resource Management. https://www.shrm.org/resourcesandtools/legal-and-compliance/employment-law/pages/trump-approves-paid-parental-leave-for-federal-workers.aspx

17. Tankersley, J., & Goldstein, D. (2021, April 28). *Biden details $1.8 trillion plan for workers, students and families. The New York Times.* https://www.nytimes.com/2021/04/28/us/politics/biden-american-families-plan.html

18. Brainerd, J. (2017, August). Paid family leave in the States. Retrieved November 9, 2021, from https://www.ncsl.org/research/labor-and-employment/paid-family-leave-in-the-states.aspx

19. Catalyst, *Working parents.* Livingston & Thomas, *Among 41 countries.*

20. Glass, J., Simon, R. W., & Andersson, M. A. (2016). Parenthood and happiness: Effects of work–family reconciliation policies in 22 OECD countries. *American Journal of Sociology, 122*(3), 886–929. Luscombe, B. (n.d.). Many parents are happier than non-parents—but not in the U.S. *Time.* https://time.com/collection/guide-to-happiness/4370344/parents-happiness-children-study/

21. Kantor, J. (2014, August 13). Working anything but 9 to 5. *The New York Times.* https://www.nytimes.com/interactive/2014/08/13/us/starbucks-workers-scheduling-hours.html. Szekely, P. (2017, July 17). *Not so fast: U.S. restaurant workers seek ban on surprise scheduling.* Reuters. https://www.reuters.com/article/us-usa-fastfood-schedules/not-so-fast-u-s-restaurant-workers-seek-ban-on-surprise-scheduling-idUSKBN1A20VC

22. New York City Department of Consumer Affairs. (2017, November 27). *City's fair workweek laws are now in effect and give workers in fast food and retail the right to predictable schedules and paychecks* [Press release]. https://www1.nyc.gov/site/dca/media/pr112717.page

23. Moskowitz, P. (2017, January 23). These cities are at the forefront of the next big labor struggle: The fight for a fair workweek. *The Nation.* https://www.thenation.com/article/archive/these-cities-are-at-the-forefront-of-the-next-big-labor-fight/

24. Kristof, N. (2020, May 8). McDonald's workers in Denmark pity us. *The New York Times.* https://www.nytimes.com/2020/05/08/opinion/sunday/us-denmark-economy.html

25. Berdahl, J. L., & Moon, S. H. (2013). Workplace mistreatment of middle class workers based on sex, parenthood, and caregiving. *Journal of Social Issues, 69*(2), 341–366. Glass, J. (2004). Blessing or curse? Work–family policies and mother's wage growth over time. *Work and Occupations, 31*(3), 367–394. Munsch, C. L. (2016). Flexible work, flexible penalties: The effect of gender, childcare, and type of request on the flexibility bias. *Social Forces, 94*(4), 1567–1591. Rudman, L. A., & Mescher, K. (2013). Penalizing men who request a family leave: Is flexibility stigma a femininity stigma? *Journal of Social Issues, 69*(2), 322–340. Vandello, J. A., Hettinger, V. E., Bosson, J. K., & Siddiqi, J. (2013). When equal isn't really equal: The masculine dilemma of seeking work flexibility. *Journal of Social Issues, 69*(2), 303–321. Williams, J. C., Blair-Loy, M., & Berdahl, J. L. (2013). Cultural schemas, social class, and the flexibility stigma. *Journal of Social Issues, 69*(2), 209–234.

26. Greenberg, D., & Landry, E. M. (2011). Negotiating a flexible work arrange-
     ment: How women navigate the influence of power and organizational context.
     Journal of Organizational Behavior, 32(8), 1163–1188. Hornung, S., Rousseau, D.
     M., & Glaser, J. (2008). Creating flexible work arrangements through idiosyncratic
     deals. *Journal of Applied Psychology, 93*(3), 655–664. Kelly, E. L., & Kalev, A. (2006).
     Managing flexible work arrangements in US organizations: Formalized discretion
     or "a right to ask." *Socio-Economic Review, 4*(3), 379–416. Rousseau, D. M. (2005).
     I-deals: Idiosyncratic deals employees bargain for themselves. M. E. Sharpe.
27. Cain Miller, C. (2019, January 25). With paid leave, Gates Foundation says there
     can be too much of a good thing. *The New York Times.*https://www.nytimes.com/
     2019/01/25/upshot/paid-parental-leave-sweet-spot-six-months-gates.html
28. Stevenson, S. (2014, May 11). Don't go to work: The management scheme that lets
     workers do whatever they want, as long as they get things done. *Slate.* https://
     slate.com/business/2014/05/best-buys-rowe-experiment-can-results-only-work-
     environments-actually-be-successful.html
29. Bhasin, K. (2013, March 18). Best Buy CEO: Here's why I killed the "results only
     work environment." *Business Insider.* https://www.businessinsider.com/best-
     buy-ceo-rowe-2013-3 Valcour, M. (2013, March 8). The end of "results only"
     at Best Buy is bad news. *Harvard Business Review.* https://hbr.org/2013/03/
     goodbye-to-flexible-work-at-be
30. Cain Miller, C. (2019, August 21). How medicine became the stealth family-friendly
     profession. *The New York Times.*https://www.nytimes.com/2019/08/21/upshot/
     medicine-family-friendly-profession-women.html
31. Bear, J. B. (2019, August). *A tale of two ambitions: Caregiving and career ambitions
     among men and women.* Academy of Management.
32. Lareau, A. (2002). Invisible inequality: Social class and childrearing in Black families
     and White families. *American Sociological Review, 67*(5), 747–776. Faircloth, C., &
     Murray, M. (2015). Parenting: Kinship, expertise, and anxiety. *Journal of Family
     Issues, 36*(9), 1115–1129.
33. Pinsker, J. (2019, January 16). "Intensive" parenting is now the norm in America.
     The Atlantic. https://www.theatlantic.com/family/archive/2019/01/intensive-hel
     icopter-parenting-inequality/580528/. Anderson, J. (2019, January 3). The much-
     hated "helicopter parenting" style has surprisingly broad appeal. *Quartz.* https://
     qz.com/1514079/much-hated-helicopter-parenting-style-is-surprisingly-popular/
34. Calhoun, A. (2020). The caregiving rack. In *Why we can't sleep: Women's new mid-
     life crisis* (p. 76). Grove Press.
35. Waverman, E. (2019, March 22). Snowplow parenting: What to know about the
     controversial technique. *Today's Parent.* https://www.todaysparent.com/blogs/
     snowplow-parenting-the-latest-controversial-technique/
36. Chua, A. (2014). On generational decline. In *Battle hymn of the tiger mother* (p. 22).
     Bloomsbury Publishing.
37. Livingston, G. (2018, September 24). *Stay-at-home moms and dads ac-
     count for about one-in-five U.S. parents.* Pew Research Center. https://www.
     pewresearch.org/fact-tank/2018/09/24/stay-at-home-moms-and-dads-
     account-for-about-one-in-five-u-s-parents/

38. Stone, P. (2008). *Opting out? Why women really quit careers and head home.* University of California Press. Blau, F. D., & Winkler, A. E. (2017). *Women, work, and family* [Working paper, National Bureau of Economic Research]. https://www. nber.org/system/files/working_papers/w23644/w23644.pdf. Goldin, C., & Katz, L. (2012, September). The most egalitarian of all professions: Pharmacy and the evolution of a family-friendly occupation [Working Paper 18410, National Bureau of Economic Research]. https://www.nber.org/papers/w18410. Pedulla, D. S., & Thébaud, S. (2015). Can we finish the revolution? Gender, work–family ideals, and institutional constraint. *American Sociological Review, 80*(1), 116–139.

   Wiswall, M., & Zafar, B. (2017). Preference for the workplace, investment in human capital, and gender. *The Quarterly Journal of Economics, 133*(1), 457–507.

39. All data reported about preferences concerning family structure are from the 2012 data set (the only year in which these questions were asked). Smith et al., *General social surveys*, 1972–2016.

40. Institute for Women's Policy Research. (2016). *Undervalued and underpaid in America: Women in low-wage, female-dominated jobs.* https://iwpr.org/wp-content/uploads/2020/09/D508-Undervalued-and-Underpaid.pdf. Treadwell, H. M. (2019). Wages and women in health care: The race and gender gap. *American Journal of Public Health, 109*(2), 208–209.

41. Rudman, L. A., & Mescher, K. (2013). Penalizing men who request a family leave: Is flexibility stigma a femininity stigma? *Journal of Social Issues, 69*(2), 322–340.

42. Menasce Horowitz, J., Parker, K., Graf, N., & Livingston, G. (2017, March 23). *How paid leave impacts gender and caregiving.* Pew Research Center. https://www.pewsocialtrends.org/2017/03/23/gender-and-caregiving/

43. Chozick, A. (2016, November 5). Hillary Clinton and the return of the (unbaked) cookies. *The New York Times.* https://www.nytimes.com/2016/11/06/us/politics/hillary-clinton-cookies.html

44. Data concerning opinions on paid leave for child care are from the 2012 data set (the most recent year with questions about this issue). Smith et al., *General Social Surveys*, 1972–2016.

45. Knickman, J. R., & Snell, E. K. (2002). The 2030 problem: Caring for aging baby boomers. *Health Services Research, 37*(4), 849–884. Newton-Small, J. (2019, February 15). A growing American crisis: Who will care for the baby boomers? *Time.* https://time.com/5529152/elderly-caregiving-baby-boomers-unpaid-caregivers-crisis/. US Census Bureau. (2019, December 10). *By 2030, all baby boomers will be age 65 or older* [America counts: Stories behind the numbers]. https://www.census.gov/library/stories/2019/12/by-2030-all-baby-boomers-will-be-age-65-or-older.html

CHAPTER 3

1. Hrdy, S. B. (2000). The milky way. In *Mother nature: Maternal instincts and how they shape the human species* (p. 121). Ballantine Books.

2. For the definition and discussion of caregiving ambition and the providing/
   provisioning dimensions, see Bear, J. B. (2019). The caregiving ambition framework. *Academy of Management Review, 44*(1), 99–125.
3. Ainsworth, M. S., & Bowlby, J. (1991). An ethological approach to personality development. *American Psychologist, 46*(4), 333–341. Bowlby, J. (1982). *Attachment
   and loss: Vol. 1. Attachment* (2nd ed.). Basic Books.
4. Mikulincer, M., & Shaver, P. R. (2007). *Attachment in adulthood: Structure, dynamics, and change.* Guilford Press. Mikulincer, M., Shaver, P. R., Gillath, O., &
   Nitzberg, R. A. (2005). Attachment, caregiving, and altruism: Boosting attachment security increases compassion and helping. *Journal of Personality and Social
   Psychology, 89*, 817–839.
5. Ainsworth, M. D. S., Blehar, M. C., Waters, E., & Wall, S. (1978). *Patterns of attachment: Assessed in the strange situation and at home.* Erlbaum. Bowlby, J. (1973).
   Attachment and loss: Vol. 2. Separation: Anxiety and anger. Basic Books.
6. Fraley, R. C., & Shaver, P. R. (2000). Adult romantic attachment: Theoretical
   developments, emerging controversies, and unanswered questions. *Review of
   General Psychology, 4*, 132–154. Mikulincer, M., Shaver, P. R., Sapir-Lavid, Y., &
   Avihou-Kanza, N. (2009). What's inside the minds of securely and insecurely attached people? The secure-base script and its associations with attachment-style
   dimensions. *Journal of Personality and Social Psychology, 97*(4), 615–632.
7. Mikulincer, & Shaver, *Attachment in adulthood.*
8. Goetz, J. L., Keltner, D., & Simon-Thomas, E. (2010). Compassion: An evolutionary
   analysis and empirical review. *Psychological Bulletin, 136*(3), 351–374.
9. Bear, J. B. (2019). The caregiving ambition framework. *Academy of Management
   Review, 44*(1), 99–125.
10. Stepler, R. (2015, November 18). *5 Facts about family caregivers.* Pew Research
    Center. https://www.pewresearch.org/fact-tank/2015/11/18/5-facts-about-
    family-caregivers/
11. Schulz, R., & Sherwood, P. R. (2008). Physical and mental health effects of family
    caregiving. *Journal of Social Work Education, 44*(3), 105–113.
12. Caputo, J., Pavalko, E. K., & Hardy, M. A. (2016). The long-term effects of care-
    giving on women's health and mortality. *Journal of Marriage and Family, 78*(5),
    1382–1398.
13. Robison, J., Fortinsky, R., Kleppinger, A., Shugrue, N., & Porter, M. (2009). A
    broader view of family caregiving: Effects of caregiving and caregiver conditions
    on depressive symptoms, health, work, and social isolation. *Journals of Gerontology
    Series B: Psychological Sciences and Social Sciences, 64*(6), 788–798.
14. Adelman, R. D., Tmanova, L. L., Delgado, D., Dion, S., & Lachs, M. S. (2014).
    Caregiver burden: A clinical review. *JAMA, 311*(10), 1052–1060.
15. Raina, P., O'Donnell, M., Schwellnus, H., Rosenbaum, P., King, G., Brehaut, J.,
    Russell, D., Swinton, M., King, S., Wong, M., Walter, S. D. & Wood, E. (2004).
    Caregiving process and caregiver burden: Conceptual models to guide research and
    practice. *BMC Pediatrics, 4*(1), 1–13. Stuart, M., & McGrew, J. H. (2009). Caregiver
    burden after receiving a diagnosis of an autism spectrum disorder. *Research in
    Autism Spectrum Disorders, 3*(1), 86–97.

16. Bertrand, M., Goldin, C., & Katz, L. F. (2010). Dynamics of the gender gap for young professionals in the financial and corporate sectors. *American Economic Journal: Applied Economics, 2*(3), 228–255. Goldin, C., & Katz, L. (2012, September). *The most egalitarian of all professions: Pharmacy and the evolution of a family-friendly occupation* [Working Paper 18410, National Bureau of Economic Research]. http://www.nber.org/papers/w18410

17. Lucas, R. (2020, February 25). *Spotlight lands on Amy Berman Jackson, judge in Stone case, after a lengthy career.* National Public Radio. https://www.npr.org/2020/02/25/808966785/after-lengthy-career-spotlight-lands-on-amy-berman-jackson-judge-in-stone-case

18. Coontz, S. (2016). Toxic parents, supermoms, and absent fathers. In *The way we never were: American families and the nostalgia trip* (p. 286). Basic Books.

19. Payton, C., Romney, M., Olson, B. H., Abatemarco, D. J., LaNoue, M., & Leader, A. E. (2019). Evaluation of workplace lactation support among employers in two Pennsylvania cities. *Business Horizons, 62*(5), 579–587.

20. Ku, L. J. E., Stearns, S. C., Van Houtven, C. H., & Holmes, G. M. (2012). The health effects of caregiving by grandparents in Taiwan: An instrumental variable estimation. *Review of Economics of the Household, 10*(4), 521–540.

21. Posadas, J., & Vidal-Fernandez, M. (2013). Grandparents' childcare and female labor force participation. *IZA Journal of Labor Policy, 2*(1), 14.

22. Herndon, J. G. (2010). The grandmother effect: Implications for studies on aging and cognition. *Gerontology, 56*(1), 73–79. https://doi.org/10.1159/000236045. Hrdy, Who cared? In *Mother nature* (p. 275). Kaptijn, R., Thomese, F., Van Tilburg, T. G., & Liefbroer, A. C. (2010). How grandparents matter. *Human Nature, 21*(4), 393–405.

23. Knudsen, K. (2012). European grandparents' solicitude: Why older men can be relatively good grandfathers. *Acta Sociologica, 55*(3), 231–250.

24. Krogstad, J. M. (2015, September 13). *5 facts about American grandparents.* Pew Research Center. https://www.pewresearch.org/fact-tank/2015/09/13/5-facts-about-american-grandparents/

25. Riley, L. A., & Glass, J. L. (2002). You can't always get what you want—Infant care preferences and use among employed mothers. *Journal of Marriage and Family, 64*(1), 2–15.

26. American Association for Retired Persons. (2019). *2018 Grandparents today national survey.* https://www.aarp.org/content/dam/aarp/research/surveys_statistics/life-leisure/2019/aarp-grandparenting-study.doi.10.26419-2Fres.00289.001.pdf

27. National Association for the Education of Young Children. (n.d.). Defining and recognizing high-quality early learning programs: NAEYC's 10 accreditation standards. Retrieved from https://www.naeyc.org/defining-recognizing-high-quality-early-learning-programs

28. Gould, E., & Cooke, T. (2015, October, 6). *High quality childcare is out of reach for working families.* Economic Policy Institute. https://www.epi.org/publication/child-care-affordability/

29. National Institute of Child Health and Human Development. (2006). *The NiCHD study of early child care and youth development: Findings for children up to 4 1/*

2 years. https://www.nichd.nih.gov/sites/default/files/publications/pubs/docume nts/seccyd_06.pdf. Glynn, S. J., Farrell, J., & Wu, N. (2013, May 8). *The importance of preschool and child care for working mothers*. Center for American Progress. https://www.americanprogress.org/issues/education-k-12/reports/2013/05/08/ 62519/the-importance-of-preschool-and-child-care-for-working-mothers/

30. Swinth, K. (2018). *Feminism's forgotten fight: The unfinished struggle for work and family*. Harvard University Press.

31. Carabillo, T., Meuli, J., & Csida, J. B. (1993). *The feminist chronicles, 1953–1993* (p. 214). Women's Graphics. Prentice, S. (2009). High stakes: The "investable" child and the economic reframing of childcare. *Signs: Journal of Women in Culture and Society, 34*(3), 687–710.

32. Mainardi, P. (1970). *The politics of housework*. New England Free Press. Stansell, C. (2011). *The feminist promise: 1792 to the present*. Random House, Modern Library.

33. Haller, S. (2018, September 19). What type of parent are you? Lawnmower? Helicopter? Attachment? Tiger? Free-range? *USA Today*. https://www.usatoday. com/story/life/allthemoms/2018/09/19/parenting-terms-explained-lawnmower- helicopter-attachment-tiger-free-range-dolphin-elephant/1357612002/

34. Doepke, M., & Zilibotti, F. (2019). *Love, money, and parenting: How economics explains the way we raise our kids*. Princeton University Press.

35. Sears, W., & Sears, M. (2001). *The attachment parenting book: A commonsense guide to understanding and nurturing your baby*. Little, Brown Spark.

36. Bear, J. (2019, August 9–13). *A tale of two ambitions: Caregiving and career ambitions among men and women* [Paper presentation]. Academy of Management Conference, Boston, MA, United States.

CHAPTER 4

1. Tronto, J. C. (2013). *Caring democracy: Markets, equality, and justice*. New York University Press.

2. Albrecht, L. (2019, December 7). *The U.S. is the no. 1 most generous country in the world for the last decade*. MarketWatch. https://www.marketwatch.com/story/ the-us-is-the-most-generous-country-but-americans-say-debt-is-keeping-them- from-giving-more-to-charity-2019-10-18

3. McPhillips, D. (2019, September 30). Aging in America, in 5 charts. *U.S. News and World Report*. https://www.usnews.com/news/best-states/articles/2019-09-30/ aging-in-america-in-5-charts

4. Turkle, S. (2011). *Alone together: Why we expect more from technology and less from each other*. Basic Books.

5. Council of Economic Advisers. (2015). *The economics of early childhood investments*. Executive Office of the President of the United States. https://obamawhitehouse. archives.gov/sites/default/files/docs/early_childhood_report_update_final_non- embargo.pdf

6. Directorate of Employment, Labour and Social Affairs. (2008). *Public spending on childcare and early education*. Organisation for Economic Co-operation and Development. http://www.oecd.org/education/school/44975840.pdf

7. Ibid.

8. Mongeau, L. (2016, July 12). Why does America invest so little in its children? *The Atlantic.* https://www.theatlantic.com/education/archive/2016/07/why-does-america-invest-so-little-in-its-children/490790/

9. Bureau of Labor Statistics. (2019). *Labor force characteristics by race and ethnicity, 2018.* US Department of Labor.https://www.bls.gov/opub/reports/race-and-ethnicity/2018/home.htm

10. Reynolds, A. J., Temple, J. A., White, B. A., Ou, S. R., & Robertson, D. L. (2011). Age 26 cost–benefit analysis of the Child-Parent Center early education program. *Child Development, 82*(1), 379–404.

11. Zero to Three. (2017, January 15). *Early head start works.* https://www.zerotothree.org/resources/477-early-head-start-works

12. Koball, H., & Jiang, H. (2018, January). *Basic facts about low-income children: Children under 18 years, 2016.* National Center for Children in Poverty, Bank Street Graduate School of Education. http://www.nccp.org/publications/pub_1194.html

13. Child Care Aware of America. (2014). *Parents and the high cost of child care: 2014 report.* https://www.childcareaware.org/wp-content/uploads/2016/12/costofcare20141.pdf

14. Office of Child Care. (2016, December 14). *Child Care and Development Fund final rule frequently asked questions.* US Department of Health and Human Services. https://www.acf.hhs.gov/occ/resource/ccdf-final-rule-faq

15. Gould, E., Austin, L. J. E., & Whitebook, M. (2017, March 29). *What does good child care reform look like?* Economic Policy Institute. https://www.epi.org/publication/what-does-good-child-care-reform-look-like/

16. Ibid.

17. Ibid.

18. Care.com. (2020, June 16). *Child care costs more in 2020, and the pandemic has parents scrambling for solutions.* https://www.care.com/c/cost-of-child-care-survey-2020-report

19. Dube, A., Lester, T. W., & Reich, M. (2014). *Minimum wage shocks, employment flows and labor market frictions.* Institute for Research and Labor and Employment. https://irle.berkeley.edu/files/2013/Minimum-Wage-Shocks-Employment-Flows-and-Labor-Market-Frictions.pdf

20. Bureau Labor of Statistics. (2020, April 10). *Childcare workers.* US Department of Labor. https://www.bls.gov/ooh/personal-care-and-service/childcare-workers.htm

21. Gould, E. (2015, November 5). *Child care workers aren't paid enough to make ends meet.* Economic Policy Institute. https://www.epi.org/publication/child-care-workers-arent-paid-enough-to-make-ends-meet/

22. Whitebook, M., Sakai, L., Gerber, E., & Howes, C. (2001). *Then and now: Changes in child care staffing, 1994–2000: Technical report.* Center for the Child Care Workforce. Thornburg, K., Raikes, H., Wilcox, B., Edwards, C. P., Torquati, J. C., Hegland, S., Peterson, C., Summers, J. A., & Atwater, J. (2005). *Policy brief: Compensation of early childhood teachers: What value do we place on young children?* Center on Children,

Families and the Law, University of Nebraska, Lincoln. https://digitalcommons.unl.edu/ccflpubs/18/

23. Whitebook et al., *Then and now*. Thornburg et al., *Policy brief*.

24. Greenberg, E., Healy, O., & Derrick-Mills, T. (2018). *Assessing quality across the center-based early care and education workforce: Evidence from the National Survey of Early Care and Education*. Urban Institute. https://www.urban.org/sites/default/files/publication/96366/assessing_quality_across_the_center-based_early_care_and_education_workforce_1.pdf

25. Directorate for Education and Skills. (2019). *Programme for international student assessment (PISA) results from PISA 2018 (U.S. country note)*. Organisation for Economic Co-operation and Development. https://www.oecd.org/pisa/publications/PISA2018_CN_USA.pdf

26. Ibid.

27. Ibid.

28. Ibid.

29. Children's Defense Fund. (2019). *Ending child poverty now*. https://www.childrensdefense.org/wp-content/uploads/2019/04/Ending-Child-Poverty-2019.pdf

30. Ibid.

31. Ibid.

32. Mongeau, Why does America invest so little?

33. Maron, D. F. (2015, June 8). Has maternal mortality really doubled in the U.S.? *Scientific American*. https://www.scientificamerican.com/article/has-maternal-mortality-really-doubled-in-the-u-s/

34. Berchick, E. R., Barnett, J. C., & Upton, R. D. (2019). *Health insurance coverage in the United States: 2018, Current population reports*. US Census Bureau. https://www.census.gov/content/dam/Census/library/publications/2019/demo/p60-267.pdf

35. Centers for Disease Control and Prevention. (2019, June 24). *Childhood obesity facts*. US Department of Health and Human Services. https://www.cdc.gov/obesity/data/childhood.html

36. Coleman-Jensen, A. (2019, December 2). *Food insecurity among children has declined overall but remains high for some groups*. Amber Waves. https://www.ers.usda.gov/amber-waves/2019/december/food-insecurity-among-children-has-declined-overall-but-remains-high-for-some-groups/

37. Children's Bureau. (2019, January 28). *Child maltreatment 2017*. US Department of Health and Human Services. https://www.acf.hhs.gov/cb/resource/child-maltreatment-2017

38. Lowrey, A. (2018). How America treats its own children. *The Atlantic*. https://www.theatlantic.com/ideas/archive/2018/06/how-america-treats-children/563306/

39. Ibid.

40. Schott, L. (2016). *Why TANF is not a model for other safety net programs*. Center on Budget and Policy Priorities. https://www.cbpp.org/sites/default/files/atoms/files/6-6-16tanf.pdf

41. Ibid.

42. Safawi, A., & Floyd, I. (2020). *TANF benefits still too low to help families, especially Black families, avoid increased hardship*. Center on Budget and Policy Priorities. https://cbpp.org/sites/default/files/atoms/files/2-2-17tanf-policybrief.pdf

43. Meyer, L., & Floyd, I. (2020). *Policy Brief: Cash assistance should reach millions more families to lesson hardship*. Center on Budget and Policy Priorities. https://www.cbpp.org/sites/default/files/atoms/files/4-5-17tanf.pdf

44. Children's Defense Fund. (2020). *The State of America's Children* 2020: Child poverty*. https://www.childrensdefense.org/policy/resources/soac-2020-child-poverty/

45. Ibid.

46. Ibid.

47. Bassuk, E. L., DeCandia, C. J., Beach, C. A., & Berman, F. (2014). *America's youngest outcasts: A report card on child homelessness*. National Center on Family Homelessness, American Institute for Research. https://www.air.org/resource/americas-youngest-outcasts-report-card-child-homelessness

48. Children's Bureau. (2020). *Foster care statistics 2018*. US Department of Health and Human Services. https://www.childwelfare.gov/pubPDFs/foster.pdf

49. Schneider, D., Hastings, O. P., & LaBriola, J. (2018). Income inequality and class divides in parental investments. *American Sociological Review, 83*(3), 475–507.

50. Campbell, A. F. (2019, August 21). Home health aides care for the elderly. Who will care for them? *Vox*. https://www.vox.com/the-highlight/2019/8/21/20694768/home-health-aides-elder-care.

51. Kane, R. A. (2001). Long-term care and a good quality of life: Bringing them closer together. *The Gerontologist, 41*(3), 293–304.

52. Board of Governors of the Federal Reserve System. (2018). *Report on the economic well-being of U.S. households in 2017*. https://www.federalreserve.gov/publications/files/2017-report-economic-well-being-us-households-201805.pdf

53. Bui, T. T. M., Button, P., & Picciotti, E. G. (2020). Early evidence on the impact of coronavirus disease 2019 (COVID-19) and the recession on older workers. *Public Policy & Aging Report, 30*(4), 154–159.

54. Gaines, A. C. (2008, July 30). *Elderly poverty: The challenge before us*. Center for American Progress. https://www.americanprogress.org/issues/poverty/reports/2008/07/30/4690/elderly-poverty-the-challenge-before-us/

55. Ibid.

56. Ibid.

57. Ungar, L., & Lieberman, T. (2019, August 28). Why America is failing to feed its aging. *Time*. https://time.com/5662200/elderly-hunger-in-america/

58. Ujvari, K., Fox-Grage, W., Houser, A., Dean, O., & Feinberg L. S. (2019, February 4). *Older Americans Act*. American Association of Retired Persons Public Policy Institute. https://www.aarp.org/ppi/info-2019/older-americans-act.html

59. Ungar & Lieberman, Why America is failing.

60. Kaiser Health News. (2019, September 3). Starving seniors: How America fails to feed its aging. *U.S. News and World Report*. https://www.usnews.com/news/healthiest-communities/articles/2019-09-03/starving-seniors-how-america-fails-to-feed-its-aging

61. Dean, O., & Flowers, L. (2018). *Supplemental Nutrition Assistance Program (SNAP) provides benefits for millions of adults ages 50 and older.* American Association of Retired Persons Public Policy Institute. https://www.aarp.org/content/dam/aarp/ ppi/2018/04/snap-provides-benefits-for-millions-of-adults-ages-50-and-older.pdf

62. Centers for Disease Control and Prevention. (2017, January 31). *Depression is not a normal part of growing older.* https://www.cdc.gov/aging/mentalhealth/depression.htm

63. Allan, C. E., Valkanova, V., & Ebmeier, K. P. (2014). Depression in older people is underdiagnosed. *The Practitioner, 258*(1771), 19–22. https://pubmed.ncbi.nlm.nih. gov/25065018/

64. Department of Public Safety. (n.d.). *Elder abuse.* State of Rhode Island Police. https://risp.ri.gov/safety/preventingviolence/elderabuse.php

65. White House. (2015, May 8). *Elder justice policy brief.* 2015 White House Conference on Aging. https://archive.whitehouseconferenceonaging.gov/home/blog/policy/ post/elder-justice-policy-brief.html

66. Ibid.

67. Rauch, J. (2010). Letting go of my father. *The Atlantic.* https://www.theatlantic.com/ magazine/archive/2010/04/letting-go-of-my-father/308001/

68. Frishberg, H. (2019, August 2). 1 in 5 millennials are lonely and have "no fri ends": Survey. *New York Post.* https://nypost.com/2019/08/02/1-in-5- millennials-are-lonely-and-have-no-friends-survey/

69. Chatterjee, R. (2018, May 1). *Americans are a lonely lot, and young people bear the heaviest burden.* NPR. https://www.npr.org/sections/health-shots/2018/05/01/606588504/ americans-are-a-lonely-lot-and-young-people-bear-the-heaviest-burden

70. Bialik, K. (2018, December 3). *Americans unhappy with family, social or finan-cial life are more likely to say they feel lonely.* Pew Research Center. https://www. pewresearch.org/fact-tank/2018/12/03/americans-unhappy-with-family-social-or-financial-life-are-more-likely-to-say-they-feel-lonely/

71. Holt-Lunstad, J., Smith, T. B., & Layton, J. B. (2010). Social relationships and mor-tality risk: A meta-analytic review. *Public Library of Science Medicine, 7*(7), Article e1000316.

72. Holt-Lunstad, J., Smith, T. B., Baker, M., Harris, T., & Stephenson, D. (2015). Loneliness and social isolation as risk factors for mortality: A meta-analytic re-view. *Perspectives on Psychological Science, 10*(2), 227–237. Alcaraz, K. I., Eddens, K. S., Blase, J. L., Diver, W. R., Patel, A. V., Teras, L. R., Stevens, V., Jacobs, E. J., & Gapstur, S. M. (2019). Social isolation and mortality in US Black and White men and women. *American Journal of Epidemiology, 188*(1), 102–109.

73. Hawkley, L. C., & Capitanio, J. P. (2015). Perceived social isolation, evolutionary fitness and health outcomes: A lifespan approach. *Philosophical Transactions of the Royal Society B: Biological Sciences, 370*(1669), Article 20140114.

74. Health Resources & Services Administration. *The "loneliness epidemic."* US Department of Health and Services. https://www.hrsa.gov/enews/past-issues/2019/ january-17/loneliness-epidemic

75. Alcaraz et al., Social isolation and mortality.

76. Caspi, A., Harrington, H., Moffitt, T. E., Milne, B. J., & Poulton, R. (2006). Socially isolated children 20 years later: Risk of cardiovascular disease. *Archives of Pediatrics & Adolescent Medicine, 160*(8), 805–811.

77. Sutin, A. R., Stephan, Y., Luchetti, M., & Terracciano, A. (2018). Loneliness and risk of dementia. *The Journals of Gerontology: Series B, 75*(7), 1414–1422.

CHAPTER 5

1. Coontz, S. (2013, June 8). Progress at work, but mothers still pay a price. *The New York Times.* https://www.nytimes.com/2013/06/09/opinion/sunday/coontz-richer-childless-women-are-making-the-gains.html

2. Hymowitz, C., & Schellhardt, T. D. (1986, March 24). The glass ceiling: Why women can't seem to break the invisible barrier that blocks them from the top job. *Wall Street Journal, 24*(1), 1573–1592.

3. Ryan, M. K., & Haslam, S. A. (2005). The glass cliff: Evidence that women are over-represented in precarious leadership positions. *British Journal of Management, 16*(2), 81–90.

4. Eagly, A., & Carli, L. L. (2007). *Through the labyrinth: The truth about how women become leaders.* Harvard Business Press.

5. Eagly, A., & Carli, L. L. (2007, September). Women and the labyrinth of leadership. *Harvard Business Review.* https://hbr.org/2007/09/women-and-the-labyrinth-of-leadership

6. Paustian-Underdahl, S. C., Walker, L. S., & Woehr, D. J. (2014). Gender and perceptions of leadership effectiveness: A meta-analysis of contextual moderators. *Journal of Applied Psychology, 99*(6), 1129–1146.

7. Eagly, A. H. (1987). *Sex differences in social behavior: A social role interpretation.* Erlbaum.

8. Eagly, A. H., & Karau, S. J. (2002). Role congruity theory of prejudice toward female leaders. *Psychological Review, 109*(3), 573–598.

9. Cuddy, A. J., Fiske, S. T., & Glick, P. (2004). When professionals become mothers, warmth doesn't cut the ice. *Journal of Social Issues, 60*(4), 701–718. Fiske, S. T., Cuddy, A. J., Glick, P., & Xu, J. (2002). A model of (often mixed) stereotype content: Competence and warmth respectively follow from perceived status and competition. *Journal of Personality and Social Psychology, 82*(6), 878–902. Heilman, M. E., & Okimoto, T. G. (2007). Why are women penalized for success at male tasks? The implied communality deficit. *Journal of Applied Psychology, 92*(1), 81–92. Okimoto, T. G., & Brescoll, V. L. (2010). The price of power: Power seeking and backlash against female politicians. *Personality and Social Psychology Bulletin, 36*(7), 923–936. Rudman, L. A., & Glick, P. (1999). Feminized management and backlash toward agentic women: The hidden costs to women of a kinder, gentler image of middle managers. *Journal of Personality and Social Psychology, 77*(5), 1004–1010.

10. Eagly, *Sex differences in social behavior.*

11. Schein, V. E., & Davidson, M. J. (1993). Think manager, think male. *Management Development Review, 6*(3), 24–28.

12. Kleven, H., Landais, C., & Søgaard, J. E. (2019). Children and gender inequality: Evidence from Denmark. *American Economic Journal: Applied Economics*, *11*(4), 181–209.

13. The statistics cited for the overall gender pay gap, as well as the gap broken down by demographic categories and internationally, are from Catalyst. Retrieved March 2, 2020. *Women's earnings—The pay gap (Quick take).* https://www.catalyst.org/research/womens-earnings-the-pay-gap/

14. Catalyst. (2020, January 15). *Pyramid: Women in S&P 500 companies (Infographic).* https://www.catalyst.org/research/women-in-sp-500-companies/

15. Zillman, C. (2019, May 16). The Fortune 500 has more female CEOs than ever before. *Fortune.* https://fortune.com/2019/05/16/fortune-500-female-ceos/

16. The statistics cited in this paragraph concerning education and work experience are reported in Blau, F. D., & Kahn, L. M. (2017). The gender wage gap: Extent, trends, and explanations. *Journal of Economic Literature*, *55*(3), 789–865.

17. Hyde, J. S. (2005). The gender similarities hypothesis. *American Psychologist*, *60*(6), 581–592. Hyde, J. S. (2014). Gender similarities and differences. *Annual Review of Psychology*, *65*, 373–398.

18. Catalyst, *Women's earnings.*

19. Goldin, C. (2014). A grand gender convergence: Its last chapter. *American Economic Review*, *104*(4), 1091–1119. Goldin, C., & Katz, L. (2012, September). *The most egalitarian of all professions: Pharmacy and the evolution of a family-friendly occupation* [Working paper 18410, National Bureau of Economic Research]. http://www.nber.org/papers/w18410

20. Olivetti, C., & Petrongolo, B. (2016). The evolution of gender gaps in industrialized countries. *Annual Review of Economics*, *8*, 405–434.

21. The statistics cited in this paragraph are reported in Blau & Kahn, The gender wage gap.

22. Bertrand, M., Goldin, C., & Katz, L. F. (2010). Dynamics of the gender gap for young professionals in the financial and corporate sectors. *American Economic Journal: Applied Economics*, *2*(3), 228–255.

23. Ibid.

24. Rotenstein, L. S., & Dudley, J. (2019, November 4). How to close the gender pay gap in U.S. medicine. *Harvard Business Review.* https://hbr.org/2019/11/how-to-close-the-gender-pay-gap-in-u-s-medicine

25. Mangurian, C., Linos, E., Sarkar, U., Rodriguez, C., & Jagsi, R. (2018, June 19). What's holding women in medicine back from leadership. *Harvard Business Review.* https://hbr.org/2018/06/whats-holding-women-in-medicine-back-from-leadership

26. Murphy, B. (2019, October 1). *These medical specialties have the biggest gender imbalances.* American Medical Association. https://www.ama-assn.org/residents-students/specialty-profiles/these-medical-specialties-have-biggest-gender-imbalances

27. Cain Miller, C. (2019, August 25). How medicine became the stealth family-friendly profession. *The New York Times.*https://www.nytimes.com/2019/08/21/upshot/medicine-family-friendly-profession-women.html?searchResultPosition=1

28. Lambert, E. M., & Holmboe, E. S. (2005). The relationship between specialty choice and gender of US medical students, 1990–2003. *Academic Medicine, 80*(9), 797–802.

29. For a discussion of women's participation in professional jobs and factors that contribute to the pay gap, see Blau & Kahn, The gender wage gap. For statistics regarding women's participation and earnings in professional jobs, as well as other job categories, see US Bureau of Labor Statistics. (2019). *Highlights of women's earnings in 2018* (Report No. 1083). US Department of Labor. https://www.bls.gov/opub/reports/womens-earnings/2018/home.htm. US Bureau of Labor Statistics. (2019). *Women in the labor force: A databook* (Report No. 1084). US Department of Labor. https://www.bls.gov/opub/reports/womens-databook/2019/home.htm

30. Acker, J. (1990). Hierarchies, jobs, bodies: A theory of gendered organizations. *Gender & Society, 4*(2), 139–158.

31. US Bureau of Labor Statistics. (2020). *Employment characteristics of families—2019* (Report No. USDL-20–0670). US Department of Labor. https://www.bls.gov/news.release/pdf/famee.pdf

32. Blau & Kahn, The gender wage gap.

33. Ruhm, C. J. (1998). The economic consequences of parental leave mandates: Lessons from Europe. *The Quarterly Journal of Economics, 113*(1), 285–317. Blau & Kahn, The gender wage gap.

34. Livingston, G. (December 20, 2013). *The link between parental leave and the gender pay gap*. Pew Research Center. https://www.pewresearch.org/fact-tank/2013/12/20/the-link-between-parental-leave-and-the-gender-pay-gap/

35. Killian, E. (2011, August 8). *Parental leave: The Swedes are the most generous*. National Public Radio. https://www.npr.org/sections/babyproject/2011/08/09/139121410/parental-leave-the-swedes-are-the-most-generous. Stanfors, M., Jacobs, J. C., & Neilson, J. (2019). Caregiving time costs and trade-offs: Gender differences in Sweden, the UK, and Canada. *SSM-Population Health, 9*(100501), 1–9.

36. McGregor, J. (2014, November 6). When "good" maternity leave programs can actually hurt women. *The Washington Post*. https://www.washingtonpost.com/news/on-leadership/wp/2014/11/06/when-good-maternity-leave-programs-can-actually-hurt-women/

37. Bear, J. B., & Glick, P. (2017). Breadwinner bonus and caregiver penalty in workplace rewards for men and women. *Social Psychological and Personality Science, 8*(7), 780–788.

38. Blau & Kahn, The gender wage gap.

39. Casper, L. M., McLanahan, S. S., & Garfinkel, I. (1994). The gender-poverty gap: What we can learn from other countries. *American Sociological Review, 59*(4), 594–605. Samuelson, R. (2018, March 18). Don't deny the link between poverty and single parenthood. *The Washington Post*. https://www.washingtonpost.com/opinions/dont-deny-the-link-between-poverty-and-single-parenthood/2018/03/18/e6b0121a-2942-11e8-b79d-f3d931db7f68_story.html

40. Correll, S. J., Benard, S., & Paik, I. (2007). Getting a job: Is there a motherhood penalty? *American Journal of Sociology, 112*(5), 1297–1338.

41. Rudman, L. A., & Mescher, K. (2013). Penalizing men who request a family leave: Is flexibility stigma a femininity stigma? *Journal of Social Issues, 69*(2), 322–340.

42. Berdahl, J. L., & Moon, S. H. (2013). Workplace mistreatment of middle class workers based on sex, parenthood, and caregiving. *Journal of Social Issues, 69*(2), 341–366. Vandello, J. A., Hettinger, V. E., Bosson, J. K., & Siddiqi, J. (2013). When equal isn't really equal: The masculine dilemma of seeking work flexibility. *Journal of Social Issues, 69*(2), 303–321.

43. Vandello, J. A., Bosson, J. K., Cohen, D., Burnaford, R. M., & Weaver, J. R. (2008). Precarious manhood. *Journal of Personality and Social Psychology, 95*(6), 1325.

44. Berdahl, J. L., Cooper, M., Glick, P., Livingston, R. W., & Williams, J. C. (2018). Work as a masculinity contest. *Journal of Social Issues, 74*(3), 422–448.

45. Levine, J. A., & Pittinsky, T. L. (1997). *Working fathers: New strategies for balancing work and family.* Addison-Wesley. Reid, E. (2015). Embracing, passing, revealing, and the ideal worker image: How people navigate expected and experienced professional identities. *Organization Science, 26*(4), 997–1017.

46. Cain Miller, C. (2014, September 6). The motherhood penalty vs. the fatherhood bonus. *The New York Times.* https://www.nytimes.com/2014/09/07/upshot/a-child-helps-your-career-if-youre-a-man.html

47. Livingston, G., & Parker, K. (2019, June 12). *8 Facts about American dads.* Pew Research Center. https://www.pewresearch.org/fact-tank/2019/06/12/fathers-day-facts/

48. Storey, A. E., Walsh, C. J., Quinton, R. L., & Wynne-Edwards, K. E. (2000). Hormonal correlates of paternal responsiveness in new and expectant fathers. *Evolution and Human Behavior, 21*(2), 79–95. Gettler, L. T., McDade, T. W., Feranil, A. B., & Kuzawa, C. W. (2011). Longitudinal evidence that fatherhood decreases testosterone in human males. *Proceedings of the National Academy of Sciences of the United States of America, 108*(39), 16194–16199.

49. Livingston & Parker, *8 Facts about American dads.*

50. Ibid.

51. Thébaud, S. (2010). Masculinity, bargaining, and breadwinning: Understanding men's housework in the cultural context of paid work. *Gender & Society, 24*(3), 330–354. Bertrand, M., Kamenica, E., & Pan, J. (2015). Gender identity and relative income within households. *The Quarterly Journal of Economics, 130*(2), 571–614.

52. Livingston & Parker, *8 Facts about American dads.* Pew Research Center. (2013, March 14). *How mothers and fathers spend their time* (Chapter 4 of *Modern Parenthood*). https://www.pewsocialtrends.org/2013/03/14/chapter-4-how-mothers-and-fathers-spend-their-time/

53. Livingston, G. (2018, May 4). *More than a million millennials are becoming moms each year.* Pew Research Center. https://www.pewresearch.org/fact-tank/2018/05/04/more-than-a-million-millennials-are-becoming-moms-each-year/

54. Pew Research Center. (2010, February 24). *Millennials: Confident. Connected. Open to change.* https://www.pewsocialtrends.org/2010/02/24/millennials-confident-connected-open-to-change/

55. The following report contains survey data both concerning different generations' views of fatherhood and concerning millennials' reported caregiving: Harrington,

B., Sabatini Fraone, J., & Lee, J. (2017). *The new dad: The career–caregiving conflict* (The New Dad Series). Boston College Center for Work & Family. https://www.bc.edu/content/dam/files/centers/cwf/research/publications/researchreports/BCCWF%20The%20New%20Dad%202017.pdf

56. Cain Miller, C. (2015, July 30). Millennial men aren't the dads they thought they'd be. *The New York Times.* https://www.nytimes.com/2015/07/31/upshot/millennial-men-find-work-and-family-hard-to-balance.html

57. Pew Research Center, *How mothers and fathers spend their time.*

58. Shaw, E., Hegewisch, A., Williams-Baron, E., & Gault, B. (2016). *Undervalued and underpaid in America: Women in low-wage, female-dominated jobs.* Institute for Women's Policy Research. https://iwpr.org/wp-content/uploads/wpallimport/files/iwpr-export/publications/D508%20Undervalued%20and%20Underpaid.pdf. Treadwell, H. M. (2019). Wages and women in health care: The race and gender gap. *American Journal of Public Health, 109*(2), 208–209.

59. Croft, A., Schmader, T., & Block, K. (2015). An underexamined inequality: Cultural and psychological barriers to men's engagement with communal roles. *Personality and Social Psychology Review, 19*(4), 343–370.

60. Eagly, A. H., Nater, C., Miller, D. I., Kaufmann, M., & Sczesny, S. (2019). Gender stereotypes have changed: A cross-temporal meta-analysis of U.S. public opinion polls from 1946 to 2018. *American Psychologist, 75*(3), 301–315.

61. Pittinsky, T. L., Bacon, L. M., & Welle, B. (2007). The great women theory of leadership? Perils of positive stereotypes and precarious pedestals. In B. Kellerman & D. Rhode (Eds.), *Women and leadership: The state of play and strategies for change* (pp. 93–125). Jossey-Bass.

62. Institute on Aging. (n.d.). See "Women as caregivers" section. https://www.ioaging.org/aging-in-america#caregivers

CHAPTER 6

1. Cellan-Jones, R. (2014, December 2). *Stephen Hawking warns artificial intelligence could end mankind.* BBC. https://www.bbc.com/news/technology/30290540

2. Smith, A., & Anderson, M. (2017, October 4). *Americans' attitudes toward robot caregivers* (Chapter 4 of *Automation in everyday life*). Pew Research Center. https://www.pewresearch.org/internet/2017/10/04/americans-attitudes-toward-robot-caregivers/

3. Geiger, A. W., Livingston, G., & Bialik, K. (2019, May 8). *6 Facts about U.S. moms.* Pew Research Center. https://www.pewresearch.org/fact-tank/2019/05/08/facts-about-u-s-mothers/

4. Raphael, R. (2019, May 27). Will robots ever be better caretakers than humans? *Fast Company.* https://www.fastcompany.com/90335808/will-robots-ever-be-better-caretakers-than-humans

5. Mather, M., Jacobsen, L. A., & Pollard, K. M. (2015). Aging in the United States. *Population Bulletin, 70*(2). https://www.prb.org/unitedstates-population-bulletin/

6. Smith & Anderson, *Americans' attitudes toward robot caregivers.*

7. Bureau of Labor Statistics. (2019, September 4). *Home health and personal care aides*. US Department of Labor. https://www.bls.gov/ooh/healthcare/home-health-aides-and-personal-care-aides.htm

8. Osterman, P. (2017). *Who will care for us? Long-term care and the long-term workforce*. Russell Sage Foundation.

9. Bureau of Labor Statistics. (2020, April 10). *Childcare workers*. US Department of Labor. https://www.bls.gov/ooh/personal-care-and-service/childcare-workers.htm

10. Wollerton, M. (2019, July 1). *Loving a robot dog is about so much more than not cleaning up poop*. CNET. https://www.cnet.com/features/loving-a-robot-dog-is-about-so-much-more-than-not-cleaning-up-poop/

11. Foster, M. (2018, March 27). *Aging Japan: Robots may have role in future of elder care*. Reuters. https://www.reuters.com/article/us-japan-ageing-robots-widerimage/aging-japan-robots-may-have-role-in-future-of-elder-care-idUSKBN1H33AB

12. Muoio, D. (2015, November 20). Japan is running out of people to take care of the elderly, so it's making robots instead. *Business Insider*. https://www.businessinsider.com/japan-developing-carebots-for-elderly-care-2015-11

13. Hamm, K., Baider, A., White, C., Robbins, K. G., Sarri, C., Stockhausen, M., & Perez, N. (2019). *America, it's time to talk about child care*. Center for American Progress. https://caseforchildcare.org/2020CaseForChildCare.pdf

14. Loudenback, T. (2016, October 12). In 33 US states it costs more to send your kid to childcare than college. *Business Insider*. https://www.businessinsider.nl/costs-of-childcare-in-33-us-states-is-higher-than-college-tuition-2016-10/

15. Hamm et al., *America, it's time to talk about child care*.

16. Muoio, Japan is running out of people.

17. Manyika, J., Chui, M., Miremadi, M., Bughin, J., George, K., Millmott, P., & Dewhurst, M. (2017). *A future that works: Automation, employment, and productivity*. McKinsey Global Institute. https://www.mckinsey.com/~/media/mckinsey/featured%20insights/Digital%20Disruption/Harnessing%20automation%20for%20a%20future%20that%20works/MGI-A-future-that-works-Executive-summary.ashx

18. Wang, S. (2018, October 8). *AI robots are transforming parenting in China*. CNN. https://www.cnn.com/2018/09/28/health/china-ai-early-education/index.html

19. Shandrow, K. L. (2016, September 30). Why parent your kids when this robot nanny can do the job for you? *Entrepreneur*. https://www.entrepreneur.com/article/283157

20. Tarantola, A. (2017, August 29). Robot caregivers are saving the elderly from lives of loneliness. *Endgadget*. https://www.engadget.com/2017-08-29-robot-caregivers-are-saving-the-elderly-from-lives-of-loneliness.html

21. Jittapong, K., & Temphairojana, P. (2016, August 15). *Firms in aging Thailand bet on demand surge for robots and diapers*. Reuters. https://www.reuters.com/article/us-thailand-ageing/firms-in-aging-thailand-bet-on-demand-surge-for-robots-and-diapers-idUSKCN10Q284

22. Muoio, Japan is running out of people.

23. Raphael, Will robots ever be better caretakers than humans?

24. Ibid.

25. Ibid.
26. Pittinsky, T. L. (2019). Technology for society. In T. L. Pittinsky (Ed.), *Science, technology, and society: New perspectives and directions* (pp. 253–262). Cambridge University Press.
27. Pittinsky, T. (2020). Algorithms and ethical diversity: Developing a more holistic view of technology and society [Commentary]. *IEEE Technology and Society Magazine, 39*(3), 20–24.
28. Gross, L. (2013, April 15). Flame retardants in consumer products are linked to health and cognitive problem. *Washington Post.* https://www.washingtonpost.com/national/health-science/flame-retardants-in-consumer-products-are-linked-to-health-and-cognitive-problems/2013/04/15/f5c7b2aa-8b34-11e2-9838-d62f083ba93f_story.html
29. Barrett, B., Muller, D., Rakel, D., Rabago, D., Marchand, L., & Scheder, J. C. (2006). Placebo, meaning, and health. *Perspectives in Biology and Medicine, 49*(2), 178–198.
30. Twenge, J. M., Cooper, A. B., Joiner, T. E., Duffy, M. E., & Binau, S. G. (2019). Age, period, and cohort trends in mood disorder indicators and suicide-related outcomes in a nationally representative dataset, 2005–2017. *Journal of Abnormal Psychology, 128*(3), 185–199.
31. Primack, B. A., Shensa, A., Sidani, J. E., Whaite, E. O., Lin, L. Y., Rosen, D., Colditz, J. B., Radovic, A., & Miller, E. (2017). Social media use and perceived social isolation among young adults in the US. *American Journal of Preventive Medicine, 53*(1), 1–8.
32. Keles, B., McCrae, N., & Grealish, A. (2020). A systematic review: the influence of social media on depression, anxiety and psychological distress in adolescents. *International Journal of Adolescence and Youth, 25*(1), 79–93.
33. Reeves W. C., Strine, T. W., Pratt L. A., Thompson, W., Ahluwalia, I., Dhingra, S. S., McKnight-Eily, L. R., Harrison, L., D'Angelo, D. V., Williams, L., Morrow, B., Gould, D., & Safran, M. A. (2011, September 2). Mental illness surveillance among adults in the United States. *Morbidity and Mortality Weekly Report, 60*(3), 1–32. http://www.cdc.gov/mmwr/preview/mmwrhtml/su6003a1.htm?s_cid=su6003a1_w
34. Ibid.
35. Suzuki, Y., Galli, L., Ikeda, A., Itakura, S., & Kitazaki, M. (2015). Measuring empathy for human and robot hand pain using electroencephalography. *Nature Scientific Reports, 5*, Article 15924.
36. Smith & Anderson, *Americans' attitudes toward robot caregivers.*
37. Raphael, Will robots ever be better caretakers than humans?
38. Span, P. (2014, June 24). When advance directives are ignored. *New York Times.* https://newoldage.blogs.nytimes.com/2014/06/24/when-advance-directives-are-ignored/
39. de Graaf, M. M. (2016). An ethical evaluation of human–robot relationships. *International Journal of Social Robotics, 8*(4), 589–598.
40. Hosseini, S. E., & Goher, K. (2017). Personal care robots for children: State of the art. *Asian Social Science, 13*(1), 169–176.
41. Pinker, S. (2013). *The village effect: How face-to-face contact can make us healthier and happier.* Spiegel & Grau.

42. Hoffman, K. M., Trawalter, S., Axt, J. R., & Oliver, M. N. (2016). Racial bias in pain assessment and treatment recommendations, and false beliefs about biological differences between Blacks and Whites. *Proceedings of the National Academy of Sciences of the United States of America*, *113*(16), 4296–4301.

43. Grother, P., Ngan, M., & Hanaoka, K. (2019). *Face recognition vendor test (FVRT) part 3: Demographic effects.* National Institute of Standards and Technology, US Department of Commerce. https://nvlpubs.nist.gov/nistpubs/ir/2019/NIST. IR.8280.pdf

44. Pittinsky, T. L. (Ed.). (2019). *Science, technology, and society: New perspectives and directions.* Cambridge University Press.

CHAPTER 7

1. Blanchard, K., Randolph, A., & Grazier, P. (2007). *Go team! Take your team to the next level.* Berrett-Koehler Publishers.

2. Kranz, G. (2009, April 16). *Tutoring benefits give employees peace of mind.* Workforce. https://www.workforce.com/news/tutoring-benefits-give-employees-peace-of-mind

3. Blair-Loy, M., & Jacobs, J. A. (2003). Globalization, work hours, and the care deficit among stockbrokers. *Gender & Society*, *17*(2), 230–249. Dumas, T. L., & Sanchez-Burks, J. (2015). The professional, the personal, and the ideal worker: Pressures and objectives shaping the boundary between life domains. *The Academy of Management Annals*, *9*(1), 803–843. Williams, J. C., Blair-Loy, M., & Berdahl, J. L. (2013). Cultural schemas, social class, and the flexibility stigma. *Journal of Social Issues*, *69*(2), 209–234.

4. Weber, M. (2002). *The Protestant ethic and the "spirit" of capitalism and other writings.* Penguin.

5. Blair-Loy, M., & Dehart, G. (2003). Family and career trajectories among African American female attorneys. *Journal of Family Issues*, *24*(7), 908–933. Dumas & Sanchez-Burks, The professional, the personal, and the ideal worker. Williams et al., Cultural schemas, social class, and the flexibility stigma.

6. Weeden, K. A. (2005). Is there a flexiglass ceiling? Flexible work arrangements and wages in the United States. *Social Science Research*, *34*(2), 454–482.

7. Williams, J. C., Berdahl, J. L., & Vandello, J. A. (2016). Beyond work–life "integration." *Annual Review of Psychology*, *67*, 515–539.

8. A notable exception is Rau, B. L., & Hyland, M. A. M. (2002). Role conflict and flexible work arrangements: The effects on applicant attraction. *Personnel Psychology*, *55*(1), 111–136.

9. Hepler, L. (2014, September 10). Silicon Valley rent too high? Google workers lived in campus parking lots with free food, amenities. *Silicon Valley Business Journal.* https://www.bizjournals.com/sanjose/news/2014/09/10/silicon-valley-rent-too-high-google-workers-lived.html

10. Ibid.

11. Lyon, D. (2017, August 31). In Silicon Valley, working 9 to 5 is for losers. *New York Times*.https://www.nytimes.com/2017/08/31/opinion/sunday/silicon-valley-work-life-balance-.html

12. Weller, C. (2017, September 17). What you need to know about egg-freezing, the hot new perk at Google, Apple, and Facebook. *Business Insider.* https://www.businessinsider.com/egg-freezing-at-facebook-apple-google-hot-new-perk-2017-9

13. Goldin, C. (1977). Female labor force participation: The origin of Black and White differences, 1870 and 1880. *Journal of Economic History, 37*(1), 87–108.

14. Banks, N. (2019, February 19). *Black women's labor market history reveals deep-seated race and gender discrimination.* Economic Policy Institute. https://www.epi.org/blog/black-womens-labor-market-history-reveals-deep-seated-race-and-gender-discrimination/

15. Hess, A. (2017, May 4). *The 20 best companies for work–life balance.* CNBC. https://www.cnbc.com/2017/05/03/the-20-best-companies-for-work-life-balance.html. Uhereczky, A. (2019, July 2). Are you missing out on the latest workplace revolution? The untapped potential of job sharing. *Fortune.* https://www.forbes.com/sites/agnesuhereczky/2019/07/02/are-you-missing-out-on-the-latest-workplace-revolution-the-untapped-potential-of-job-sharing/#476965b73403

16. Armour, S. (2020, March 4). Coronavirus response plan exposes vulnerabilities in U.S. health-care system. *Wall Street Journal.* https://www.wsj.com/articles/coronavirus-response-plan-exposes-vulnerabilities-in-u-s-health-care-system-11583323754

17. Bureau of Labor Statistics. (2019, February 26). *Employee benefits survey.* US Department of Labor. https://www.bls.gov/ncs/ebs/factsheet/family-leave-benefits-fact-sheet.htm

18. Kruse, M. M. (2016, March 14). *The social security con: How stay-at-home moms (or dads) lose their social security disability.* Huffpost. https://www.huffpost.com/entry/the-social-security-con-h_b_9369742

19. Tamborini, C. R., & Whitman, K. (2007). Women, marriage, and social security benefits revisited. *Social Security Bulletin, 67*(4). https://www.ssa.gov/policy/docs/ssb/v67n4/67n4p1.html

20. Bauer, E. (2018, March 16). (How) Should we make social security fairer for moms? *Forbes.* https://www.forbes.com/sites/ebauer/2018/03/16/how-should-we-make-social-security-fairer-for-moms/#1efdb96e6040

21. Konda, S. (2019, June 12). *A brief history of when (and why) women started wearing pants.* Medium. https://medium.com/@snehako/a-brief-history-of-women-and-pants-a5c81ac4e245

22. McLaughlin, K. (2014, August 25). *5 Things women couldn't do in the 1960s.* CNN. https://www.cnn.com/2014/08/07/living/sixties-women-5-things/index.html

23. Bianchi, J. (n.d.). *What is a returnship? (Hint: Something you probably want to check out if you're returning to the workforce).* The Muse. https://www.themuse.com/advice/what-is-a-returnship-hint-something-you-probably-want-to-check-out-if-youre-returning-to-the-workforce

24. Ibid.

25. Hewlett Packard. (n.d). *Your path forward at HPE*. https://www.pathforward.org/
     your-path-forward-at-hpe/
26. Ibid.
27. Glassdoor. (2019, July 9). *Companies offering returnship programs*. https://www.
     glassdoor.com/blog/6-companies-offering-returnship-programs/
28. Wingard, J. (2019, February 13). Are returnships the key to relaunching your career?
     Forbes.   https://www.forbes.com/sites/jasonwingard/2019/02/13/are-returnships-
     the-key-to-relaunching-your-career/#473545ce3cdf
29. Ibid.
30. Sammer, J. (2020, January 6). *4 Lessons about unlimited vacation: Early adopters
     share what they've learned so far*. Society for Human Resource Management.
     https://www.shrm.org/resourcesandtools/hr-topics/benefits/pages/4-lessons-
     about-unlimited-vacation.aspx
31. Ibid.
32. Ibid.
33. Ibid.
34. Keynes, J. M. (2010). Economic possibilities for our grandchildren. In *Essays in
     Persuasion* (pp. 321–332). Palgrave Macmillan.
35. Unilever. Unilever NZ to trial four-day work week at full pay. (2020). https://
     www.unilever.com.au/news/press-releases/2020/unilever-nz-to-trial-
     four-day-work-week-at-full-pay/
36. Baltes, B. B., Briggs, T. E., Huff, J. W., Wright, J. A., & Neuman, G. A. (1999).
     Flexible and compressed workweek schedules: A meta-analysis of their effects on
     work-related criteria. *Journal of Applied Psychology*, 84(4), 496–513. Beauregard, T.
     A., & Henry, L. C. (2009). Making the link between work–life balance practices and
     organizational performance. *Human Resource Management Review*, 19(1), 9–22.
37. Graeber, D. (2018). *Bullshit jobs*. Simon & Schuster Paperbacks.
38. Turits, M. (2017, January 17). *What's the best plan for a radical new workday?*
     BBC.   https://www.bbc.com/worklife/article/20210113-whats-the-best-
     plan-for-a-radical-new-workday
39. Mercer. (n.d.). *Mercer Global*. https://www.mercer.us/our-thinking/healthcare/
     new-survey-finds-employers-adding-fertility-benefits-to-promote-dei.html
40. Rosemberg, J. (2019, April 5). Great eggspectations. *New York Times*. https://www.
     nytimes.com/2019/04/05/well/family/great-eggspectations.html
41. Williams, J. C., Blair-Loy, M., & Berdahl, J. L. (2013). Cultural schemas, social class,
     and the flexibility stigma. *Journal of Social Issues*, 69(2), 209–234.
42. Lott, Y., & Chung, H. (2016). Gender discrepancies in the outcomes of schedule
     control on overtime hours and income in Germany. *European Sociological Review*,
     32(6), 752–765.
43. Burnford, J. (2019, May 28). Flexible working: The way of the future. *Forbes*. https://
     www.forbes.com/sites/joyburnford/2019/05/28/flexible-working-the-way-of-the-
     future/#355e2f184874
44. Wingard, J. (2020, March 6). 94% of workers want this benefit (and most leaders
     are screwing it up). *Forbes*. https://www.forbes.com/sites/jasonwingard/2020/

03/06/94-of-workers-want-this-benefit-and-most-leaders-are-screwing-it-up/#63b9b87a451f

45. Guyot, K., & Sawhill, I. V. (2020, April 6). *Telecommuting will likely continue long after the pandemic.* The Brookings Institution. https://www.brookings.edu/blog/up-front/2020/04/06/telecommuting-will-likely-continue-long-after-the-pandemic/

46. Gould, E., & Shierholz, H. (2020, March 19, 2020). *Not everybody can work from home.* Economic Policy Institute. https://www.epi.org/blog/black-and-hispanic-workers-are-much-less-likely-to-be-able-to-work-from-home/

47. Ibanez, M. R., Clark, J. R., Huckman, R. S., & Staats, B. R. (2018). Discretionary task ordering: Queue management in radiological services. *Management Science, 64*(9), 4389–4407.

48. Murphy, A. P. (2003, May 28). *Split-shift parents cut childcare costs.* ABC News. https://abcnews.go.com/GMA/AmericanFamily/story?id=125137&page=1

49. Ibid.

50. Ibid.

51. Goodman, C. K. (2011, October 24). Shift work's 24/7 challenges; odd hours can affect health, relationships. *Buffalo News.* https://buffalonews.com/2011/10/24/shift-works-247-challenges-odd-hours-can-affect-health-relationships/

52. Gajendran, R. S., & Harrison, D. A. (2007). The good, the bad, and the unknown about telecommuting: Meta-analysis of psychological mediators and individual consequences. *Journal of Applied Psychology, 92*(6), 1524–1541.

53. Lee, M. D., MacDermid, S. M., Williams, M. L., Buck, M. L., & Leiba-O'Sullivan, S. (2002). Contextual factors in the success of reduced-load work arrangements among managers and professionals. *Human Resource Management, 41*(2), 209–223.

54. Gariety, B. S., & Shaffer, S. (2001). Wage differentials associated with flextime. *Monthly Labor Review, 124,* 68–75. Weeden, Is there a flexiglass ceiling?

55. Blair-Loy, M., & Wharton, A. S. (2002). Employees' use of work–family policies and the workplace social context. *Social Forces, 80*(3), 813–845.

56. Council of Economic Advisers. (2014). *Work–life balance and the economics of workplace flexibility.* Executive Office of the President of the United States. https://obamawhitehouse.archives.gov/sites/default/files/docs/updated_workplace_flex_report_final_0.pdf

57. Glass, J. (2004). Blessing or curse? Work–family policies and mother's wage growth over time. *Work and Occupations, 31*(3), 367–394. Leslie, L. M., Manchester, C. F., Park, T. Y., & Mehng, S. A. (2012). Flexible work practices: A source of career premiums or penalties? *Academy of Management Journal, 55*(6), 1407–1428. Wharton, A. S., Chivers, S., & Blair-Loy, M. (2008). Use of formal and informal work–family policies on the digital assembly line. *Work and Occupations, 35*(3), 327–350. Judiesch, M. K., & Lyness, K. S. (1999). Left behind? The impact of leaves of absence on managers' career success. *Academy of Management Journal, 42*(6), 641–651.

58. Leslie et al., Flexible work practices.

59. Bourdeau, S., Ollier-Malaterre, A., & Houlfort, N. (2019). Not all work–life policies are created equal: Career consequences of using enabling versus enclosing work-life policies. *Academy of Management Review, 44*(1), 172–193.

60. Pittinsky, T. L. (2001). *Knowledge nomads: Commitment at work* [Unpublished doctoral dissertation]. Harvard University.

CHAPTER 8

1. Fuller, J., & Raman, M. (2019). *The caring company* (p. 28). Harvard Business School. https://www.hbs.edu/managing-the-future-of-work/Documents/The_Caring_Company.pdf
2. Vermeulen, F. (2009, April 13). The case for work/life programs. *Harvard Business Review.* https://hbr.org/2009/04/the-case-for-worklife-programs.html
3. Arthur, M. M. (2003). Share price reactions to work–family initiatives: An institutional perspective. *Academy of Management Journal, 46*(4), 497–505. Arthur, M. M., & Cook, A. (2004). Taking stock of work–family initiatives: How announcements of "family-friendly" human resource decisions affect shareholder value. *ILR Review, 57*(4), 599–613.
4. Henn, S. (2015, August 6). *Netflix's parental leave plan is groundbreaking—and unlikely to spread.* National Public Radio. https://www.npr.org/2015/08/06/429911928/netflixs-parental-leave-plan-is-groundbreaking-and-unlikely-to-spread
5. Oxford University Press. (n.d.). Business case. In *Oxford English dictionary.* https://www.lexico.com/definition/business_case
6. Hewlett, S. A., & Luce, C. B. (2006, December). Extreme jobs: The dangerous allure of the 70-hour workweek. *Harvard Business Review.* https://hbr.org/2006/12/extreme-jobs-the-dangerous-allure-of-the-70-hour-workweek. Suneson, G., & Stebbins, S. (2018, June 15). What are the worst companies to work for? New report analyzes employee reviews. *USA Today.* https://www.usatoday.com/story/money/business/2018/06/15/worst-companies-to-work-for-employee-reviews/35812171/
7. Sanders, S. (2015, August 6). *Netflix's new, generous parental leave policy leaves some employees out.* National Public Radio. https://www.npr.org/sections/thetwo-way/2015/08/06/430069888/netflixs-new-generous-parental-leave-policy-leaves-some-employees-out
8. Alba, D. (2015, December 9). Netflix adds hourly workers to its general parental leave plan. *Wired.* https://www.wired.com/2015/12/netflix-adds-hourly-workers-to-its-generous-parental-leave-plan/
9. Coontz, S. (2016). *The way we never were: American families and the nostalgia trap.* Basic Books.
10. Green, H. (2012). *The company town: The industrial edens and satanic mills that shaped the American economy.* Basic Books.
11. Guilford, G. (2017, December 30). The 100-year capitalist experiment that keeps Appalachia poor, sick, and stuck on coal. *Quartz.* https://qz.com/1167671/the-100-year-capitalist-experiment-that-keeps-appalachia-poor-sick-and-stuck-on-coal/. Khazan, S. (2015, August 20). Life in the sickest town in America. *The Atlantic.* https://www.theatlantic.com/health/archive/2015/01/life-in-the-sickest-town-in-america/384718/

12. The Henry Ford. (n.d.). *Checking on Ford employees home conditions, views from "Factory Facts from Ford," 1917*. https://www.thehenryford.org/collections-and-research/digital-collections/artifact/109833

13. Coontz, Bra burners and family bashers. In *The way we never were*.

14. Gordon, A. M., & Browne, K. W. (2013). *Beginnings & beyond: Foundations in early childhood education*. Delmar Learning.

15. Swinth, K. (2018). *Feminisms forgotten fight: The unfinished struggle for work and family*. Harvard University Press.

16. Levine, J. A., & Pittinsky, T. L. (1997). *Working fathers: New strategies for balancing work and family*. Addison-Wesley.

17. Friedman, M. (1975). *Capitalism and freedom*. University of Chicago Press.

18. Harter, J. K., Schmidt, F. L., & Hayes, T. L. (2002). Business-unit-level relationship between employee satisfaction, employee engagement, and business outcomes: A meta-analysis. *Journal of Applied Psychology, 87*(2), 268–279.

19. Judge, T. A., Thoresen, C. J., Bono, J. E., & Patton, G. K. (2001). The job satisfaction–job performance relationship: A qualitative and quantitative review. *Psychological Bulletin, 127*(3), 376–407.

20. Carsten, J. M., & Spector, P. E. (1987). Unemployment, job satisfaction, and employee turnover: A meta-analytic test of the Muchinsky model. *Journal of Applied Psychology, 72*(3), 374–381. Spector, P. E. (1997). *Job satisfaction: Application, assessment, causes, and consequences*. Sage.

21. Bateman, T. S., & Organ, D. W. (1983). Job satisfaction and the good soldier: The relationship between affect and employee "citizenship." *Academy of Management Journal, 26*(4), 587–595. Miles, D. E., Borman, W. E., Spector, P. E., & Fox, S. (2002). Building an integrative model of extra role work behaviors: A comparison of counterproductive work behavior with organizational citizenship behavior. *International Journal of Selection and Assessment, 10*(1–2), 51–57.

22. Arthur, Share price reactions to work-family initiatives. Arthur & Cook, Taking stock of work–family initiatives.

23. Kaplan, R. S., & Norton, D. P. (1996). Linking the balanced scorecard to strategy. *California Management Review, 39*(1), 53–79.

24. Levine & Pittinsky, *Working fathers*. Reid, E. (2015). Embracing, passing, revealing, and the ideal worker image: How people navigate expected and experienced professional identities. *Organization Science, 26*(4), 997–1017.

25. Wademan Dowling, D. (2019). Balance parenting and work stress. In S. Friedman, E. G. Saunders, P. Bregman, & D. Wademan Dowling (Eds.), *HBR guide to work–life balance* (pp. 161–168). Harvard Business Review Press.

26. Kelly, E. L., & Moen, P. (2020). *Overload: How good jobs went bad and what we can do about it*. Princeton University Press.

27. Kelly, E. L., & Moen, P. (2020). Dual-agenda work redesign: Understanding STAR at TOMO. In *Overload* (p. 80).

28. Kelly, E. L., & Moen, P. (2020). The business impacts of work redesign. In *Overload* (p. 141).

29. Del Ray, J. (2020, February 24). *Amazon tells Sanders and Warren that warehouse workers can pee whenever they want*. Vox. https://www.vox.com/recode/2020/2/

24/21151296/amazon-warehouse-bathroom-breaks-workers-senators-letter-bezos-warren-sanders

30. Kantor, J., & Streitfeld, D. (2015, August 15). Inside Amazon: Wrestling big ideas in a bruising workplace. *The New York Times.* https://www.nytimes.com/2015/08/16/technology/inside-amazon-wrestling-big-ideas-in-a-bruising-workplace.html

31. Dastin, J., & Rana, A. (2020, July 30). *Amazon posts biggest profit ever at height of pandemic in U.S.* Reuters. https://www.reuters.com/article/us-amazon-com-results/amazon-posts-biggest-profit-ever-at-height-of-pandemic-in-u-s-idUSKCN24V3HL

32. Toh, M. (2020, August 27). *Jeff Bezos is now worth a whopping $200 billion.* CNN Business. https://www.cnn.com/2020/08/27/tech/jeff-bezos-net-worth-200-billion-intl-hnk/index.html

33. Campbell, A. F. (2019, April 4). *Google will extend some benefits to contract workers after internal protest.* Vox. https://www.vox.com/2019/4/4/18293900/google-contractors-benefits-policy

34. Hrdy, S. B. (2011). *Mothers and others: The evolutionary origins of mutual understanding.* Belknap Press.

35. O'Connell, B. (2020, May 30). *COVID-19 spurs expanded paid leave.* Society for Human Resource Management. https://www.shrm.org/hr-today/news/all-things-work/pages/covid-19-spurs-expanded-paid-leave.aspx

36. New York State. (n.d.). *New paid leave for COVID-19.* https://paidfamilyleave.ny.gov/COVID19. US Department of Labor. (n.d.). *Families First Coronavirus Response Act: Employee paid leave rights.* https://www.dol.gov/agencies/whd/pandemic/ffcra-employee-paid-leave

37. Kurtzleben, D. (2015, July 15). *Lots of other countries mandate paid leave. Why not the U.S.?* National Public Radio. https://www.npr.org/sections/itsallpolitics/2015/07/15/422957640/lots-of-other-countries-mandate-paid-leave-why-not-the-us.Pinsker, J. (2019, July 25). The conservative argument over paid family leave. *The Atlantic.* https://www.theatlantic.com/family/archive/2019/07/family-leave-conservatives/594838/

38. Linskey, A., & Viser, M. (2020, July 21). Biden unveils $775 billion plan for universal preschool, child care and elder care. *The Washington Post.* https://www.washingtonpost.com/politics/biden-to-unveil-775-billion-plan-for-universal-preschool-child-care-and-elder-care/2020/07/20/e273dabc-cae7-11ea-91f1-28aca4d833a0_story.html. Wilkie, C. (2020, July 21). *Biden announces $775 billion plan to fund universal child care and in-home elder care.* CNBC. https://www.cnbc.com/2020/07/21/biden-to-unveil-775-billion-plan-to-fund-child-care-and-elder-care.html

39. US Congress. (2019, December 4). *Advancing Support for Working Families Act.* https://www.congress.gov/bill/116th-congress/senate-bill/2976?q=%7B%22search%22%3A%5B%22The+Skills+Act%22%5D%7D&s=1&r=2

40. Flowers, A. (2016, February 18). *Marco Rubio's paid family leave plan may not work.* FiveThirtyEight. https://fivethirtyeight.com/features/marco-rubios-paid-family-leave-plan-may-not-work/. Flynn, A. (2015, October 7). A GOP-style approach to parental leave. *The Atlantic.* https://www.theatlantic.com/business/archive/2015/10/rubio-parental-leave/409285/

41. Maltin, E. (2019, January 8). What successful public–private partnerships do. *Harvard Business Review.* https://hbr.org/2019/01/what-successful-public-private-partnerships-do

42. Fuller & Raman, *The caring company* (p. 28).

CHAPTER 9

1. Hammer, M., & Champy, J. (1993). *Reengineering the corporation: Manifesto for business revolution* (p. 226). HarperBusiness.

2. Butts, M. M., Becker, W. J., & Boswell, W. R. (2015). Hot buttons and time sinks: The effects of electronic communication during nonwork time on emotions and work-nonwork conflict. *Academy of Management Journal, 58*(3), 763–788. Wright, K. B., Abendschein, B., Wombacher, K., O'Connor, M., Hoffman, M., Dempsey, M., Krull, C., Dewes, A., & Shelton, A. (2014). Work-related communication technology use outside of regular work hours and work life conflict: The influence of communication technologies on perceived work life conflict, burnout, job satisfaction, and turnover intentions. *Management Communication Quarterly, 28*(4), 507–530.

3. Festinger, L. (1954). A theory of social comparison processes. *Human Relations, 7*(2), 117–140.

4. Appel, H., Gerlach, A. L., & Crusius, J. (2016). The interplay between Facebook use, social comparison, envy, and depression. *Current Opinion in Psychology, 9,* 44–49.

5. Irvine, W. B. (2009). *A guide to the good life.* Oxford University Press. Pigliucci, M. (2017). *How to be a stoic: Ancient wisdom for modern living.* Random House.

6. Smith, R. H., & Kim, S. H. (2007). Comprehending envy. *Psychological Bulletin, 133*(1), 46–64.

7. Cardozo, A. R. (1986). *Sequencing.* Atheneum Books.

8. Hewlett, S. A. (2007). *On ramps and off ramps.* Harvard Business Press.

9. Stone, P., & Lovejoy, M. (2019). *Opting back in: What really happens when mothers go back to work.* University of California Press.

10. Plant, J. (2006, May 4). Practice makes "sequencing" look less perfect. *Women's eNews.* https://womensenews.org/2006/05/practice-makes-sequencing-look-less-perfect/. Slaughter, A. M. (2012, July/August). Why women still can't have it all. *The Atlantic.* https://www.theatlantic.com/magazine/archive/2012/07/why-women-still-cant-have-it-all/309020/

11. Swinth, K. (2018). *Feminisms forgotten fight: The unfinished struggle for work and family.* Harvard University Press.

12. Tuna, C., & Lublin, J. S. (2009, July 14). Welch: "No such thing as work–life balance." *The Wall Street Journal.* https://www.wsj.com/articles/SB124726415198325373

13. Gilovich, T., Medvec, V. H., & Chen, S. (1995). Commission, omission, and dissonance reduction: Coping with regret in the "Monty Hall" problem. *Personality and Social Psychology Bulletin, 21*(2), 182–190.

14. Nietzsche, F. W. (1974). *The gay science* (W. Kaufmann, Trans.). Vintage Books.

15. Lutz, J. (2018, January 11). It's time to kill the fantasy that is work–life balance. *Forbes.* https://www.forbes.com/sites/jessicalutz/2018/01/11/its-time-to-kill-the-fantasy-that-is-work-life-balance/#397c32f970a1

16. Phillips, A. (2010). *On balance*. Farrar, Straus, & Giroux.
17. Deci, E. L., & Ryan, R. M. (2000). The "what" and "why" of goal pursuits: Human needs and the self-determination of behavior. *Psychological Inquiry, 11*, 227–268. Freud, S. (1930). *Civilization and its discontents* (J. Riviere, Trans.) Hogarth.
18. Ryan, R. M., & Deci, E. L. (2000). Self-determination theory and the facilitation of intrinsic motivation, social development, and well-being. *American Psychologist, 55*, 68–78.
19. Slaughter, A. M. (2016). *Unfinished business*. Random House. Moravcsik, A. (2015, October). Why I put my wife's career first. *The Atlantic*. https://www.theatlantic.com/magazine/archive/2015/10/why-i-put-my-wifes-career-first/403240/
20. Sandberg, S. (2013). *Lean in: Women, work, and the will to lead*. Random House. Orr, M. (2019). *Lean out: The truth about women, power, and the workplace*. HarperCollins Leadership.
21. Yoe, J. (2019). *Why are older people working longer?* Monthly Labor Review, US Bureau of Labor Statistics. https://www.bls.gov/opub/mlr/2019/beyond-bls/why-are-older-people-working-longer.htm

Conclusion

1. Damon, W. (2003). Purpose at work: Discovering your calling. In *Noble purpose: The joy of living a meaningful life* (p. 22). Templeton Foundation Press.
2. Bowlby, J. (1982). *Attachment and loss: Vol. 1. Attachment* (2nd ed.). Basic Books. Mikulincer, M., & Shaver, P. R. (2007). *Attachment in adulthood: Structure, dynamics, and change*. Guilford Press.
3. Pollack, J. M., Ho, V. T., O'Boyle, E. H., & Kirkman, B. L. (2020). Passion at work: A meta-analysis of individual work outcomes. *Journal of Organizational Behavior, 41*(4), 311–331.
4. Brooks, K. (2018). *Small animals: Parenting in the age of fear*. Flatiron Books.
5. Miller, C. C., & Streitfeld, D. (2015, September 1). Big leaps for parental leave, if workers actually take it. *The New York Times*. http://www.nytimes.com/2015/09/02/upshot/big-leaps-for-parental-leave-if-workers-actually-follow-through.html?_r=0

For the benefit of digital users, indexed terms that span two pages (e.g., 52–53) may, on occasion, appear on only one of those pages.

Tables are indicated by *t* following the page number